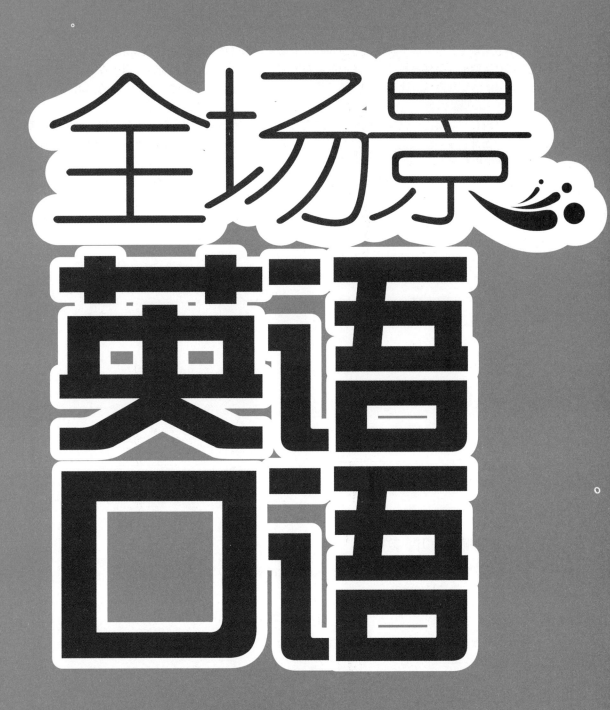

全场景英语口语

郑小俐 编著

U0336853

机械工业出版社
CHINA MACHINE PRESS

本书覆盖了日常生活中高频发生的 600 多个场景，均以真实情景中的实际需求为切入点展开话题，以对话的形式呈现该场景下必备的英语知识和口语表达，对学习者而言相当于直接参与实战训练，学习能够更加高效。此外，每个场景的内容都是独立的，学习者可以根据自己的需求有针对性地学习某个场景的内容。

本书内容与时俱进，包含大量与近年互联网高速发展密切相关的高频新话题（如手机拍照、手机投屏、面部识别、滤镜美颜、地图导航、在线转账和支付等），能让学习者即学即用，在日常工作、生活中更自如地用英语来表达与交流。

本书配备纯正美式发音音频，可供学习者跟读模仿，反复磨耳朵，快速提升英语听力和口语水平。

图书在版编目（CIP）数据

全场景英语口语 / 郑小俐编著. — 北京：机械工业出版社，2023.11（2024.9重印）
ISBN 978-7-111-74340-8

Ⅰ.①全… Ⅱ.①郑… Ⅲ.①英语 – 口语 – 自学参考资料 Ⅳ.①H319.9

中国国家版本馆CIP数据核字（2023）第227976号

机械工业出版社（北京市百万庄大街22号 邮政编码100037）
策划编辑：尹小云 责任编辑：尹小云
责任校对：苏筛琴 责任印制：单爱军
保定市中画美凯印刷有限公司印刷
2024年9月第1版第3次印刷
184mm×260mm·16.75印张·1插页·381千字
标准书号：ISBN 978-7-111-74340-8
定价：68.00元

电话服务 网络服务
客服电话：010-88361066 机 工 官 网：www.cmpbook.com
　　　　　010-88379833 机 工 官 博：weibo.com/cmp1952
　　　　　010-68326294 金 书 网：www.golden-book.com
封底无防伪标均为盗版 机工教育服务网：www.cmpedu.com

序 言

亲爱的读者，

　　你是否曾梦想过用流利的英语自如地沟通交流，却在开口时感到困难重重？你是否在尝试学习英语多年后，仍然发音不准确，无法说出地道的英语？或许你已经有了自己的孩子，而他／她经常在英语听力测试中丢分或是不能自信大胆地开口讲英语？如果你或你的孩子有这样的困惑，那么这本书就是为你们量身定做的。

　　我出生于普通的农村，但是有幸通过努力考上了香港中文大学，有幸获得了优质的教育资源，也有幸告别了"哑巴英语"。毕业后，我决定成为一名自媒体工作者。我把生活中的各种场景拍摄成英文小视频发布到网上，迅速获得了无数网友的点赞和转发，而我也收获了 600 万粉丝。

　　我深知学习英语的重要性，也深知课本上的英语知识有时是与现实生活中的沟通需求脱节的。而我更加了解的是，很多普通家庭的孩子享受的优质教育资源十分有限。因此，我想通过这本书，帮助那些学习英语多年却仍然无法说出流利英语的人以及那些普通家庭的孩子们迅速突破口语和听力，告别"哑巴英语"。

　　《全场景英语口语》是一本涵盖了 12 大主题的口语宝典，包含了 600 多个生活中常见的场景，从饮食、科技到职场、交通、旅游和购物等一应俱全。此外，本书特别注重实用性和与时俱进。例如，手机和电脑是我们在日常生活中几乎每天都会用到的，但是当大家想要表达"手机没电""信号弱""充电宝""卡顿"或"刷屏"等时，大脑中往往一片空白。所以，我特意将这些内容包含在"科技生活"部分，让大家能轻松掌握，进而在日常生活中能更加自如地用英语来表达自己。

　　此外，为了让大家的学习更加高效，全书配备了纯正的美音音频。你可以在学会地道表达的同时，通过美国播音员的朗读音频，反复磨耳朵，提升听力，自信大胆地开口讲英语。

　　让我们一起开启这段英语学习之旅吧！希望这本书能成为你学习英语口语的得力助手，让你在生活和工作中更加自信、流利地说英语。

　　祝你学习愉快！

晓莉老师

目 录

Part 2

Technological Life
科技生活

Part 3   Working Life
职场生活

Part 4　Travelling
旅游出行

Part 5　Foods and Drinks
饮食生活

Part 6　Choosing a Hotel
选择酒店

Part 7　Transportation
交通出行

Part 8　Consumer Life
消费生活

Part 9　Banking Business
银行业务

Part 1   Social Life
社交生活

Unit 1 Greetings 打招呼

Scene 1　初次见面

A: Hi, I'm Tom. Nice to meet you.

B: Hi, I'm Mary. Nice to meet you too.

A: How are you doing today?

B: I'm good. Thanks. And you?

A: I'm doing well. Thanks. Where are you from?

B: I'm from London. How about you?

A: I'm from New York.

A：嗨，我是汤姆，很高兴认识你。

B：嗨，我是玛丽，也很高兴认识你。

A：你今天怎么样?

B：我很好，谢谢。你呢?

A：我也很好，谢谢。你来自哪里?

B：我来自伦敦。你呢?

A：我来自纽约。

Scene 2　好久不见

A: Hi Sam! It's been a long time!

B: Yeah, it has. How have you been?

A: Same old, same old. How about you?

B: Can't complain. What have you been up to lately?

A: Just working and trying to stay busy.

A：嗨，萨姆! 好久不见!

B：是啊，确实很久了。你最近怎么样?

A：一如既往，没什么变化。你呢?

B：我没什么好抱怨的。你最近在忙什么呢?

A：只是在工作，尽量保持忙碌状态。

Unit 2 Saying Goodbye 道别

Scene 1　离别之际

A: It's tough to say goodbye to everyone.

B: Yeah, but we'll stay connected.

A: I'll miss you all so much.

B: Farewell doesn't mean forever.

A: I guess you're right. Goodbye for now.

A：向每个人告别真令人难受。

B：是啊，但我们会保持联系的。

A：我会很想念大家的。

B：告别并不代表永别。

A：我想你说得对。再见。

重点词汇及表达

☐ How are you doing today?
你今天怎么样?

☐ same old 一如既往

☐ can't complain 没什么好抱怨的

☐ farewell n. 告别

Scene 2　与家人告别

A: Bye, Dad.

B: I'll miss you. Take care of yourself. Have a safe trip!

A: No worries. I'll call you as soon as I get home.

B: Sounds good. Let me know when you arrive.

A: Definitely will. Bye!

B: Bye, sweetie, take care.

A：再见，爸爸。

B：我会想你的。照顾好自己。一路顺风!

A：不用担心，我到家后会立即给你打电话的。

B：好的，一定要让我知道你到家了。

A：当然会的。再见!

B：再见，亲爱的，注意安全。

Scene 3　出国告别

A: Hey, I'm leaving for abroad.

B: Really? When?

A: Tomorrow. I'm going to miss you.

B: It won't be the same without you here.

A: We'll still keep in touch. Let's plan a video call soon to catch up.

B: Definitely! Let's keep in touch.

A：嘿，我要出国了。

B：真的吗? 什么时候?

A：明天。我会想念你的。

B：你不在，一切就都不一样了。

A：我们还会保持联系的。我们尽快安排一次视频电话，到时候好好聊聊吧。

B：当然! 保持联系。

003

Unit 3　Making an Apology 道歉

Scene 1　撞到别人

A: Oh my god. I'm so sorry! Are you alright?

B: Yeah, I'm fine. It's all good. Don't worry.

A: Let me help you up. Here, give me your hand.

B: No need. I'm good. Just watch your step next time.

A: Yeah, I will. I'm really sorry, though.

B: It's all good. No harm done. Take care now.

A：哦，天哪，太抱歉了! 你还好吗?

B：还好，我没事。都挺好。别担心。

A：我扶你起来吧。来，把手给我。

B：不用了。我没事。下次走路小心点就行了。

A：好的，我会注意的。不过真的很抱歉。

B：没事的，我没受伤。你保重。

□ take care 当心，保重

□ keep in touch 保持联系

□ catch up 叙旧

□ watch one's step 小心脚下

Scene 2 摔坏手机

A: Oh no, I can't believe I broke your phone screen! I'm so sorry!

B: Ugh, it's totally shattered. You owe me a new phone. You know that, right?

A: Yes, I understand. I feel terrible about what happened. Let me make it right and pay for a new one.

B: Yeah, you better. My phone is really important to me.

A: I promise I'll make it up to you. I'll get you a new phone. I'm truly sorry.

A：哦，不，我真不敢相信我弄坏了你的手机屏幕! 非常抱歉!

B：哎呀，屏幕完全裂开了。你得赔我一部新手机，知道吗?

A：是的，我知道。我对此感到非常抱歉。让我弥补过失，买一部新手机给你。

B：嗯，你最好这么做。我的手机对我而言非常重要。

A：我保证，我会补偿你的。我会给你买一部新手机。真的很抱歉。

Scene 3 看电影迟到

A: I'm sorry I'm late.

B: You missed the start of the movie!

A: I hope you can forgive me.

B: It's OK, but don't let it happen again.

A: I won't. Thanks for waiting.

A：抱歉，我迟到了。

B：你错过了这部电影的开头!

A：希望你能原谅我。

B：没关系，但是不要有下次哦。

A：我不会的。谢谢你等我。

Scene 4 会面迟到

A: I'm sorry I missed our meeting.

B: I had to reschedule everything!

A: I hope you can forgive me.

B: It's OK, but it was inconvenient.

A: I'll be there next time. Sorry again.

A：抱歉，我错过会面的时间了。

B：我得重新安排所有的事情!

A：我希望你能原谅我。

B：没事，但是这确实给我带来了不便。

A：下次我一定赶到。再次道歉。

重点词汇
及表达

□ shatter v. 粉碎；（使）破碎

□ owe v. 欠；归功于

□ miss v. 错过

□ reschedule v. 重新安排

□ inconvenient adj. 不方便的

Scene 5 伤到别人

A: Oh shoot! Did I hurt you? I'm so sorry!

B: Yeah, you bumped into me pretty hard. Watch where you're going, will you?

A: Yeah, I totally understand. I owe you an apology for being so clumsy.

B: It's fine. Just be more careful next time, OK?

A: Absolutely, I will. Thanks for understanding, and sorry again for running into you.

A：哎呀! 我伤到你了吗？太抱歉了!

B：是啊，你狠狠地撞了我一下。下次走路要注意，知道吗？

A：嗯，我知道了。很抱歉我笨手笨脚的。

B：没事。下次要更小心一点，好吗？

A：当然，我会的。谢谢你的理解，再次抱歉撞到你。

Unit 4 Expressing Thanks 表达感谢

Scene 1 感谢妈妈做的晚餐

A: Wow! Everything looks delicious! Did you make all of this?

B: Yes, I did. I'm glad you like it.

A: Thank you so much for cooking all of this. It tastes incredible!

B: You're welcome. I'm just happy to see you enjoy it.

A: Mom, I just wanted to say thank you again for this amazing meal. It really means a lot to me.

B: Of course, dear. It's my pleasure. Enjoy every bite!

A：哇! 所有的东西看起来都很美味! 这些都是您做的吗？

B：是的，是我做的。我很高兴你喜欢。

A：非常感谢您做了所有这些食物。味道真的很棒!

B：不客气，我很高兴看到你喜欢吃。

A：妈妈，我只是想再次感谢您为我做了这么棒的一顿饭。这对我来说真的很重要。

B：当然，亲爱的。我很乐意为你做饭。好好享受每一口食物吧!

☐ bump into 撞上

☐ owe sb an apology 向某人道歉

☐ clumsy *adj.* 笨拙的

☐ run into 撞上

☐ delicious *adj.* 美味的

☐ incredible *adj.* 不可思议的

☐ mean *v.* 意味着

社交生活

Scene 2　感谢帮忙找手机

A: Hi, I lost my phone earlier. Have you seen it?

B: Yeah, actually, I found it earlier and kept it safe for you.

A: Oh my god, that's such a relief! Thank you so much for finding it!

B: No worries. I'm just happy to help.

A: Can I give you a little something to show my appreciation?

B: No need, but I appreciate the offer. Have a good day!

A：嗨，我刚刚丢了手机。你看到了吗？

B：看到了。事实上，我之前就找到了，而且帮你保管着。

A：哦，天哪，真是松了一口气！非常感谢你找到了我的手机！

B：不客气，我很乐意帮忙。

A：我能送你一点东西表达感激吗？

B：不用了，但是感谢你的好意。祝你拥有美好的一天！

Scene 3　感谢帮忙换零钱

A: Hey there, sorry to bother you, but do you happen to have change for a five?

B: Ah, sorry. I don't have any change on me right now.

A: Shoot, I don't have any smaller bills. Looks like I'm out of luck.

B: Hey, no worries. I'll cover for you this time.

A: Wow, you're too kind. Thank you so much!

B: Of course, happy to help.

A: That really means a lot. Thanks again!

A：嗨，不好意思打扰你，你有零钱换一下五元的钞票吗？

B：哦，抱歉。我现在身上没有零钱。

A：糟糕，我没有更小面额的钞票了。看来我的运气真差。

B：嘿，没关系。这次我帮你付吧。

A：哇，你太好了。非常感谢！

B：不客气，我乐意帮忙。

A：这对我而言真的很重要。再次感谢！

Scene 4　感谢邀请

A: I heard you're getting married. Congratulations!

B: Thanks. I'm really excited.

A：我听说你们要结婚了，恭喜！

B：谢谢。我特别激动。

- relief *n.* 轻松
- show one's appreciation 表达感激
- change *n.* 零钱
- out of luck 运气不好

006

A: I'm honored to be invited. Thank you!

B: Oh, we can't wait to celebrate with you.

A: I'll be there with bells on. Wouldn't miss it!

B: Great! It's going to be a wonderful day.

A：能够受邀参加婚礼真是荣幸。谢谢!

B：哦，我们很期待和你一起庆祝。

A：我非常乐意参加，我不会错过这么重要的日子!

B：太好了! 那一定会是美好的一天。

Scene 5　感谢同事

A: Thanks so much for your help with the project. I really appreciate it.

B: No problem at all. It was a team effort.

A: I'm really grateful for your support, Boss.

B: Hey, you did a great job. I'm happy to help.

A: Thanks again. I couldn't have done it without you.

B: Anytime, that's what colleagues are for. Happy to lend a hand.

A：特别感谢您对这个项目的帮助。我真的非常感激。

B：不客气。这是团队合作的结果。

A：老板，我真的很感谢您的支持。

B：嘿，你做得很好。我很高兴能够帮助你。

A：再次感谢您。没有您我不可能完成这个项目。

B：不用谢，同事之间就该互帮互助。我很乐意帮忙。

Scene 6　感谢老师和同学

A: Congratulations on graduating!

B: Thank you! I'm deeply thankful for our teachers and classmates.

A: Yeah, they helped us a lot.

B: Absolutely, I couldn't have done it without them.

A: Same here. Let's keep in touch.

B: Sure thing. Let's grab some drinks sometime!

A：恭喜你毕业了!

B：谢谢! 非常感谢我们的老师和同学们。

A：是啊，他们给了我们很多帮助。

B：没错，没有他们我毕不了业。

A：我也是。我们保持联系。

B：当然会的。有机会我们一起去喝点东西吧!

☐ honor *v.* 尊敬，感到荣幸

☐ with bells on　乐意地，渴望地

☐ grateful *adj.* 感激的

☐ lend a hand 帮忙

☐ thankful *adj.* 感激的

☐ grab some drinks 喝点东西

Scene 7　感谢礼物

A: Hey, I just wanted to take a moment to say thank you!

B: For what?

A: For the gift you gave me. It was so thoughtful.

B: Ah, no worries at all. I'm really glad you like it!

A: Yeah, it's amazing. Thank you so much!

B: Hey, it was my pleasure.

A：嘿，我只是想花一点时间说声"谢谢"！

B：为什么呢？

A：谢谢你送给我的礼物。你太体贴了。

B：啊，没事。我很高兴你喜欢它！

A：是啊，这礼物真是太棒了。非常感谢！

B：嘿，这是我的荣幸。

Unit 5　Talking About Hobbies 交流喜好

Scene 1　读书

A: Do you like reading books?

B: Yes, I do. How about you?

A: Same here! What type of books do you enjoy?

B: I love reading mystery novels. What about you?

A: I'm a big fan of non-fiction books, especially about science and history.

B: That's interesting. Any recommendations?

A：你喜欢读书吗？

B：是的，我喜欢读书。你呢？

A：我也喜欢！你喜欢什么类型的书？

B：我喜欢悬疑小说。你呢？

A：我非常喜欢非虚构类图书，尤其是科学和历史类图书。

B：那很有意思。你有什么推荐的吗？

Scene 2　看电影

A: What kind of movies are you into?

B: I enjoy action and adventure films. And you?

A: I like romantic comedies and dramas.

B: Ah, gotcha. Any favorites?

A: Definitely *The Notebook* and *Crazy Rich Asians*. How about you?

A：你喜欢什么类型的电影？

B：我喜欢惊险动作片。你呢？

A：我喜欢浪漫喜剧和戏剧。

B：啊，明白了。有最喜欢的吗？

A：当然是《恋恋笔记本》和《摘金奇缘》。你呢？

重点词汇
及表达

☐ thoughtful *adj.* 体贴的

☐ no worries at all 完全不用担心

☐ How about you? 你怎么样？

☐ What about you? 你怎么样？

☐ be into 喜欢

☐ gotcha（got you）明白你的意思

B: I'm a big fan of the *Indiana Jones* series.

A: Nice! Those are some classics.

B：我是《夺宝奇兵》系列的超级粉丝。

A：好极了！这些都是经典作品。

Scene 3　追星

A: Who is your favorite movie star?

B: Definitely Emma Watson. How about you?

A: I'm a big fan of Tom Hanks. His acting skill is incredible.

B: Oh yeah. Tom Hanks is amazing! Have you seen *Forrest Gump*?

A: Yes, I love that movie. He really knows how to bring a character to life.

B: Definitely. Have you watched any recent movies with him?

A: Yeah, I saw *News of the World* recently. He was great in that too.

B: I haven't seen that one yet, but I've heard good things about it. I'll definitely watch this movie sometime.

A：你最喜欢的电影明星是谁？

B：当然是艾玛·沃特森。你呢？

A：我是汤姆·汉克斯的超级粉丝。他的演技令人难以置信。

B：哦，是的。汤姆·汉克斯太棒了！你看过《阿甘正传》吗？

A：看过，我超爱那部电影。他真的很清楚如何把角色演得栩栩如生。

B：没错。你看过他最近演的电影吗？

A：看过，我最近看了《世界新闻报》。他在这部影片中表现得也很出色。

B：我还没看过这部电影，但我听说它很不错。我一定会找时间去看的。

Unit 6　Making a Self-introduction 自我介绍

Scene 1　小学生的自我介绍

A: Hello there! My name is Jimmy, and I'm 10 years old. I'm in Grade 4, Class 17. I come from a family of five, which includes my grandparents, parents, and of course, myself. In my free time, I enjoy playing basketball and drawing. It's my great honor to be here. I hope we can be friends. Thank you!

A：大家好！我叫吉米，今年10岁。我在四年级17班。我来自一个五口之家，我的家人包括祖父母、父母，当然，还有我自己。在空闲时间里，我喜欢打篮球和画画。我很荣幸来到这里。我希望我们能成为朋友。谢谢！

☐ a big fan of ……的超级粉丝

☐ definitely *adv.* 明确地，肯定地

☐ honor *n.* 荣幸

社交生活

Scene 2　大学生的自我介绍

A: Hey there, my name is Jack. I'm currently a student at the University of Hong Kong. My major is Computer Science. I'm crazy about technology and I enjoy coding in my free time. I'm excited to be here today. It's great to connect with like-minded people.

A: 大家好，我叫杰克。我现在是香港大学的学生。我的专业是计算机科学。我对技术很着迷。我喜欢在空闲时间里写代码。今天我很高兴来到这里。很高兴能与志同道合的人建立联系。

Scene 3　职场新人的自我介绍

A: Hi, my name is Emily. I'm a recent graduate of Harvard University. I earned my bachelor's degree in Business Administration. I'm a detail-oriented person. I have a great passion for strategic planning and problem-solving. In my free time, I enjoy hiking, reading, and exploring new places. I'm excited to be here today and look forward to meeting you all.

A: 嗨，我叫艾米丽。我最近刚从哈佛大学毕业。我获得了工商管理学士学位。我是一个注重细节的人。我对战略规划和解决问题有着极大的热情。在空闲时间里，我喜欢徒步旅行、阅读和探索新的地方。今天，我很高兴来到这里，我一直期待着与大家见面。

010

Scene 4　游客的自我介绍

A: Hello, my name is Lily. I come from China. I'm currently visiting New York. I love reading and traveling. Nice to meet you. May I ask your name?

B: Hey, Lily. My name is Jackie. Welcome to New York. It's a great city. How long do you plan to stay in New York?

A: I plan to stay for one week. Do you have any recommendations? Any place I should go or visit?

B: One week? That's a good amount of time to explore the city. There's so much to see and do. Have you been to Central Park yet?

A: 你好，我叫莉莉。我来自中国。我现在正在纽约旅行。我喜欢阅读和旅行。很高兴见到你。请问你的名字是？

B: 嘿，莉莉。我叫杰基。欢迎来到纽约。这是一个很棒的城市。你打算在纽约待多久？

A: 我打算待一周。你有什么建议吗？有我应该去或参观的地方吗？

B: 一周？用一周时间来探索这个城市非常合适。要看的和要做的有很多。你去过中央公园吗？

重点词汇
及表达

□ connect with 与……联系

□ bachelor *n.* 学士

□ look forward to (sth/doing sth)
期待（某事/做某事）

□ recommendation *n.* 推荐，建议

A: No, I haven't. Is it a must-see place?

B: Definitely! Central Park is a beautiful park. It's in the heart of Manhattan. You can go for a walk, rent a bike, and have a picnic. It's a great place to spend a day.

A: That sounds amazing. I'll definitely check it out. Do you have any favorite restaurants in the city?

B: Yes, I love this little Italian restaurant called Patsy's Pizza. It's been around since 1933, and they make amazing pizza. If you're interested, I can give you the address.

A: That sounds great! Thank you so much for your help, Jackie. I really appreciate it.

B: No problem, Lily. Enjoy your stay in New York!

A：没有，我没去过。那是必须去的地方吗？

B：当然！中央公园是一个美丽的公园。它位于曼哈顿的中心。你可以去散步、租一辆自行车，还可以野餐。那是一个度过一天的好地方。

A：听起来太棒了。我一定会去看看的。你在这个城市有最喜欢的餐厅吗？

B：有，我喜欢这家名叫"帕齐比萨"的意大利小餐厅。它从 1933 年就开始营业了，他们做的比萨饼很棒。如果你感兴趣，我可以给你地址。

A：听起来不错！非常感谢你的帮助，杰基。我真的很感激。

B：不客气，莉莉。祝你在纽约过得愉快！

社交生活

Unit 7 Making a Date 约会

Scene 1 介绍相亲对象

A: Hey, I know someone I think you might like.

B: Oh really? Tell me more.

A: He's smart, funny, and has a great sense of humor.

B: Sounds interesting. What's he like?

A: He's a teacher and loves to travel.

B: That sounds great. Can you introduce us sometime?

A: Sure thing! I'll set it up.

A：嘿，我认识一个人，我想你可能会喜欢。

B：哦，真的吗？跟我具体说说。

A：他聪明、风趣，而且很有幽默感。

B：听起来很有趣。他是个什么样的人？

A：他是一名教师，喜欢旅行。

B：听起来不错。你什么时候能介绍我们认识一下？

A：没问题！我来安排。

☐ must-see *adj.* 必看的

☐ check out 查看

☐ sense of humor 幽默感

☐ set up 安排

Scene 2　见面交谈

A: So you're the girl Mrs. Li introduced me to for the blind date?

B: Yes.

A: OK. But to be honest, I don't have an apartment or a car.

B: It doesn't matter. If you don't have a car, there's always the subway or the bus. If you don't have an apartment, just rent one.

A: But I don't look good.

B: I don't mind. Appearances are not that important.

A: I don't even have any savings.

B: It's not a big deal. You know you can save some as time goes by.

A: You really don't mind?

B: Of course I don't mind. It's not like I'm going to marry you.

A：你就是李太太介绍我相亲的那个女孩？

B：是的。

A：但说实话，我既没有房子也没有车。

B：没关系。如果没有车，你可以乘坐地铁或公交车。如果没有公寓，你可以租房。

A：但我也不帅。

B：我不介意。外表并不那么重要。

A：我连一点积蓄都没有。

B：没什么大不了的。你知道，随着时间的推移，你可以存下钱的。

A：你真的不介意吗？

B：当然，我不介意。我又不是要嫁给你。

012

Scene 3　约人成功

A: Hey, do you want to hang out with me sometime?

B: Yeah, I'd love to! What did you have in mind?

A: I thought we could have a picnic in the park. What do you think?

B: That sounds like a great idea. What do we need to bring?

A: I'll grab a blanket and make some sandwiches. Would you mind bringing some drinks and snacks?

B: Not at all. I can definitely do that. Can't wait!

A：嘿，你想什么时候和我一起出去玩吗？

B：嗯，我很想去！你有什么想法吗？

A：我想我们可以去公园野餐。你觉得呢？

B：听起来是个好主意。我们需要带些什么？

A：我会带条毯子，做些三明治。你介意带些饮料和零食吗？

B：当然不介意。完全没问题。我都等不及了！

重点词汇
及表达

☐ blind date 相亲

☐ to be honest 说实话

☐ It's not a big deal. 没什么大不了的。

☐ hang out 闲逛

☐ have...in mind 想，考虑

☐ mind v. 介意

Scene 4 约人失败

A: Hey, would you like to grab dinner together tonight?

B: I'm sorry. I can't make it tonight. Can I take a rain check?

A: Sure. When is a good time for you?

B: I'm really busy this week. Maybe next week?

A: Sure. Next week works for me. Let's plan for that.

B: Sounds good. I'll check my schedule and let you know.

A: 嘿，你今晚想一起吃晚饭吗？

B: 抱歉。我今晚去不了。能改天再约吗？

A: 当然可以。你什么时候方便？

B: 我这周真的很忙。下周怎么样？

A: 很好。下周我可以。我们计划一下吧。

B: 听起来不错。我先查一下我的日程安排，然后告诉你。

Scene 5 约会地点

A: Hey, where are you at?

B: I'm waiting at the entrance. Where are you?

A: I'm here, but I can't seem to find you. Where exactly are you standing?

B: I'm near the fountain, right next to the coffee shop.

A: Got it. I'm on my way over there.

B: Alright, see you in a bit!

A: 嘿，你在哪儿？

B: 我在入口处等着呢。你在哪儿？

A: 我在这里，但我好像找不到你。你到底站在哪儿呢？

B: 我在喷泉附近，就在咖啡店旁边。

A: 知道了。我现在就过去。

B: 好的，一会儿见!

Unit 8 Making Suggestions 提建议

Scene 1 不要在电梯里吸烟

A: Excuse me. Smoking is not allowed in the elevator.

B: Oh, sorry about that.

A: It's dangerous. Please don't do it again.

B: I understand. Thanks for reminding me.

A: No problem. Have a good day!

A: 打扰了，电梯里不允许吸烟。

B: 哦，抱歉。

A: 太危险了。请不要再这么做了。

B: 我知道了。谢谢你提醒我。

A: 不客气。祝你过得愉快!

☐ grab dinner 用餐

☐ make it 成功；及时赶上参加

☐ rain check 延期，改天

☐ fountain *n.* 喷泉

☐ allow *v.* 允许

Scene 2　不要大声喧哗

A: Hey, sorry to interrupt. Could you please lower your voice?

B: Oh, my bad. I didn't even realize I was being loud.

A: Yeah, we're in a library, and folks are trying to focus on their studies.

B: Ah, gotcha. I'll keep it down from now on.

A: Thanks for being understanding.

A：嘿，抱歉打断你。你能小声点吗？

B：哦，我的错。我没意识到我弄出的声响太大了。

A：嗯，我们是在图书馆里，大家都在专心学习。

B：好的，明白了。从现在开始我会小声点的。

A：谢谢你的理解。

Unit 9　Talking About Weather 谈论天气

Scene 1　希腊天气

A: Where do you come from?

B: I come from Greece.

A: What's the climate like in your country?

B: It's very pleasant.

A: What's the weather like in spring?

B: It's often windy in March. It's always warm in April and May, but it rains sometimes.

A: What's it like in summer?

B: It's always hot in June, July, and August. The sun shines every day.

A: Is it cold or warm in autumn?

B: It's always warm in September and October. It's often cold in November, and it rains sometimes.

A: Is it very cold in winter?

B: It's often cold in December, January, and February. It snows sometimes.

A：你来自哪里？

B：我来自希腊。

A：你们国家的气候怎么样？

B：非常宜人。

A：春天的天气怎么样？

B：三月经常刮风。四月和五月总是很暖和，但有时会下雨。

A：夏天怎么样？

B：六月、七月和八月总是很热。每天都阳光灿烂。

A：秋天的天气是冷还是暖？

B：九月和十月总是很暖和。十一月通常很冷，有时还会下雨。

A：冬天很冷吗？

B：十二月、一月和二月通常很冷。有时会下雪。

□ interrupt v. 打断

□ focus on 集中

□ climate n. 气候

□ pleasant adj. 愉快的，宜人的

Scene 2　英国天气

A: Where do you come from?

B: I come from England.

A: What's the climate like in your country?

B: It's mild. But it's not always pleasant. The weather's often cold in the North and windy in the East. It's often wet in the West and sometimes warm in the South.

A: Which seasons do you like best?

B: I like spring and summer. The days are long, and the nights are short. The sun rises early and sets late. I don't like autumn and winter. The days are short, and the nights are long. The sun rises late and sets early. Our climate is not very good, but it's certainly interesting. It's our favorite subject of scene.

A：你是哪里人？

B：我来自英国。

A：你们国家的气候怎么样？

B：很温和，但并不总是很宜人。北部时常很冷，东部经常刮风。西部时常潮湿，南部有时暖和。

A：你最喜欢哪个季节？

B：我喜欢春天和夏天。白天很长，夜晚很短。太阳升得早，落得晚。我不喜欢秋天和冬天。白天短，夜晚长。太阳升得晚而落得早。我们的气候不是很好，但确实很有趣。天气是我们最喜欢的话题。

社交生活

Scene 3　连续下雨

A: What a miserable day!

B: Yeah, it's been raining non-stop.

A: I can't believe how dark it is outside.

B: I know. It feels like it's already night-time.

A: I hope it stops soon.

B: Me too. I'm getting tired of the rain.

A：多么糟糕的一天啊！

B：是啊，雨一直下个不停。

A：我真不敢相信外面的天色这么暗。

B：是呀。感觉已经是晚上了。

A：我希望雨快点停。

B：我也是。我对雨天感到厌倦了。

Scene 4　各种雨天

A: What a drizzle today!

B: Yeah, but I love this misty rain.

A: I prefer a heavy rainstorm.

B: Oh, I hate being soaked!

A: How about a light rain?

B: That's fine. A romantic walk, maybe?

A：今天毛毛雨下了一天了！

B：是啊，但我喜欢这种蒙蒙细雨。

A：我更喜欢暴风雨。

B：哦，我讨厌浑身被淋湿！

A：小雨怎么样？

B：挺好的。也许可以来一次浪漫的雨中漫步？

☐ mild *adj.* 温和的

☐ subject *n.* 话题

☐ miserable *adj.* 糟糕的

☐ non-stop *adv.* 不停地

☐ drizzle *n.* 毛毛细雨

☐ rainstorm *n.* 暴风雨

Scene 5　天气放晴

A: Finally, the sun is out after days of rain!

B: Yeah, it's a perfect day to go out.

A: Do you have any plans for today?

B: Let's go for a hike or a picnic.

A: That sounds like a great idea!

A：下了几天雨后，太阳终于出来了！

B：是啊，今天是外出的好天气。

A：你今天有什么安排吗？

B：我们去远足或者野餐吧。

A：听起来是个好主意！

Scene 6　天冷添衣

A: It's getting cold. Do you need a jacket?

B: Yes. I forgot to bring one.

A: Here, take mine. It's warm.

B: Thanks, that's very kind of you.

A: No problem. We should stay warm in this weather.

B: Definitely. Thanks again for your help.

A：天变冷了。你需要夹克衫吗？

B：需要。我忘了带。

A：给你，穿我的吧。这件夹克衫很暖和。

B：谢谢，你真是太好了。

A：别客气。这种天气我们应该注意保暖。

B：没错。再次感谢你的帮助。

Scene 7　是否使用空调

A: It's so hot. Should we turn on the air conditioner?

B: But it's expensive. Maybe a fan is enough.

A: I don't know. I can't stand this heat.

B: Let's compromise and use the fan first.

A: Alright, but if it doesn't work, we'll have to use the air conditioner.

A：太热了。我们应该开空调吗？

B：但是开空调费用太高了。也许开电风扇就够了。

A：我不确定。我无法忍受这种炎热的天气。

B：我们折中一下，先用电风扇吧。

A：好吧，但如果还是很热，我们就得开空调。

Scene 8　春夏天气

A: Spring is my favorite season. What about you?

B: Me too. It's always sunny and warm.

A: And the flowers start to bloom.

B: Yeah, everything looks so colorful and alive.

A：春天是我最喜欢的季节。你呢？

B：我也是。春天天气总是晴朗而且温暖。

A：花儿也开始绽放了。

B：是啊，一切看起来都那么丰富多彩、生机勃勃。

重点词汇
及表达

☐ hike *n.* 远足，徒步旅行

☐ picnic *n.* 野餐

☐ No problem. 没问题。

☐ stand *v.* 忍受

☐ compromise *v.* 折中

☐ bloom *v.* 开花

☐ alive *adj.* 有生气的

A: Summer is nice too, but it can be too hot.

B: I agree. I prefer spring's mild weather.

A：夏天也很好，但是太热了。

B：没错。我更喜欢春天温和的天气。

Scene 9   秋冬天气

A: The weather is getting cooler. It feels like autumn.

B: Yeah, the leaves are changing color too.

A: I love the cool breeze and sweater weather.

B: Me too. But winter will be cold and snowy.

A: True, it's going to be tough to get out of bed.

B: We'll need extra layers and hot drinks.

A：天气越来越凉了。感觉像是秋天。

B：是啊，树叶也在变黄。

A：我喜欢凉爽的微风和穿毛衣的天气。

B：我也是。但是冬天会很冷，会下雪。

A：没错，起床会很困难。

B：我们需要多穿几件衣服，多喝热饮。

Scene 10   天气预报

A: Hello, this is Mia. Welcome to today's weather report. Let's look at today's weather. It's a sunny day today, with a slight chance of light rain in the late afternoon. The high of today will be 73 degrees, with a low of 33 degrees this evening. Tomorrow will be overcast, so be careful of UV rays. It's supposed to rain heavily this weekend. My name is Mia. See you tomorrow.

A：大家好，我是米娅。欢迎收听今天的天气预报。我们来看看今天的天气。今天是晴天，下午晚些时候可能会有小雨。今天最高气温是 73 华氏度，夜间最低气温是 33 华氏度。明天是阴天，所以要小心紫外线。这周末应该会下大雨。我是米娅。明天见。

社交生活

017

☐ breeze *n.* 微风

☐ tough *adj.* 困难的

☐ chance *n.* 机会

☐ overcast *adj.* 多云的

☐ UV ray 紫外线

Part 2
Technological Life
科技生活

Unit 1 Using a Smartphone 使用手机

Scene 1 开机与关机

A: Can you turn off your phone, please?   A：请问您能把手机关机吗？

B: Sure. Do you need it off for a while?   B：当然可以。是需要关机一段时间吗？

A: Yes, we're going into a meeting.   A：是的，我们要开会了。

B: Okay, I'll turn it off now.   B：好的，我现在就关机。

A: Thanks. And don't forget to turn it back on later.   A：谢谢。待会别忘了开机。

B: Got it.   B：明白。

Scene 2 接电话与打电话

A: The phone's ringing. Can you answer it?   A：电话响了。你能接听一下吗？

B: Sure, hello?   B：当然可以。喂？

A: Who's calling?   A：是谁打来的？

B: It's John from accounting.   B：是会计部的约翰。

A: Okay, I'll take it. Hand me the phone.   A：好的，我来接听。把电话给我。

B: Here you go.   B：给你。

Scene 3 挂电话与回拨

A: Can you hang up the phone?   A：你能挂断电话吗？

B: Sorry, I was on hold.   B：抱歉，我在等待接通。

A: It's been 10 minutes. Can you try calling back later?   A：你已经等了10分钟了。可以晚点再打回去吗？

B: Good idea. I'll try again tomorrow.   B：好的，我明天再试试。

A: Thanks. I need to make a call now.   A：谢谢。我现在需要打个电话。

B: Sure, I'll give you some privacy.   B：没问题，我会给你一些私人空间。

Scene 4 打错电话

A: Hello?   A：喂？

B: Hi, can I speak to John?   B：嗨，我可以和约翰讲话吗？

□ turn off 关掉

□ Got it. 明白了。

□ accounting *n.* 会计

□ privacy *n.* 隐私

020

全场景英语口语

A: Sorry, wrong number. Who are you trying to reach?

B: I'm looking for John. Is this not his number?

A: No, sorry. You must have dialed the wrong number.

B: Okay, my apologies. Have a good day.

A: No problem. You too, take care.

A：抱歉，你拨错电话号码了。你要找谁？

B：我找约翰。这不是他的电话号码吗？

A：抱歉，不是。你肯定拨错电话号码了。

B：哦，不好意思。祝你生活愉快!

A：没关系。你也是，保重。

Scene 5 转告电话信息

A: Hi, can I speak to John?

B: Sorry, he's not available right now. Can I take a message?

A: Yes, please tell him that Jane called.

B: Sure, I'll let him know. Is there anything else?

A: No, that's it. Thanks.

B: You're welcome. Have a good day.

A: You too. Goodbye.

A：嗨，我可以和约翰讲话吗？

B：抱歉，他现在没空。需要我帮你捎话吗？

A：需要，请转告他，简给他打过电话。

B：好的，我会告诉他的。还有别的事吗？

A：没有了，就这些。谢谢。

B：不客气。祝你过得愉快。

A：你也是。再见。

021

Scene 6 手机卡顿

A: My phone is so slow. It keeps freezing.

B: Have you tried clearing some space?

A: I have, but I don't know what else to do.

B: You could try deleting apps you don't use.

A: That's a good idea. Do you know any good storage apps?

B: I use one called CCleaner. It works pretty well.

A: Thanks. I'll give it a try.

A：我的手机太慢了，老是卡住不动。

B：你试过清理出一些储存空间吗？

A：试过，但我不知道还能做些什么。

B：你可以试试删除你不用的软件。

A：好主意。你知道有什么好用的存储空间管理软件吗？

B：我用的是 CCleaner。非常好用。

A：谢谢。我会试试。

☐ dial *v.* 拨号

☐ available *adj.* 有空的

☐ take a message 带个口信

☐ clear some space 清理空间

☐ delete *v.* 删除

☐ CCleaner 一款存储空间管理软件

Scene 7 检查网络连接

A: Hey, did you send me a message earlier?

B: Yeah, I did. Did you get it?

A: No, I haven't received anything.

B: That's weird. I'll send it again.

A: Okay, let me know if it goes through.

B: Sure thing. Did you check your connection?

A: Yeah, everything seems fine on my end.

B: Alright, let me try sending it again.

A：嘿，你之前给我发信息了吗？

B：发了，给你发过了。你收到了吗？

A：没有，我什么都没收到。

B：真奇怪。我再发一次。

A：行，如果发出了请告诉我。

B：好的。你检查过网络连接吗？

A：检查过，我这边看起来一切都很正常。

B：好的，我再试着发送一次。

Scene 8 没有信号

A: I'm not getting any signal on my phone.

B: Did you try turning it off and on again?

A: Yeah, still nothing.

B: You could try resetting your network settings.

A: How do I do that?

B: Go to Settings > General > Reset > Reset Network Settings.

A: Okay, I'll try that. Thanks for your help.

B: No problem. Let me know if that works.

A：我的手机没有信号。

B：你试过关机重启吗？

A：试过了，还是没有信号。

B：你可以尝试重置网络设置。

A：怎么操作呢？

B：进入"设置 > 常规 > 重置 > 重置网络设置"。

A：知道了，我试试。谢谢你的帮助。

B：不客气。如果成功了记得告诉我。

Scene 9 信号微弱

A: Hey, can you hear me?

B: Yeah, I can hear you, but the reception is really weak. Can you speak up a bit?

A: Sure, can you hear me now?

B: It's still a bit fuzzy.

A: Sorry about that. Is there a better spot for you to get a stronger signal?

B: Let me try moving around a bit. How about now? Is it any better?

A：嘿，你能听到我说话吗？

B：能，我能听到，但信号特别弱。你能大声点说吗？

A：好的，你现在能听到吗？

B：还是有点听不清。

A：抱歉，那你能找个信号更好的地方吗？

B：我试着换个位置。现在能听到吗？好点了吗？

022

重点词汇
及表达

□ send v. 发送

□ connection n. 连接

□ signal n. 信号

□ reset v. 重置

□ reception n. 接收效果

□ weak adj. 微弱的

A: Yeah, that sounds clearer. Maybe you should try going outside.

B: Good idea. Hang on a sec. (pauses) Can you hear me now?

A: Yes, that's much better. Thanks for trying.

B: No problem. Sorry about the weak reception earlier.

A: It's all good. So, what did you want to talk about?

A：嗯，听得清楚些了。也许你应该走到室外试试看。

B：好主意。等我一下。（停顿）你现在能听到我说话吗？

A：能，清楚多了。谢谢你的尝试。

B：不客气。之前的信号不好，抱歉。

A：没事。嗯，你想聊些什么呢？

Scene 10 手机话费

A: Hey, how's your phone bill this month?

B: Not bad, just $30.

A: Really? Mine was $60 last month.

B: Did you use a lot of data?

A: Yeah, I watched too many videos.

B: That can get expensive.

A：嘿，你这个月的话费多少？

B：还行，只有 30 美元。

A：是吗？我上个月的话费是 60 美元。

B：你使用了很多流量吗？

A：是的，我看了太多视频。

B：那样话费可能确实会很高。

Scene 11 流量套餐

A: I'm thinking about changing my data plan.

B: Do you need more or less data?

A: I'm not sure. I don't want to pay for more than I need.

B: You could check your usage in Settings > Cellular.

A: Good idea. How much data do you have?

B: I have 10 GB, but I hardly use all of it.

A: Okay, thanks for the advice. I'll check my usage.

A：我在考虑换一种流量套餐。

B：你需要更多还是更少的流量？

A：我不确定。流量够用就可以了。

B：你可以在"设置 > 蜂窝移动网络"中查看你的流量使用情况。

A：好主意。你有多少流量？

B：我有 10GB，但我很难用完这么多流量。

A：好的，谢谢你的建议。我会查一下我的流量使用情况。

□ bill *n.* 账单

□ data *n.* 数据，流量

□ cellular *n.* 蜂窝移动网络

Scene 12　屏幕损坏

A: Oh no, my screen is cracked.

B: That's too bad. Is it still functional?

A: It still works, but the cracks are getting worse.

B: You might want to take it to a repair shop.

A: Do you know any good ones?

B: There's a shop downtown that's pretty reputable.

A: Thanks. I'll check it out.

A：哦，天哪，我的手机屏幕裂了。

B：太糟糕了。它还能用吗？

A：还能用，但是裂痕越来越大了。

B：你最好把它拿到修理店去修理。

A：你知道有什么好的店吗？

B：市中心有一家声誉很好的修理店。

A：谢谢。我打算去看看。

Scene 13　沉迷手机

A: Hey, can you stop playing on your phone?

B: Sorry, I'm almost done.

A: You've been on it for an hour now.

B: I know. I just got caught up in something.

A: You should take a break. It's not good for your eyes.

B: You're right. I'll put it away for a bit.

A: Good idea. Let's do something else.

A：嘿，你能不能别玩手机了？

B：抱歉，我马上就好了。

A：你已经玩了一个小时。

B：我知道。我只是沉迷进去了。

A：你应该休息一下。玩手机对你的眼睛不好。

B：你说得对。我先把手机放一放。

A：好的。我们做点别的事情吧。

024

Unit 2　The Functions of a Smartphone 手机功能

Scene 1　手机密码

A: Do you use Face ID or Touch ID?

B: I use Face ID. What about you?

A: I prefer Touch ID. It's more reliable for me.

B: That's true, but I like the convenience of Face ID.

A: I also use a passcode, just in case.

B: Me too. You can never be too careful.

A：你用人脸识别还是指纹识别？

B：我用人脸识别。你呢？

A：我更喜欢用指纹识别。对我来说它更可靠。

B：没错，但我喜欢人脸识别的便捷性。

A：我也设置了密码，以防万一。

B：我也是。再怎么小心也不为过。

重点词汇
及表达

□ crack v. 破裂

□ functional adj. 工作的，运转的

□ take a break 休息

□ put away 放在一边

□ Face ID 人脸识别

□ Touch ID 指纹识别

□ reliable adj. 可靠的

Scene 2 接收与发送消息

A: Hey, did you receive my message?

B: Yeah, I did. Thanks.

A: Did you get the attachment as well?

B: Yes, it opened just fine.

A: Great. Just let me know if you need anything else.

B: Will do. Thanks again.

A：嘿，你收到我的信息了吗？

B：嗯，收到了。谢谢。

A：你也收到附件了吗？

B：收到了，打开之后没什么问题。

A：太好了。如果你还需要什么就告诉我。

B：好的。再次感谢。

Scene 3 调节音量

A: Can you turn up the volume?

B: Is that better?

A: A little more, please.

B: How about now?

A: Perfect, thanks. It was too low before.

B: No problem. Let me know if you need anything else.

A: Will do. Thanks again.

A：你能把音量调大吗？

B：这样好些了吗？

A：请再调大一点。

B：现在怎么样？

A：很好，谢谢。之前音量太小了。

B：不客气。如果你还需要什么，请告诉我。

A：好的。再次感谢。

Scene 4 静音与飞行模式

A: Can you put your phone on silent, please?

B: Sure, it's on silent now.

A: Thanks.

B: I usually forget to do that in meetings.

A: No problem. Have you tried the airplane mode?

B: Yeah, but it disconnects my Wi-Fi.

A: It's useful during flights, though.

B: Good point. I'll use it on my next trip.

A：你能把手机调成静音吗？

B：当然可以，现在是静音了。

A：谢谢。

B：开会的时候我经常忘记设置静音。

A：没关系。你试过飞行模式吗？

B：试过，但是它会断开我的网络连接。

A：不过它在乘坐飞机的时候很有用。

B：没错。下次旅行时我会设置成飞行模式。

025

科技生活

☐ message *n.* 信息

☐ attachment *n.* 附件

☐ turn up the volume 调大音量

☐ put...on silent 将……设置为静音

☐ mode *n.* 模式

Scene 5　询问时间

A: What time is it?

B: Let me check. It's 2:45 pm.

A: Thanks. I need to be somewhere at 3:00 pm.

B: Do you want me to set the alarm?

A: No, it's okay. I'll keep an eye on the time.

B: Alright. Let me know if you need anything else.

A: Will do. Thanks for checking the time.

A：现在几点了？

B：我看一下。下午 2 点 45 分。

A：谢谢。我下午 3 点得去个地方。

B：需要我定闹钟吗？

A：不用了。我会留意时间的。

B：好的。如果你还需要什么就告诉我。

A：好的。谢谢你帮我查看时间。

Scene 6　设定闹钟

A: Did you set your alarm?

B: Yeah, it's set for 6:30 am.

A: I always forget to set mine.

B: You can ask your phone's assistant to do it.

A: Really? I didn't know that.

B: Yeah, it's super helpful. Just say, "Set an alarm for 7:00 am."

A: Thanks for the tip. I'll try it tonight.

A：你定闹钟了吗？

B：定了，定在早晨 6 点 30 分。

A：我总是忘记定我的。

B：你可以让你的手机助手帮你定。

A：是吗？我不知道还有这个功能。

B：有的，这个功能非常好用。你只用说，"把闹钟定在早晨 7 点。"

A：谢谢你的建议。我今晚试试。

026

Scene 7　下载与上传

A: How's your Internet speed?

B: It's pretty fast. Why do you ask?

A: I need to download a large file, but my speed is slow.

B: You could try pausing any other downloads or uploads.

A: That's a good point. Should I also reset my modem?

B: That could help, but it might take a few minutes to reconnect.

A: Okay, thanks for the advice.

A：你的网速怎么样？

B：挺快的。你为什么问这个？

A：我需要下载一个大文件，但是我的网速很慢。

B：你可以试试暂停其他的下载或上传。

A：好主意。我也应该重置调制解调器吗？

B：这可能有帮助，但重新连接可能需要几分钟。

A：知道了，谢谢你的建议。

重点词汇
及表达

☐ somewhere *adv.* 在某处

☐ keep an eye on 留意

☐ super *adv.* 特别，格外

☐ download *v.* 下载

☐ file *n.* 文件

☐ upload *n.* 上传

Scene 8　拍照美颜

A: Could you take a picture of me?

B: Sure. Do you want it in landscape or portrait mode?

A: Landscape, please.

B: Okay. How about this?

A: Looks good! Can you add some filters?

B: Sure. Which one do you want?

A: How about the black and white one?

B: Great choice. Do you want me to smooth out your skin with the beauty filter?

A: Yes, please.

B: Alright, all set! Let's take a few more, just in case. By the way, did you know that the front camera is also very clear? You can easily take selfies with it.

A：你能帮我拍张照片吗?

B：没问题。你想要横屏模式还是竖屏模式的?

A：横屏模式的。

B：好的。这张怎么样?

A：看起来很不错!能加一些滤镜效果吗?

B：当然可以。你想要哪种?

A：黑白滤镜怎么样?

B：很不错。你想让我用美颜滤镜给你磨皮吗?

A：好呀。

B：好的，都弄好了!我们再拍几张，以防万一。对了，你知道吗?前置摄像头也很清晰。你用它自拍很方便。

Scene 9　发送照片

A: Can you send me that photo?

B: Sure. Do you want me to email it to you?

A: That works, or you can send it through social media.

B: Okay, which one do you prefer?

A: How about Instagram? I can add it to my collection.

B: Sounds good. I'll send it to you now.

A：你能把那张照片发给我吗?

B：当然可以。我通过电子邮件发送给你，可以吗?

A：可以，你也可以通过社交软件发送。

B：好的。你喜欢哪种方式?

A："照片墙"怎么样?我可以把它加入我的收藏夹。

B：好呀。我现在就发送给你。

Scene 10　截屏与录屏

A: Can you show me how to take a screenshot?

B: Sure, just press the power button and volume up button together.

A：你能教我怎么截屏吗?

B：当然可以，只要同时按下电源键和音量增大键就可以了。

☐ filter *n.* 滤镜

☐ take selfies 自拍

☐ social media 社交媒体

☐ collection *n.* 收藏

☐ screenshot *n.* 截屏

☐ power button 电源键

科技生活

A: Thanks. How about recording the screen?

B: You can add it to your control center and press the record button.

A: Awesome! I didn't know you could do that.

B: It's really useful for sharing moments with friends.

A: Definitely. I'll have to try it out.

A：谢谢。录屏怎么操作？

B：你可以把屏幕录制功能添加到控制中心，然后按录制键。

A：太棒了！我不知道还能这么操作。

B：在与朋友分享精彩时刻的时候，它真的很有用。

A：没错。我得试试。

Scene 11　手机投屏

A: Can you help me project my phone screen?

B: Sure. Do you have a TCL TV or Skyworth TV?

A: I have a TCL TV.

B: Great. Just swipe down and tap on "Screen Mirroring".

A: Okay, got it. Wow, this is so cool.

B: Yeah, it's a great way to share photos and videos.

A：你能帮我把手机投屏吗？

B：当然可以。你有 TCL 或创维品牌的电视吗？

A：我有一台 TCL 电视。

B：太好了。只需要向下滑动并点击"屏幕镜像"。

A：好的，知道了。哇，这太棒了。

B：是的，这是分享照片和视频的好方法。

Scene 12　蓝牙与隔空投送

A: Can you connect your bluetooth to the speaker?

B: Sure, let me try.

A: Got it. Can you play some music?

B: How about this song?

A: Nice! Have you tried AirDrop for file transfer?

B: Yeah, it's so convenient. I use it all the time.

A: Me too. It's amazing how fast it is.

A：你能把蓝牙连接到扬声器上吗？

B：当然，我试试。

A：好的。你能播放点音乐吗？

B：这首歌怎么样？

A：很不错！你试过隔空投送传输文件吗？

B：试过，非常方便。我一直在用。

A：我也在用。它的速度快得惊人。

Scene 13　手机地图

A: How do I get to the museum?

B: Use your phone's map app.

A：去博物馆怎么走？

B：你可以使用手机里的地图软件。

重点词汇及表达

☐ record the screen 录屏
☐ project v. 投射
☐ swipe down 下滑
☐ tap on 点击

☐ bluetooth n. 蓝牙
☐ transfer n. 传输

A: I'm not good at using it.

B: Type in the museum's address.

A: Got it. Is it far?

B: Not too far, about a 10-minute walk.

A: 我不太会用。

B: 输入博物馆的地址就可以了。

A: 好的。离这里远吗？

B: 不是很远，步行大约 10 分钟。

Scene 14　手机购物

A: Have you ever shopped on your phone?

B: Yes, I use it all the time.

A: What's your favorite app or website?

B: I like using Taobao, but sometimes I check out other sites too.

A: I'll have to try it. Is it easy to use?

B: Very user-friendly. You should give it a shot.

A: 你在手机上购过物吗？

B: 购过，我一直都在手机上购物。

A: 你最喜欢的购物软件或者网站是什么？

B: 我喜欢用淘宝，但有时我也会去其他网站看看。

A: 我一定要试试。它用起来简单吗？

B: 非常好用。你应该试试。

Scene 15　手机扫码

A: Hey, can I add you on social media?

B: Sure. What's your username?

A: It's hard to spell. Can I just scan your code?

B: Yeah, let me pull it up for you.

A: Got it, thanks! I'll add you now.

B: Sounds good. I'll accept it right away.

A: 嘿，我能添加你的社交媒体账号吗？

B: 当然可以。你的用户名是什么？

A: 我的用户名很难拼写。我可以就扫描一下你的二维码吗？

B: 可以，我给你打开。

A: 好的，谢谢！我现在加你。

B: 没问题。我马上就接受。

Scene 16　手机支付

A: Hey, do you have cash for the movie tickets?

B: No, I don't. Can I pay you through my phone?

A: Sure. What app do you use?

B: WeChat Pay or Alipay, which one do you prefer?

A: WeChat Pay works for me.

A: 嘿，你有现金买电影票吗？

B: 没有。我可以用手机付款给你吗？

A: 当然可以。你用什么支付？

B: 微信支付或支付宝，你喜欢哪一种？

A: 微信支付。

☐ type v. 打字

☐ address n. 地址

☐ website n. 网站

☐ user-friendly adj. 用户界面友好的

☐ give it a shot 尝试一下

☐ username n. 用户名

☐ code n. 代码

☐ prefer v. 更喜欢

Scene 17　手机转账

A: Hey, can I borrow some money?

B: Sure, how much?

A: $50. Can you transfer it to me?

B: Yeah, sure. What's your bank account info?

A: Let me check my phone. It's 123456789.

B: Got it; just sent the money.

A: Thanks. Got it!

A：嘿，我能找你借点钱吗？

B：当然可以。你要借多少钱？

A：50美元。你可以转给我吗？

B：当然可以。你的银行账户信息是什么？

A：我在手机上查一下。我的账号是123456789。

B：知道了。我把钱转过去了。

A：谢谢。收到了！

Scene 18　手机电影

A: Want to watch a movie tonight?

B: Sure, what do you have in mind?

A: I have a few on my phone.

B: Can we connect to the TV?

A: Yeah, let me grab my HDMI cable.

B: Awesome. Let's get cozy and watch!

A：今晚想看电影吗？

B：当然想。你有什么想法？

A：我的手机里有几部电影。

B：我们能连接上电视吗？

A：能，我拿一下HDMI高清连接线。

B：太棒了！我们舒舒服服地看吧！

030

Scene 19　刷短视频

A: Have you heard of TikTok?

B: Yeah, it's a short-video app.

A: I'm addicted to it.

B: Me too. Can't stop swiping.

A: It's like a black hole.

B: I know. I lose track of time.

A: Let's set a timer for ourselves next time.

A：你听说过抖音吗？

B：当然听说过，它是一款短视频软件。

A：我玩抖音上瘾了。

B：我也是。刷短视频刷得停不下来。

A：它就像一个黑洞。

B：是呀，刷着刷着就忘了时间。

A：下次我们给自己计时吧。

重点词汇
及表达

□ transfer v. 转账

□ bank account 银行账户

□ connect v. 连接

□ HDMI（High Definition Multimedia Interface）高清多媒体接口

□ cozy adj. 舒适的

□ short-video n. 短视频

□ be addicted to 对……上瘾

□ swipe v. 刷

□ black hole 黑洞

Scene 20　手机直播

A: Have you seen the live stream for the music festival?

B: No, not yet. Where can I find it?

A: You can download the app "MusicFest Live" and watch it there.

B: Thanks. I'll check it out.

A: It's really cool. You can even interact with the artists during the show.

B: That sounds amazing! I can't wait to watch it.

A: Yeah, let's plan a virtual watch party with our friends.

B: Great idea, I'll invite them all. Thanks for telling me about it.

A：你看音乐节的直播了吗?

B：还没呢。我在哪儿可以看?

A：你可以下载一款名为"音乐节直播"的软件，然后在那上面看。

B：谢谢。我会去看看。

A：真的很酷。你甚至可以在演出期间与艺术家互动。

B：听起来太棒了!我等不及要看了。

A：哦，我们和朋友们一起计划一次虚拟观影派对吧。

B：好主意，我会邀请他们所有人。谢谢你告诉我。

Scene 21　手机备份

A: Hey, you got a new phone! Did you back up your old one?

B: Yeah, I did. Everything transferred smoothly.

A: Good job. I always forget to do it.

B: It's important. I don't want to lose anything.

A: Agreed. How did you back it up?

B: I used the cloud. It's so convenient.

A：嘿，你有新手机了!你把旧手机上的内容备份了吗?

B：嗯，我备份了。全部内容都转存得很顺利。

A：很好。我总是忘记备份。

B：备份很重要。我不想丢失任何东西。

A：没错。你是怎么备份的?

B：我使用云盘备份。特别方便。

Scene 22　放大与缩小

A: Wow, this photo looks amazing! How did you take it?

B: Thanks! I used my new phone. You can zoom in and out with just a pinch.

A: That's so cool. Can you show me?

A：哇，这张照片看起来棒极了!你是怎么拍的?

B：谢谢!我用我的新手机拍的。你只需用手指捏一捏，就能放大和缩小。

A：太棒了。你能给我演示一下吗?

□ live stream 直播

□ virtual *adj.* 虚拟的

□ back up 备份

□ cloud *n.* 云盘

□ zoom in and out
　放大和缩小

031

科技生活

B: Sure. Let me find the photo. Here it is. See, you can pinch to zoom in like this.

A: Wow, that's incredible. I need to get a new phone with this feature.

B: Definitely! It's so much easier to get a good shot with the right tools.

A: Thanks for showing me. I can't wait to try it out myself.

B：当然可以。我找找照片。找到了。看，你可以像这样捏一捏来放大。

A：哇，太不可思议了。我需要买一部具有这种功能的新手机。

B：当然！有了合适的工具，拍一张好照片就简单多了。

A：谢谢你展示给我看。我迫不及待要自己试试了。

Scene 23　复制粘贴

A: Hey, check out this cool article I found online.

B: Sure. Can you send me the link?

A: Sure, let me copy and paste it for you.

B: Thanks. Got it!

A: No problem. It's a really interesting read.

B: I'll check it out. Thanks for sharing.

A：嘿，看看我在网上找到的这篇特别棒的文章。

B：好啊。你能把链接发给我吗？

A：当然可以，我复制粘贴给你。

B：谢谢。收到了！

A：不客气。这篇文章读起来很有趣。

B：我要读一下。谢谢分享！

Scene 24　撤回消息

A: Oops, I sent the wrong message!

B: What did you say?

A: Can you please ignore it?

B: Sure, I won't say anything.

A: Actually, I think I can recall it.

B: How do you do that?

A: I just need to tap on the message and choose "Recall".

B: Oh, cool. It disappeared.

A：哎呀，我发错信息了！

B：你发了些什么？

A：你能忽略它吗？

B：当然，我什么都不会说的。

A：事实上，我想我能撤回信息。

B：你怎么撤回？

A：我只需要点击信息，然后选择"撤回"。

B：哦，太好了。信息消失了。

Scene 25　添加书签

A: Hey, what are you reading on your phone?

A：嘿，你在手机上看什么呢？

032

重点词汇
及表达

☐ feature *n.* 功能

☐ link *n.* 链接

☐ copy and paste 复制粘贴

☐ share *v.* 分享

☐ ignore *v.* 忽略

☐ recall *v.* 撤回

B: Just an interesting article. Want me to send it to you?

A: Sure, thanks! Can you also teach me how to bookmark it?

B: No problem. Just tap the star icon, and it'll be saved in your bookmarks.

A: Great, that's so helpful. I always forget how to do it.

B: It's a useful feature, especially for saving important messages too.

A: Oh yeah, I should try that. Thanks again!

B：一篇有趣的文章。想要我发给你吗？

A：当然，谢谢！你能教我如何把它添加在书签里吗？

B：没问题。只要点击星号图标，就能把它保存在你的书签里。

A：太好了，这太好用了。我总是忘记怎么做。

B：这是一项很有用的功能，保存重要信息时尤其好用。

A：嗯，是的，我应该试试。再次感谢！

Scene 26 使用扬声器

A: Wow, your new phone has great sound quality!

B: Yeah, the built-in speakers are amazing.

A: Do you use the phone's speaker when making calls?

B: Sometimes, but I prefer using earphones.

A: I get it. I don't like holding my phone to my ear, either.

B: Plus, using the speaker in public can be disruptive.

A: Good point, but it's nice to have the option.

A：哇，你的新手机音质真好！

B：是的，内置扬声器很棒。

A：你打电话的时候使用手机扬声器吗？

B：有时候用，但我更喜欢使用耳机。

A：理解。我也不喜欢把手机放在耳边。

B：另外，在公共场合使用扬声器可能会打扰别人。

A：没错，但有这个选择也挺好。

Scene 27 共享位置

A: Hey, where are you? Can't find you!

B: I'm at the coffee shop.

A: Which one? I don't see you.

B: Hang on. Let me send my location.

A: Oh, there you are! Thanks!

B: No problem. Next time wear your glasses.

A：嘿，你在哪儿？我找不到你！

B：我在咖啡店。

A：哪家咖啡店？我没看见你。

B：稍等。我发送一下我的位置。

A：哦，看到你了！谢谢！

B：不客气。你下次戴好眼镜。

▢ bookmark v. 添加书签

▢ star icon 星号图标

▢ built-in speaker 内置扬声器

▢ disruptive adj. 破坏的，扰乱的

▢ hang on 稍等

▢ location n. 位置，定位

Scene 28　发送定位

A: Hey, where are you? I can't find you.

B: I'm at the park.

A: Could you share your location with me?

B: Sure thing. I'll send it over.

A: Thanks! You're a lifesaver.

B: No problem. Always here to help.

A：嘿，你在哪儿？我找不到你。

B：我在公园里。

A：你能把你的位置共享给我吗？

B：当然可以。我把定位发给你。

A：谢谢。你是我的救星。

B：不客气。我随时乐意帮忙。

Unit 3　Mobile Phone Accessories 手机配件

Scene 1　手机壳

A: Nice phone case!

B: Thanks! It's durable, just like my phone.

A: Ha! Have you ever dropped it?

B: Yeah, but I've got a screen protector too.

A: Looks like you've got it covered.

B: Yeah, I'm not taking any chances.

A: I can't blame you. Phone repairs are expensive.

A：这个手机壳真不错！

B：谢谢！它很耐用，就像我的手机一样。

A：哈！你的手机摔过吗？

B：摔过，但是我的手机也贴了屏幕保护膜。

A：看来你都做好防护了。

B：是的，我可不想冒任何风险。

A：这不能怪你。修手机费用很高。

034

Scene 2　手机支架

A: Hey, do you know what I got for my birthday?

B: No. What did you get?

A: A phone stand for my car!

B: Oh wow, that's a game-changer!

A: Yeah, no more dropping my phone while driving.

B: And no more buying new phone screens!

A: True. Best birthday gift ever.

A：嘿，你知道我收到了什么样的生日礼物吗？

B：不知道。你收到什么了？

A：车载手机支架！

B：哦，哇，那真是个超级棒的礼物！

A：是的，开车的时候手机再也不会掉了。

B：也不用再换新的手机屏幕了！

A：没错。这真是最棒的生日礼物。

重点词汇
及表达

☐ share one's location 共享定位

☐ lifesaver *n.* 救星

☐ phone case 手机壳

☐ screen protector 屏幕保护膜

☐ take any chances 冒险

☐ phone stand 手机支架

☐ phone screen 手机屏幕

B: I'll remember that for next year.

B: 明年我会记住这个的。

Scene 3　移动充电器

A: My phone's almost dead.

A: 我的手机快没电了。

B: Use my portable charger.

B: 你可以用我的移动充电器。

A: Thanks! How long does it last?

A: 谢谢! 它可以充多久?

B: Around 2-3 full charges.

B: 大约可以充 2~3 次。

A: That's impressive. I need one of these.

A: 太棒了! 我需要一个这样的充电器。

B: Yeah, they're a lifesaver on-the-go.

B: 是的，它们就是旅途中的救星。

A: I'll definitely buy one soon.

A: 我肯定不久之后也会买一个。

Scene 4　共享充电宝

A: Oh, my god, my phone died.

A: 哦，天哪，我的手机没电了。

B: Do you have a charger?

B: 你有充电器吗?

A: I forgot it at home. It's completely out of power.

A: 我把它忘在家里了。我的手机完全没电了。

B: Do you have a power bank or a spare battery?

B: 你有充电宝或备用电池吗?

A: No, I don't have those either. I should have been more prepared.

A: 没有，这两样都没有。我应该做好准备的。

B: Don't worry. We can find a charger (shared power bank) somewhere.

B: 别担心。我们应该可以在什么地方找到充电器 (共享充电宝)。

Scene 5　充电器与插座

A: Can I borrow your charger?

A: 我能借用一下你的充电器吗?

B: Sure, here you go.

B: 当然可以，给你。

A: Do you have a wall socket?

A: 墙上有插座吗?

B: Yeah, it's over there.

B: 有，就在那边。

A: Thanks. I always forget to charge my phone.

A: 谢谢。我老是忘了给手机充电。

B: A portable charger might be useful too.

B: 也许你也用得上移动充电器。

A: Good idea. I'll have to get one soon.

A: 好主意。我得尽快买一个。

035

- ☐ dead *adj.* 没电的
- ☐ portable charger 移动充电器
- ☐ on-the-go 在旅途中
- ☐ die *v.* 电量耗尽

- ☐ out of power 没电
- ☐ power bank 充电宝
- ☐ spare battery 备用电池
- ☐ socket *n.* 插座

- ☐ portable *adj.*
  可移动的，便携式的

Unit 4 Using a Computer 电脑操作

Scene 1　电脑开机

A: Good morning! Ready to start the day?

B: Yep, I just need to turn on my computer.

A: Me too. I love the sound it makes when it starts up.

B: Yeah, it's like music to my ears.

(Computer chimes)

A: Ah, there it is. Let's get to work!

A：早上好！准备好开始新的一天了吗？

B：准备好了，我只需要打开我的电脑。

A：我也是。我喜欢电脑启动时发出的声音。

B：是啊，这对我来说就像音乐。

（电脑开机声）

A：啊，打开了。我们开始工作吧！

Scene 2　重启电脑

A: Ugh, my computer crashed. Can you help me?

B: Sure. Did you try restarting it?

A: No, how do I do that?

B: Just hold down the power button for a few seconds.

(Computer restarts)

A: Hey, it worked! Thanks for your help.

B: No problem. Glad I could assist.

A：啊，我的电脑死机了。你能帮帮我吗？

B：当然。你试过重启吗？

A：没有，怎么重启？

B：只需要长按电源键几秒钟。

（电脑重启）

A：嘿，正常运行了！谢谢你的帮助。

B：不客气。很高兴能帮上忙。

Scene 3　电脑关机

A: Hey, it's getting late. Time to shut down.

B: Yeah, let me save my work first.

A: Okay, I'll go grab a drink.

(5 minutes later)

A: You done yet?

B: Just a sec...okay, all set!

A: Great, let's shut it down and call it a night.

A：嘿，时间不早了。该关电脑收工了。

B：好的，我先保存一下我的工作内容。

A：好的，我去拿点喝的。

（5分钟后）

A：你弄完了吗？

B：等一下……好了，都完成了！

A：太好了，我们关电脑收工吧。

重点词汇
及表达

☐ turn on 打开

☐ start up 启动

☐ restart v. 重启

☐ assist v. 帮忙

☐ shut down 停工

☐ call it a night 到此为止

036

Scene 4 鼠标操作

A: How do I select the file?

B: Click the file with the left mouse button.

A: And how do I open it?

B: Double-click it with the left mouse button.

A: How about renaming it?

B: Right-click the file and select "Rename".

A：我应该怎样选择文件?

B：用鼠标左键点击文件。

A：怎样打开呢?

B：双击鼠标左键。

A：怎么给它重命名?

B：右键单击文件，选择"重命名"。

Scene 5 清理电脑桌面

A: Your desktop looks so organized. How do you do it?

B: It's easy. Just create folders for different categories.

A: Hmm, I should try that. Mine's a mess.

B: You can do it! Start by deleting what you don't need.

A: Okay, I'm going to give it a go.

(15 minutes later)

A: Wow, what a difference! Thanks for the tip.

B: No problem. Happy to help.

A：你的桌面看起来很整洁。你是怎么做到的?

B：这很容易。分类创建文件夹就行了。

A：嗯，我应该试试。我的桌面简直一团糟。

B：你也能让桌面变整洁! 从删除你不需要的文件开始。

A：好的，我试试。

(15分钟后)

A：哇，很不一样了! 谢谢你的小窍门。

B：不客气。我很乐意帮忙。

037

Unit 5 Computer Configuration 电脑配置

Scene 1 电脑配置

A: Hey, nice setup! What are your specs?

B: Thanks! Just a basic build. How about you?

A: I went all out on my rig. Top-tier specs.

B: Wow, that must be awesome for gaming.

A：嘿，装配得不错! 你的电脑配置是怎样的?

B：谢谢! 只是基本的配置。你的呢?

A：我在配置上全力以赴。顶级配置。

B：哇，打游戏一定很棒。

☐ file *n.* 文件

☐ click *v.* 点击

☐ rename *v.* 重命名

☐ desktop *n.* 桌面

☐ folder *n.* 文件夹

☐ give it a go 尝试一下

☐ setup *n.* 安装

☐ go all out on one's rig 全力以赴

☐ top-tier *adj.*
    顶级的；质量最好的

A: It is. Worth the investment.

B: Maybe I should upgrade my setup sometime.

A: Definitely worth considering.

A：是的。值得投资。

B：也许改天我应该升级一下我的设备。

A：绝对值得考虑。

Scene 2 电脑浏览器

A: This website won't load. Should I refresh?

B: Yeah, try it. Hit F5 or click the refresh button.

(Chrome browser refreshes)

A: It's still not working. What's the website?

B: It's *www.example.com.* Let me try in Firefox.

(Opens Firefox browser)

B: Hmm, it's working here. Maybe it's a Chrome issue.

A: Okay, I'll switch to Firefox. Thanks for your help!

A：这个网站无法加载。我要刷新一下吗？

B：是的，试试看。按 F5 键或者单击刷新按钮。

（刷新谷歌浏览器）

A：还是不行。网址是什么？

B：是 www.example.com. 我用火狐浏览器试试。

（打开火狐浏览器）

B：嗯，这个浏览器能加载。也许是谷歌浏览器的问题。

A：好的，我换成火狐浏览器。谢谢你的帮助！

038

Scene 3 显示器和主机

A: I'm having trouble connecting my monitor to my computer.

B: Did you make sure the cable is plugged in properly?

A: Yes, but the screen is still black.

B: Is the computer turned on?

A: Oh...I forgot to turn it on.

B: Try turning it on now and see if it works.

A: It's working now. Thank you!

A：我的显示器和电脑连接有问题。

B：你确定电源线接好了吗？

A：接好了，但屏幕还是黑的。

B：电脑开机了吗？

A：哦……我忘了开机。

B：现在试着开机，看看能不能运行。

A：现在可以了。谢谢你！

Scene 4 键盘和鼠标

A: I hate using this keyboard. It's so loud!

A：我讨厌使用这个键盘。声音太大了！

□ upgrade *v.* 升级

□ refresh *v.* 刷新

□ browser *n.* 浏览器

□ monitor *n.* 显示器

□ cable *n.* 电源线

□ keyboard *n.* 键盘

B: Want to switch to a quieter one?

A: That would be great. Do you have an extra?

B: Sure, and I also have a wireless mouse.

A: Awesome! Let's make the switch.

(10 minutes later)

B: Much better, right?

A: Absolutely. Thanks for the upgrade!

Scene 5 网络和路由器

A: Why is the Internet so slow today?

B: Maybe the router needs to be reset. Have you tried that?

A: No. How do I do it?

B: Just unplug it for 10 seconds and plug it back in.

A: Okay, let me try that.

(After resetting)

A: Wow, it's so much faster now! Thanks!

B: No problem. Glad it worked.

B: 要换一个声音小点的吗？

A: 那就太好了。你有多余的吗？

B: 有，而且我还有一个无线鼠标。

A: 太棒了！我们换一下吧。

（10分钟后）

B: 好多了，对吧？

A: 没错。谢谢你帮我升级！

A: 今天网速为什么这么慢？

B: 也许路由器需要重置。你试过重置吗？

A: 没试过。我该怎么做？

B: 拔掉电源插头10秒钟，然后再插回去。

A: 好的，我试试。

（调整后）

A: 哇，现在快多了！谢谢！

B: 不客气。很高兴重置路由器有用。

科技生活

Unit 6 Computer Types 电脑类型

Scene 1 笔记本电脑和台式机

A: What kind of computer do you have?

B: I have a laptop and a desktop.

A: Which one do you use more often?

B: I use my laptop for work and my desktop for gaming.

A: That makes sense. Do you prefer the keyboard on one over the other?

A: 你用什么样的电脑？

B: 我有一台笔记本电脑和一台台式机。

A: 你更常用哪一台？

B: 我用笔记本电脑工作，用台式机玩游戏。

A: 很合理。你更喜欢哪台电脑的键盘？

☐ wireless mouse 无线鼠标 ☐ unplug v. 拔掉电源插头 ☐ desktop n. 台式机

☐ upgrade n. 升级 ☐ plug v. 插上电源插头 ☐ make sense 有道理

☐ router n. 路由器 ☐ laptop n. 笔记本电脑

B: I prefer my laptop's keyboard for typing.

A: Got it. Do you have a favorite brand?

B: I like Huawei for laptops and Shenzhou for desktops.

B：我更喜欢用笔记本电脑的键盘打字。

A：明白了。你有最喜欢的品牌吗？

B：我喜欢华为笔记本电脑和神舟台式机。

Scene 2 平板电脑

A: Have you seen my new tablet?

B: No, let me see it.

A: Here it is. It's so thin and light.

B: Wow, it's really nice.

A: And the screen is so clear.

B: How long does the battery last?

A: About 10 hours.

A：你看过我的新平板电脑吗？

B：没有。让我看看。

A：给你。它又薄又轻。

B：哇，真漂亮。

A：屏幕也很清晰。

B：电池能用多久？

A：大约 10 个小时。

知识拓展

电脑按键

☐ Control key 控制键

☐ Alt key 替换键

☐ Caps Lock key 大写锁定键

☐ Enter key 回车键

☐ Delete key 删除键

☐ Home key 主页键

☐ Page Up key 向上翻页键

☐ Arrow keys 方向键

☐ Function keys 功能键

☐ Scroll Lock key 滚动锁定键

☐ Shift key 切换键

☐ Tab key 制表键

☐ Esc key 退出键

☐ Backspace key 退格键

☐ Insert key 插入键

☐ End key 结束键

☐ Page Down key 向下翻页键

☐ Windows key 视窗键

☐ Print Screen key 打印屏幕键

☐ Pause/Break key 暂停/中断键

重点词汇
及表达

☐ tablet *n.* 平板电脑

☐ battery *n.* 电池

常见软件及程序名称

- Windows Explorer Windows 资源管理器
- Internet Explorer IE 浏览器
- Microsoft Edge 微软浏览器
- Windows Media Player Windows 媒体播放器
- Windows Photo Viewer Windows 照片查看器
- Windows Live Mail Windows 邮件
- Microsoft Office 微软办公软件（包括 Word，Excel，PowerPoint 等）
- Microsoft OneNote 微软笔记软件
- Windows Defender Windows 防病毒软件
- Windows Update Windows 系统更新程序
- Windows Remote Desktop Connection Windows 远程桌面连接
- Snipping Tool 截图工具
- Paint 画图工具
- Notepad 记事本程序
- Command Prompt 命令提示符
- Task Manager 任务管理器
- Control Panel 控制面板
- Device Manager 设备管理器
- Disk Cleanup 磁盘清理
- Disk Defragmenter 磁盘碎片整理程序

Part 3　Working Life

职场生活

# Unit 1 Interviews 面试

Scene 1 面试自我介绍

A: Tell me about yourself.

B: Hello, my name is Judy, and I have five years of experience in sales. I'm hard-working and passionate about sales. During my career, I have repeatedly exceeded my targets. Besides, I have helped my team members achieve their goals. As a result, I'm confident that I can be a great fit for this sales position.

A：请介绍一下你自己。

B：您好，我叫朱迪，我有五年的销售经验。我工作努力，对销售充满热情。在我的职业生涯中，我多次超额完成目标。此外，我帮助我的团队成员实现了他们的目标。因此，我相信我非常适合这个销售岗位。

Scene 2 雇用理由

A: Why should we hire you?

B: Well, first, I have the skills and experience needed for this job. Besides, I'm a hard worker and a quick learner, and I'm always willing to go the extra mile. I'm passionate about this industry, and I'm committed to achieving success. I believe I can contribute to your team and help the company grow.

A：我们为什么要雇用你？

B：嗯，首先，我有这份工作所需要的技能和经验。此外，我工作努力、学习能力强，总是愿意付出额外的努力。我对这个行业充满热情，我致力于取得成功。我相信我能为贵公司的团队做出贡献，为公司的发展助力。

Scene 3 个人优点

A: What is your greatest strength?

B: I'm a skilled salesperson with over ten years' experience. I've exceeded my sales goals every quarter by at least 20%, and I've earned a bonus each year since I started with my current employer.

A：你最大的优点是什么？

B：我是一名熟练的销售人员，有着十多年的工作经验。我每个季度都至少超额完成销售目标的20%，而且自从我入职现在的公司以来，我每年都拿到了奖金。

重点词汇
及表达

- passionate *adj.* 热情的
- target *n.* 目标
- achieve one's goal 实现某人的目标
- be committed to (sth/doing sth) 致力于（某事／做某事）
- contribute to 对……做贡献
- strength *n.* 优势
- exceed *v.* 超出
- bonus *n.* 奖金

044

Scene 4　个人弱点

A: What is your greatest weakness?

B: Being organized wasn't always my strongest skill, but I found a way to improve. I started using a time management system that helped me better manage my workload. Now I'm much more organized. I feel much more confident in my ability to prioritize my work effectively.

A：你最大的弱点是什么？

B：我做事不太有条理，但我找到了改进的方法。我开始使用时间管理系统来帮助我更好地管理我的工作量。现在我更有条理了。我对自己有效划分工作优先级的能力更有信心了。

Scene 5　工资期望

A: What are your salary expectations?

B: I'm open to discussing what you believe to be a fair salary for the position. But based on my previous salary and my knowledge of the industry, I would expect a salary in the range of 13,000 to 15,000. Again, I'm open to discussing it with you.

A：你期望的薪资是多少？

B：我愿意和您讨论您觉得这个职位适合的薪资。但根据我之前的工资和我对该行业的了解，我期望工资在13000至15000元之间。我愿意再次与您讨论这个问题。

045

Scene 6　职业规划和期望

A: What are your career plans and expectations?

B: I love sales. So, I wanna stay in sales for the foreseeable future. My goal is to become a leading sales manager and be recognized as a product expert in this industry.

A：你的职业规划和期望是什么？

B：我喜欢销售。所以，我想在可预见的未来继续从事销售。我的目标是成为一名优秀的销售经理，成为业界公认的产品专家。

Scene 7　选择理由

A: Why do you wanna work here?

B: I want to work here because I believe that this company shares my values and goals. I'm impressed with the work that this company is doing, and I feel that I can make a meaningful contribution to the team. I'm also excited about the potential for growth and learning opportunities within this team.

A：你为何选择在这里工作？

B：我想在这里工作，因为我相信这家公司和我有着共同的价值观和目标。贵公司的工作给我留下了深刻的印象，我觉得我能对团队做出有意义的贡献。这个团队的成长潜力和学习机会也让我感到兴奋。

职场生活

☐ weakness *n.* 弱点

☐ workload *n.* 工作量

☐ prioritize *v.* 划分优先顺序

☐ salary expectation 薪资期望

☐ range *n.* 范围

☐ career plan 职业规划

☐ foreseeable *adj.* 可预见的

☐ value *n.* 价值，价值观

☐ goal *n.* 目标

☐ potential *n.* 潜力

Scene 8　如何应对压力

A: How do you handle stress and pressure?

B: I'm not a person who has a difficult time with stress. When I'm under pressure, I focus and get the job done. From a personal perspective, I manage stress by visiting the gym very often. It's a great stress reducer.

A：你是如何处理压力的？

B：我不是一个容易被压力困扰的人。当我有压力时，我会集中精力完成工作。就个人而言，我经常去健身房缓解压力。这是一种很好的减压方式。

Scene 9　为何换工作

A: Why did you leave your previous job?

B: I left my previous job because of family reasons. To be specific, my children needed to attend school in this area, so I needed to relocate. While I enjoyed working at my previous job, family comes first, and I'm excited to find a new opportunity in this area.

A：你为什么辞去之前的工作？

B：出于家庭原因，我辞去了上一份工作。具体来说，我的孩子需要在这个地区上学，所以我需要搬家。虽然我喜欢上一份工作，但家庭是第一位的，我很期待能在这个地区找到一个新的机会。

046

Unit 2　A Business Trip 出差

Scene 1　出差安排

A: When and where is the business trip?

B: Next Monday to Wednesday in London.

A: Who will be attending?

B: You, me, and the CEO.

A: Great，let's make sure we have everything planned.

B: Agreed. I'll send over the details for the trip.

A：你什么时候去出差？去哪儿？

B：下周一到周三在伦敦。

A：哪些人去？

B：你，我，还有总裁。

A：好的，我们要确保规划好一切。

B：是的。我会把此次行程的细节发给你。

重点词汇
及表达

- □ stress *n.* 压力
- □ pressure *n.* 压力
- □ from a personal perspective
  从个人角度来看
- □ previous *adj.* 之前的
- □ relocate *v.* 搬家
- □ business trip 出差
- □ detail *n.* 细节

Scene 2 注意事项

A: Do you have any tips for when we arrive at our destination?

A: 到达目的地后，你有什么建议吗？

B: Make sure to have your important documents on hand.

B: 一定要把重要的文件放在手边。

A: What about local customs or etiquette?

A: 那么当地的风俗和礼仪呢？

B: It's always best to research those beforehand.

B: 最好事先研究一下。

A: Do we need to be aware of any safety concerns?

A: 我们需要注意安全问题吗？

B: Yes, pay attention to any warnings from the hotel or locals.

B: 需要，要注意酒店或当地人的警告。

A: Thanks for the advice. I'll keep it in mind.

A: 谢谢你的建议。我会记住的。

Scene 3 费用报销

A: What documents do I need for expense reimbursement?

A: 报销费用时需要什么文件？

B: You'll need receipts and a completed expense report.

B: 需要收据和一份完整的费用报告。

A: When is the deadline for submission?

A: 提交文件的截止日期是什么时候？

B: Expenses must be submitted within 30 days of the trip.

B: 费用报告必须在出差后的 30 天内提交。

A: Can I submit the expenses online?

A: 我可以在网上提交吗？

B: Yes, you can submit them through the company's online portal.

B: 可以。你可以通过公司的在线门户网站提交。

047

职场生活

Unit 3 Resignation 辞职

Scene 1 提出辞职

A: Hey, Boss, can I talk to you for a moment?

A: 嘿，老板，我能和您谈谈吗？

B: Sure. What's on your mind?

B: 当然可以。你想谈什么？

☐ destination *n.* 目的地

☐ on hand 在手边

☐ beforehand *adv.* 提前

☐ expense reimbursement 费用报销

☐ deadline *n.* 截止日期

☐ submission *n.* 提交

☐ portal *n.* 门户网站

A: So, I don't know if you know this, but I recently had a baby.

B: Wow, congratulations! That's great news.

A: Thanks, I'm really excited. But I've been thinking about it a lot. And I've decided that I want to focus on my family more and resign from my position here.

B: I understand. When do you plan on leaving?

A: I'm thinking in about a month or so.

B: Okay. We'll miss you, but family comes first, and I support your decision. Let's discuss a smooth transition.

A: 嗯，我不知道您是否知道，我的孩子最近出生了。

B: 哇，恭喜你！真是好消息。

A: 谢谢，我真的很兴奋。但我一直在想一件事。我已经决定，我要更多地关注我的家庭，辞去我在这里的职位。

B: 我理解。你打算什么时候离职？

A: 我想大约一个月后。

B: 好的。我们会想你的，但家庭是第一位的，我支持你的决定。我们讨论一下如何平稳地交接工作吧。

Scene 2 办理手续

A: Hi, I'm here to process my resignation.

B: Okay. Please fill out this form.

A: Do I need to provide any other documents?

B: Your resignation letter and company property.

A: When can I expect to receive my final paycheck?

B: Within two weeks. We'll email you.

A: Thank you for your help.

B: You're welcome. Good luck in your future endeavors.

A: 你好，我是来办理离职手续的。

B: 好的。请填写这张表。

A: 我还需要提供其他文件吗？

B: 还需要提交你的辞职信和归还公司物品。

A: 我什么时候能拿到最后一笔工资？

B: 两周内。我们会给你发送电子邮件。

A: 谢谢你的帮助。

B: 不客气。祝你未来的日子一帆风顺。

Scene 3 辞职感受

A: Hey, I quit my job.

B: Really? Do you regret it?

A: Sometimes, but I needed a change.

B: That's understandable. What's next for you?

A: I'm not sure yet. Maybe travel for a bit.

A: 嘿，我辞职了。

B: 真的吗？你后悔吗？

A: 有时候会后悔，但我需要改变一下。

B: 可以理解。你的下一步计划是什么？

A: 还不确定。也许会去旅行一段时间。

重点词汇
及表达

□ resign from 从……离职

□ position n. 职位

□ transition n. 交接

□ process one's resignation 办理离职

□ company property 公司物品

□ paycheck n. 工资

□ quit one's job 辞职

□ regret v. 后悔

B: That sounds like a good plan. Don't worry. You'll figure it out.

B：听起来是个好计划。别担心。你会想清楚的。

 # Unit 4 Working Overtime 加班

Scene 1 临时加班

A: Boss just informed us to work overtime tonight.

A：老板刚通知我们今晚加班。

B: What happened? Any urgent changes to the plan?

B：怎么了？计划有紧急变动吗？

A: The client made some unexpected modifications to the proposal.

A：客户对方案做了一些意料之外的修改。

B: Okay. I'll stay and work on it with you.

B：好的。我留下来和你一起加班。

A: Thanks for your help. Let's get started.

A：谢谢你的帮助。我们开始工作吧。

Scene 2 周末加班

A: Who's available for weekend overtime?

A：谁能周末加班？

B: I am. What time?

B：我能来。什么时间？

A: Let's meet at the office at 8:00 am.

A：我们早晨 8 点在办公室见。

B: Okay. Who else will be there?

B：好的。还有谁会来？

A: Tom and Jerry confirmed already. Waiting on Mary.

A：汤姆和杰瑞已经确认要来了。我还在等玛丽回复。

B: Got it. I'll let you know if I hear from Mary.

B：知道了。如果有玛丽的消息，我会通知你的。

Scene 3 加班福利

A: Can we discuss the overtime pay and benefits?

A：我们能谈谈加班费和福利吗？

B: Sure, what do you have in mind?

B：当然可以。你有什么想法？

A: I think we deserve higher pay for working extra hours.

A：我认为我们加班应该得到更高的报酬。

B: I understand. Let's see what we can do.

B：我明白。看看我们能争取到些什么。

049

职场生活

□ work overtime 加班
□ modification *n.* 修改
□ proposal *n.* 方案
□ confirm *v.* 确认

□ overtime pay 加班费
□ benefit *n.* 福利

A: Also, can we get additional benefits like health insurance?

B: Let me check the company policy and get back to you.

A: Thank you. I appreciate it.

A：还有，我们能得到健康保险之类的额外福利吗？

B：我查一下公司政策，然后回复你。

A：谢谢。非常感谢。

Unit 5 Having Meetings 开会

Scene 1 会议主题

A: What should we discuss in the meeting?

B: How about the new product launch?

A: Good idea. Any other suggestions?

B: Maybe we can also talk about marketing strategy.

A: Alright, let's put these two topics on the agenda.

A：我们在会上应该讨论什么？

B：讨论新品发布怎么样？

A：好主意。还有其他建议吗？

B：也许我们还可以讨论营销策略。

A：好的，我们把这两个话题提上议程。

Scene 2 会议重点

A: So, what's the focus of the meeting?

B: I think we need to address the budget issue.

A: Agreed. What else?

B: Maybe we can also review the progress of ongoing projects.

A: That sounds good. Let's make it a two-point agenda.

A：那么，这次会议的重点是什么？

B：我认为我们需要解决预算问题。

A：同意。还有什么？

B：也许我们还可以看看进行中项目的进展情况。

A：听起来不错。那我们提出两点议程吧。

Scene 3 会议安排

A: When should we schedule the meeting?

B: How about next Monday at 10:00 am?

A: That works for me. Where should we have it?

A：我们什么时候安排会议？

B：下周一上午10点怎么样？

A：我没问题。我们应该在哪儿开会呢？

重点词汇
及表达

□ health insurance 健康保险

□ company policy 公司政策

□ new product launch 新品发布

□ marketing strategy 营销策略

□ agenda n. 议程

□ budget issue 预算事宜

□ ongoing project 进行中的项目

B: Let's use the conference room on the third floor.

B: 我们使用三楼的会议室吧。

A: Great! I'll send out a calendar invite with the details.

A: 好的。我会给你发一份包含详情的日历邀请函。

B: Thanks. Looking forward to it.

B: 谢谢。我很期待。

Scene 4　参会人员

A: Who do we have confirmed for the meeting?

A：我们确定谁参加会议了吗？

B: So far, we have John, Sarah, and Tom.

B：到目前为止，有约翰、萨拉和汤姆。

A: Anyone else we need to invite?

A：我们还需要邀请其他人吗？

B: Maybe we should invite Jane and Mark as well.

B：也许我们还应该邀请简和马克。

A: Sounds good. When should we send the invitation?

A：听起来不错。我们什么时候发出邀请函？

B: Let's send them out by the end of the day.

B：我们在今天结束前把邀请函发出去吧。

051

Scene 5　参会邀请

A: Have you sent out the invitations yet?

A：你发出邀请函了吗？

B: Not yet. Who should we invite?

B：还没有。我们应该邀请谁？

A: Let's invite the department heads and project leads.

A：邀请部门主管和项目负责人吧。

B: Should we also invite our clients?

B：我们是不是也应该邀请我们的客户？

A: Yes, we should. When should we send the invitations?

A：是的，应该邀请。我们什么时候发出邀请函？

B: I think we should send them by the end of this week.

B：我想我们应该在本周末之前发出。

Scene 6　会议总结

A: Let's summarize the meeting content.

A：我们来总结一下会议内容。

B: Okay. What were the key points?

B：好的。重点内容有哪些？

□ conference *n.* 会议

□ calendar *n.* 日历

□ invite *n.* 邀请；请柬

□ invitation *n.* 邀请函

□ client *n.* 客户

□ summarize *v.* 总结

A: We discussed the project timeline and budget.

B: Right, and we agreed on the next steps.

A: I'll send out a meeting summary email.

B: Great. Thanks for taking care of that.

A：我们讨论了项目时间表和预算。

B：没错，我们也就下一步的行动达成了一致。

A：我会发出一封会议纪要邮件。

B：太好了，谢谢你处理这件事情。

Unit 6 Asking for Leave 请假

Scene 1 病假（1）

A: I'm feeling sick. I need to take a sick day.

B: Oh no. What's wrong?

A: I have a fever.

B: Okay. Rest up and take care of yourself.

A: Thanks. I will.

A：我觉得不舒服。我需要请一天病假。

B：哦，天哪。怎么了？

A：我发烧了。

B：好的。好好休息，好好照顾自己。

A：谢谢。我会的。

Scene 2 病假（2）

A: I'm not feeling well. Can I ask for sick leave?

B: Sure, dear. What seems to be the issue?

A: I have a terrible headache，and my nose keeps running.

B: I see. Please take the time you need to rest and recover.

A: Thank you. I appreciate it.

A：我感觉不舒服。我可以请病假吗？

B：当然，亲爱的。你怎么了？

A：我头痛得厉害，而且一直流鼻涕。

B：我明白了。你慢慢休息和恢复。

A：谢谢。感谢您的关照。

Scene 3 事假

A: I need to take some time off. My relative passed away.

B: I'm so sorry to hear that. How long do you need?

A：我需要请假一段时间。我的亲戚去世了。

B：听到这个消息我很难过。你需要请多长时间的假？

重点词汇
及表达

☐ project timeline 项目时间表

☐ summary n. 总结

☐ take a sick day 请一天病假

☐ rest up 休息

☐ ask for sick leave 请病假

☐ recover v. 恢复

☐ take some time off 请假

A: Probably a week or so.

B: Of course. Take all the time you need. Let me know if there's anything I can do.

A: Thank you. I appreciate it.

B: No problem. Take care of yourself.

Scene 4 调休

A: Can I take a day off next week?

B: Sure. Do you want to use your vacation days?

A: No, I'd like to use my comp time.

B: Okay. Just make sure to check with our supervisor first.

A: Will do. Thanks for your help.

B: No problem! Enjoy your day off!

A：大约一周左右吧。

B：当然可以。你需要多少时间都行。有什么我能做的尽管说。

A：谢谢您。我很感激。

B：不客气。照顾好自己。

A：我下周可以请一天假吗？

B：当然可以。你想用你的带薪假期吗？

A：不，我想调休。

B：好的。一定要先和我们的主管确认一下。

A：好的。谢谢你的帮助。

B：不客气。好好享受休假吧!

职场生活

☐ comp time 补偿时间；调休

☐ supervisor *n.* 主管

Part 4　Travelling
旅游出行

Unit 1 Making Preparations 出行准备

Scene 1 旅行前咨询

A: Excuse me. Could you recommend some Hawaii tours?

B: Sure, we have several options available. When would you like to go?

A: Sometime in June. What do you suggest?

B: Our 10-day Maui tour is popular this time of year. Would you like more information?

A: Yes, please. What's included in the tour package?

B: Round-trip airfare, accommodations, daily breakfast, and sightseeing tours. It starts at $2,500 per person.

A: Sounds good.

A: 打扰一下，你能推荐一些夏威夷旅游线路吗？

B: 当然，我们有几种选择。您想什么时候去？

A: 六月的某个时候。你有什么建议？

B: 每年这个时候，我们的毛伊岛 10 天之旅都很受欢迎。您想了解更多的信息吗？

A: 想。旅行套餐包括什么？

B: 往返机票、住宿费、每日早餐和观光旅游。起价为每人 2500 美元。

A: 听起来不错。

Scene 2 提交材料

A: Do we need to submit our passport and visa to the travel agency?

B: Yes, we do. They'll need them for booking.

A: When do they need them?

B: They'll let us know, maybe before the trip.

A: Alright. I'll prepare them in advance.

B: That's a good idea. Better safe than sorry.

A: 我们需要把护照和签证交给旅行社吗？

B: 需要。他们要用这些来订票。

A: 他们什么时候需要？

B: 他们会通知我们的，也许是在出行之前。

A: 好的。我会提前准备好的。

B: 很好。有备无患。

Scene 3 咨询导游

A: Hi, do you know any local tour guides?

A: 嗨，你认识当地的导游吗？

重点词汇
&表达

☐ recommend *v.* 推荐
☐ option *n.* 选择
☐ tour package 旅行套餐
☐ passport *n.* 护照

☐ visa *n.* 签证
☐ in advance 提前
☐ Better safe than sorry. 有备无患。
☐ tour guide 导游

B: Yes, I'm a local tour guide. What do you need?

A: We want to discuss some tour suggestions and prices.

B: Sure, I can suggest some places and prices based on your budget.

A: Great! We have a budget of $500.

B: That should be enough for a full-day tour. We can visit the historical sites and try some local food.

B: 认识。我就是当地导游。请问您需要什么？

A: 我们想讨论一些旅行建议和价格。

B: 好的，我可以根据你们的预算提一些地点和价格方面的建议。

A: 太棒了！我们的预算是 500 美元。

B: 这应该够玩一整天了。我们可以参观历史遗迹，品尝当地的食物。

Scene 4　购买境外手机卡

A: Hi, I want to buy a phone card. Can you help me?

B: Sure, we have a variety of options. Do you have any preferences?

A: Yes, I'm looking for a monthly plan with unlimited data.

B: Great, we have several options for that. Here are the plans and prices.

A: That looks good. Can you help me sign up for the plan?

B: Of course. Let me just grab some paperwork, and we can get started.

A: 你好，我想买一张手机卡。你能帮我吗？

B: 当然可以，我们有多种选择。请问您有什么偏好吗？

A: 哦，我想订不限流量的包月套餐。

B: 好的，我们有几种包月套餐选择。这是套餐项目和价格。

A: 那个套餐看起来不错。你可以帮我开通吗？

B: 当然可以。我去取一些文件，然后就可以开通了。

057

Scene 5　携带物品

A: What are you packing for the trip?

B: Just the essentials, clothes, toiletries, and my camera.

A: Do you think we need to bring snacks or a first-aid kit?

A: 你准备带什么去旅行？

B: 只带必需品、衣服、洗漱用品和我的相机。

A: 你认为我们需要带零食或急救箱吗？

☐ budget *n.* 预算

☐ historical site 历史遗迹

☐ unlimited data 不受限的流量

☐ paperwork *n.* 文书

☐ essential *n.* 必需品

☐ first-aid kit 急救箱

旅游出行

B: Yeah. That's a good idea. And maybe some extra batteries for our devices.

A: Agreed, let's make sure we have everything we need before we leave.

B：需要。这是个好主意。也许还应该给我们的设备多准备一些电池。

A：没错，我们在出发前要确保准备好我们需要的物品。

Unit 2 Exchanging Foreign Currency 外币兑换

Scene 1　人民币兑换美元

A: Exchange currency, please.

B: What kind of currency do you want to exchange?

A: I want to exchange RMB to USD.

B: The exchange rate is 1 USD to 6.5 RMB today. How much do you want to exchange?

A: 1000 RMB.

B: Here's your 153.85 USD.

A：我想兑换货币。

B：您要兑换哪种货币？

A：我想把人民币兑换成美元。

B：今天的汇率是 1 美元兑换 6.5 元人民币。您要兑换多少？

A：1000 元人民币。

B：这是您的 153.85 美元。

Scene 2　英镑兑换美元

A: Hi, can you tell me the exchange rate for GBP to USD?

B: It's 1.38 USD for 1 GBP.

A: I'd like to change 1,000 GBP. Can you give me 50 USD bills?

B: Sorry, we only have 20 USD bills.

A: That's OK. 20 USD bills are fine.

A：你好，你能告诉我英镑兑换美元的汇率吗？

B：1 英镑兑换 1.38 美元。

A：我想兑换 1000 英镑。能换成面值为 50 美元的纸币吗？

B：抱歉，我们只有面值为 20 美元的纸币。

A：没关系。换成面值为 20 美元的纸币也行。

重点词汇
及表达

☐ exchange currency 货币兑换

☐ exchange rate 汇率

☐ bill *n.* 钞票，纸币

Scene 3 美元兑换欧元

A: How much is the exchange rate for USD to EUR?

B: It's 0.84 EUR for 1 USD.

A: Can I change 500 USD into 100 EUR bills?

B: Sure, but we also have 50 EUR bills.

A: 100 EUR bills are fine. Thanks.

A：美元兑换欧元的汇率是多少？

B：1 美元兑换 0.84 欧元。

A：我可以把 500 美元兑换成面值为 100 欧元的纸币吗？

B：当然可以，不过我们也有面值为 50 欧元的纸币。

A：换成面值为 100 欧元的纸币就可以了。谢谢。

Scene 4 美元兑换人民币

A: Good morning, Ma'am. How can I help you?

B: I need some Chinese RMB.

A: Certainly, Ma'am. What kind of foreign currency do you have?

B: US dollars. What's today's exchange rate for US dollars?

A: It's 680 RMB for 100 US dollars.

B: I'd like to exchange 100 US dollars.

A: Oh, that is 680 RMB in all. Would you please fill in this foreign currency exchange declaration form?

B: OK. Done. Here you are.

A: What denominations would you like to have?

B: I would like 6 100-RMB bills and coins for the rest.

A: Would you please sign the memo?

B: Sure.

A: Thank you, Ma'am. Here is your money, and here is your memo.

A：早上好，女士。有什么我能帮您的吗？

B：我需要一些人民币。

A：没问题，女士。您持有哪种外币？

B：美元。今天美元兑换人民币的汇率是多少？

A：100 美元兑换 680 元人民币。

B：我想兑换 100 美元。

A：好的，一共 680 元人民币。请您填写这张外币兑换申报表，好吗？

B：好的。填好了。给你。

A：您想要什么面值的？

B：我要 6 张 100 元的纸币，其余的钱要硬币。

A：请您在这张兑换单上签字，好吗？

B：好的。

A：谢谢您，女士。这是您的钱，这是您的兑换单。

□ change...into... 把……换成……

□ foreign currency 外币

□ sign the memo 在兑换单上签字

旅游出行

059

Unit 3 The Destination 旅行目的地

Scene 1　讨论目的地

A: When do we have a vacation?

B: In two weeks. Where should we go?

A: How about the beach?

B: Good idea. Should we drive or take a plane?

A: Let's drive. It's cheaper.

B: OK! Let's plan our route.

A：我们什么时候去度假？

B：两周后。我们去哪儿呢？

A：去海滩怎么样？

B：好主意。我们开车还是乘飞机去？

A：我们开车去吧。开车费用更低。

B：好的！我们规划一下路线。

Scene 2　办理落地签

A: Hi, what documents do I need to apply for a visa on arrival?

B: You need a valid passport, a passport photo, and proof of your travel plan.

A: OK. Thanks.

B: No problem. Let me know if you have any other questions.

A: Actually, what kind of proof of itinerary do I need?

B: Any document that shows your travel plans, such as flight tickets, hotel reservations, or tour bookings.

A: Got it. Thanks for your help.

B: You're welcome. Have a safe trip!

A：您好，请问申请落地签需要什么文件？

B：需要有效护照、护照照片和旅行计划证明。

A：好的。谢谢。

B：不客气。如果您还有其他问题，请告诉我。

A：实际上，我需要什么样的行程证明呢？

B：任何显示您的旅行计划的文件，比如机票、酒店预订或旅游预订文件。

A：明白了。谢谢您的帮助。

B：不客气。一路平安！

重点词汇
及表达

☐ have a vacation 度假

☐ apply for a visa 申请签证

☐ valid *adj.* 有效的

☐ itinerary *n.* 行程

060

Scene 3　当地景点

A: Hi, what are some popular local tourist spots?

B: The national park and historic district are top attractions.

A: Interesting. Are there any other places you recommend?

B: Yes, the local zoo and art museum are also worth visiting.

A: Thanks for the suggestions.

B: No problem. Let me know if you need any help planning your visit.

A: I appreciate it.

B: Enjoy your time here!

A：嗨，当地有哪些热门旅游景点？

B：国家公园和历史街区是最吸引人的地方。

A：听起来挺有趣的。还有其他推荐的地方吗？

B：有，当地的动物园和美术馆也值得一游。

A：谢谢你的建议。

B：不客气。如果您需要我帮忙安排行程，请告诉我。

A：我很感激。

B：在这里玩得开心哦!

旅游出行

Scene 4　当地美食

A: Excuse me. Do you know any local restaurants with authentic cuisine?

B: Yes, there's a great place down the street.

A: Can you recommend any specific dishes?

B: Their specialty is the local seafood stew. It's a must-try.

A: Sounds delicious! Do you know how to get there?

B: Sure, it's a ten-minute walk from here. Let me show you on the map.

A：打扰一下，你知道当地有什么食物正宗的餐厅吗？

B：知道，这条街上有一家很棒的餐厅。

A：你能具体推荐一些菜肴吗？

B：他们的特色菜是当地的海鲜炖菜。必须去尝尝。

A：听起来很美味! 你知道怎么去那里吗？

B：知道，从这里步行10分钟就到了。我在地图上指给你看。

☐ tourist spot 旅游景点

☐ attraction *n.* 向往的地方

☐ authentic cuisine 正宗的食物

☐ specialty *n.* 特色菜

05

Part 5
Foods and Drinks
饮食生活

Unit 1　At a Restaurant 在餐厅

Scene 1　约见用餐

A: Hey, do you want to go out to eat tonight?

B: Sure, where do you want to go?

A: How about that new sushi place downtown?

B: Sounds good to me. What time should we meet up?

A: How about 7:00 pm?

B: Works for me. See you at 7:00 at the restaurant.

A：嘿，你今晚想出去吃饭吗？

B：想啊。你想去哪儿吃？

A：去市中心新开的那家寿司店怎么样？

B：听起来不错。我们约在什么时候碰面？

A：晚上 7 点怎么样？

B：我没问题。7 点餐厅见。

Scene 2　个人口味

A: What's your favorite type of dish?

B: I really like Italian food. How about you?

A: I prefer Chinese food, especially spicy dishes.

B: That's cool. I can't handle too much spice.

A: Yeah, it's definitely not for everyone.

A：你最喜欢什么菜？

B：我特别喜欢意大利菜。你呢？

A：我更喜欢中国菜，尤其是辣的。

B：太酷了。我吃不了太辣的。

A：嗯，当然不是每个人都能吃辣的。

Scene 3　辣味食品

A: Is that spicy? It looks really spicy.

B: Not at all. It's very good. Try it.

A: Are you sure?

B: It's not spicy at all. Try it. Trust me.

A: Really?

B: Have some water. But it's not spicy at all. Really?

A: Where are you from?

B: Hunan Province.

A：辣吗？看起来真的很辣。

B：一点也不辣。非常美味。你尝尝。

A：你确定吗？

B：一点也不辣。尝尝看。相信我。

A：真的吗？（注：外国人以为不辣，吃了一口，结果辣得流泪了。）

B：喝点水。但是一点也不辣。不是吗？

A：你是哪里人？

B：我是湖南人。

重点词汇
及表达

☐ sushi *n.* 寿司
☐ meet up 见面
☐ type *n.* 类型

☐ spicy *adj.* 辛辣的
☐ Not at all. 一点也不。

Scene 4　预订餐位

A: Hi, can I make a reservation for tonight?

B: Yes, of course. How many people are at your party?

A: There are four of us.

B: Great, and what time would you like to come in?

A: Around 7:00 pm, if possible.

B: OK. I have you down for a party of four at 7:00 pm. See you tonight!

A：你好，我可以预订今晚的餐位吗？

B：当然可以。你们一共多少人？

A：我们有四个人。

B：好的，你们想什么时候来？

A：如果可以的话，晚上 7 点左右。

B：好的。我为您安排了晚上 7 点的四人位。晚上见!

Scene 5　预订餐厅

A: Hello, welcome to Mia's restaurant. Do you have a reservation?

B: Yes, under the name of Lily at 7:00 pm. Do you have a table for two?

A: Yes, right over here.

A：您好，欢迎光临米娅的餐厅。请问您预订了吗？

B：预订了，晚上 7 点，用莉莉的名字预订的。你们有两人位吗？

A：有，这边请。

Scene 6　选择座位

A: Hi, welcome to the restaurant. How many are at your party?

B: There are four of us.

A: Great, we do have a few tables available. Would you like a booth or a table?

B: A booth would be nice if you have one available.

A: Sure thing. Follow me, please. Here's a booth for four. Is this OK?

B: Yes, this is perfect. Thank you.

A: You're welcome. Enjoy your meal!

A：您好，欢迎光临。请问你们有多少人？

B：我们有四个人。

A：好的，我们确实还有几个空位。您要卡座还是普通桌子？

B：如果你们有卡座的话，那就再好不过了。

A：当然有。请跟我来。这是四人卡座。可以吗？

B：哦，完美。谢谢你!

A：不客气。祝您用餐愉快!

065

饮食生活

☐ make a reservation 预订

☐ under the name of 以……的名字

☐ booth *n.* 卡座

Scene 7　更换座位

A: Good evening, sir. Welcome to our restaurant.

B: Good evening. I made a reservation under the name of Tim at 7:30 pm.

A: OK. This way, please.

B: Excuse me. The dazzling lights outside the window are hurting my eyes. Could I change tables?

A: I'll draw the curtains for you, sir.

B: I'd rather change a table. It's too cold here. Could you turn the air-conditioning down a bit?

A: I'm sorry. I can't turn down the air-conditioning because our hotel is centrally air-conditioned. Would you mind putting on your coat?

B: Well, I don't particularly enjoy eating with my coat on.

A: How about sitting over there?

B: There is a vacant table in the corner, where I can enjoy the band pretty well. I'd prefer the table in the corner. Can you arrange it?

A: No problem, sir. This way, please.

A: 晚上好，先生。欢迎光临我们的餐厅。

B: 晚上好。我用蒂姆的名字预订了晚上 7 点 30 分的餐位。

A: 好的。请这边走。

B: 打扰一下，窗外耀眼的灯光刺得我眼睛疼。我可以换张桌子吗？

A: 先生，我帮您拉上窗帘。

B: 我还是想换张桌子。这里太冷了。你能把空调的冷气调小一点吗？

A: 抱歉。我不能调小，因为我们酒店安装的是中央空调。您介意穿上外套吗？

B: 哦，可是我不太喜欢穿着外套吃饭。

A: 您觉得去那边坐怎么样？

B: 角落里有张空桌子，在那里我可以很好地欣赏乐队演奏。我喜欢角落里的那张桌子。你能安排一下吗？

A: 没问题，先生。请这边走。

Scene 8　餐厅等位

A: Excuse me. How long is the wait for a table? I've been waiting for a while.

B: I'm sorry. We're quite busy.

A: Oh, OK. Is it possible to get a menu while we wait?

B: Of course. Let me grab one for you.

A: Thank you so much.

A: 打扰一下，等位要多久？我已经等了很久了。

B: 抱歉。我们特别忙。

A: 哦，好吧。我们等待的时候能不能拿一份菜单过来？

B: 当然可以。我去给您拿一份。

A: 非常感谢。

重点词汇及表达

☐ draw the curtain 拉上窗帘

☐ change a table 换张桌子

☐ vacant *adj.* 空着的

☐ busy *adj.* 忙碌的

☐ menu *n.* 菜单

Scene 9   点西餐

A: Hi, do you know what you want to drink?

B: Water, please. And could you recommend a dish?

A: Our specialty is the grilled salmon. It's really popular.

B: That sounds great. I'll have the grilled salmon, please.

A: Sure. Anything else?

B: No, that's it. Thank you.

A：您好，请问您想喝点什么？

B：请给我一杯水。你能推荐一道菜吗？

A：我们的特色菜是烤三文鱼。这道菜很受欢迎。

B：听起来不错。我要一份烤三文鱼。

A：好的。请问您还要别的吗？

B：不要了，就要这个。谢谢！

Scene 10   点中餐

A: What do you want to order?

B: Let me see the menu.

A: Sure, take your time.

B: I'll have the Kung Pao chicken.

A: Great choice. Anything else?

B: Yes, I'd also like some fried rice with an egg.

A: Got it. Anything to drink?

B: Just water for me.

A: OK. I'll put in your order.

A：请问您想要点什么？

B：我看看菜单。

A：好的，您慢慢看。

B：我要一份宫保鸡丁。

A：不错的选择。请问还要别的吗？

B：嗯，我还要一份蛋炒饭。

A：好的。请问您要喝点什么？

B：只要水。

A：好的。我这就为您下单。

Scene 11   点饮品

A: Here is our menu. What would you like to drink to start with?

B: Oh, my god. Coffee is 38, soda is 9, and orange juice is 19. It's a rip-off. Just water, please.

A：这是我们的菜单。您想先喝点什么？

B：哦，天哪。咖啡 38 元，苏打水 9 元，橙汁 19 元。这是敲竹杠。请给我一杯水。

饮食生活

□ recommend *v.* 推荐

□ popular *adj.* 受欢迎的

□ take one's time 慢慢来

□ order *n.* 订单

□ soda *n.* 苏打水

□ It's a rip-off. 这是敲竹杠。

Scene 12　点蛋炒饭

A: Excuse me?

B: Yes, are you ready to order?

A: Yes.

B: What would you like?

A: I don't know. What do you recommend?

B: Well, today we have a combo special. It's roast beef with vegetables.

A: How much is it?

B: It's 299.

A: 299? Em, I think I will just get fried rice with an egg.

B: Anything else?

A: No, that's it.

B: That's it? I thought you had a friend coming.

A: Actually, the fried rice with an egg is for him. I just need the water.

B: OK.

A：打扰了。

B：没事，请问您准备好点餐了吗?

A：是的。

B：请问您要点什么?

A：我不知道。你有什么推荐的吗?

B：嗯，今天我们有特价套餐：烤牛肉配蔬菜。

A：多少钱?

B：299 元。

A：299 元? 嗯，我想我就要一份蛋炒饭好了。

B：还要别的吗?

A：不要了，我就要这个。

B：就这个吗? 我以为你有朋友要来。

A：事实上，蛋炒饭是给他的。我只需要水。

B：好的。

Scene 13　点酒水

A: What kind of drink do you want?

B: I'd like a glass of red wine.

A: We have several options. Do you have a preference?

B: I'll go with the house red, please.

A: Got it. Anything else for now?

B: No, that's all for now. Thank you.

A：请问您想要哪种饮品?

B：我想喝杯红葡萄酒。

A：我们有几种选择。请问您有什么偏好吗?

B：就选你们的招牌红葡萄酒吧!

A：好的。现在还要点别的吗?

B：不要了，现在就点这个。谢谢!

Scene 14　选择牛排

A: Hey, I'll be your waitress today. Would you like something to drink to start with?

A：您好，今天我来为您服务。请问您想先喝点什么吗?

□ a combo special 特价套餐

□ option *n.* 选择

□ preference *n.* 偏好

B: Yes, I'll have iced tea, please.

A: OK. Are you ready to order, or do you need a few minutes?

B: I think I'm ready. I'll have tomato soup to start with. For the main course, I'd like to have sirloin steak with mashed potatoes and peas.

A: How would you like your steak to be cooked? Rare, medium rare, medium, medium well, or well done?

B: Medium well. Thanks.

B：嗯，我要一杯冰茶。

A：好的。请问您准备好点餐了吗？或者说还需要再考虑几分钟？

B：我想我准备好点餐了。我先来一份西红柿汤。主菜我要西冷牛排配土豆泥和豌豆。

A：请问您的牛排要几分熟？一分熟，三分熟，五分熟，七分熟，还是全熟？

B：七分熟。谢谢。

Scene 15　点牛排和煎蛋

A: How do you want your steak cooked?

B: I want it medium rare.

A: And would you like a fried egg with that?

B: Yes, please. Sunny-side up, please.

A: Great, I'll make a note of that for the chef.

A：请问您的牛排要几分熟？

B：我要三分熟的。

A：要搭配一个煎蛋吗？

B：要。要一面煎的太阳蛋。

A：好的，我会给厨师做个备注。

Scene 16　等待食物

A: Excuse me. I've been waiting for a while. I was wondering if my order is ready.

B: Let me check for you. Oh, fried rice with an egg?

A: Right. I ordered 2 minutes ago.

B: Eh, I'm afraid it's gonna take more than 2 minutes, even for fried rice with an egg.

A: I have to say...I'm kind of disappointed with the efficiency of your restaurant.

B: I apologize, Miss. Let me check with the kitchen for you.

A: Thank you.

A：抱歉，我已经等了一会儿了。我想知道我点的餐做好了吗？

B：我帮您看一下。哦，是蛋炒饭吗？

A：是的，我两分钟前就点餐了。

B：嗯，即使是蛋炒饭，恐怕也不止两分钟。

A：我不得不说……我对你们餐厅的效率有点失望。

B：抱歉，女士。我去厨房帮您看一下。

A：谢谢。

☐ soup *n.* 汤

☐ main course 主菜

☐ medium rare 三分熟

☐ sunny-side up 太阳蛋（只煎一面，看起来像太阳）

☐ make a note of 做笔记

☐ chef *n.* 厨师

☐ ready *adj.* 准备好的

☐ efficiency *n.* 效率

Scene 17　比较食物

A: What's the difference between the regular burger and the combo meal?

B: The combo meal comes with fries and a drink. The regular burger doesn't include any sides or drinks.

A: Oh, I see. How much is the combo meal?

B: It's $10 for the combo meal and $5 for just the burger.

A：普通汉堡和套餐有什么区别？

B：套餐里有薯条和饮料。单个普通汉堡不包括任何小食或饮料。

A：哦，我明白了。套餐多少钱？

B：套餐10美元，单个汉堡5美元。

Scene 18　素食套餐

A: Excuse me. Do you have any vegetarian set meals?

B: Yes, we do. Our vegetarian set meal includes a salad, soup, and a main course.

A: That sounds perfect. Can I please order that?

B: Of course. I'll put in your order right away.

A：打扰一下，请问你们有素食套餐吗？

B：有。我们的素食套餐包括沙拉、汤和主菜。

A：听起来很不错。我可以点一份吗？

B：当然可以。我马上给您下单。

Scene 19　推荐美食

A: Have you tried that new Italian restaurant downtown?

B: No, I haven't. Is it any good?

A: Yeah, the pasta is delicious.

B: I'll have to check it out. Have you been to that sushi place near your house?

A: Yes, I have. The sushi rolls there are amazing.

B: I'll have to try it. Thanks for the recommendation.

A：你去过市中心那家新开的意大利餐厅吗？

B：没有，我没去过。那里的食物好吃吗？

A：好吃，那里的意大利面很好吃。

B：我得去看看。你去过你家附近的那家寿司店吗？

A：去过。那里的寿司卷很好吃。

B：我一定要去吃吃看。谢谢你的推荐。

Scene 20　打包外带

A: Hi, can I place an order for takeout, please?

B: Of course. What would you like to order?

A：你好，请问我可以点餐带走吗？

B：当然可以。您想要点什么？

重点词汇
及表达

☐ regular *adj.* 常规的
☐ combo meal 套餐
☐ side *n.* 小食

☐ vegetarian *adj.* 素食的
☐ set meal 套餐
☐ downtown *adv.* 在市中心

☐ recommendation *n.* 推荐
☐ place an order 下订单
☐ takeout *n.* 外卖食品

A: I'd like a chicken sandwich, a side of fries, and a Coke, please.

B: Alright, that'll be ready in about 10 minutes. Would you like to pay now or when you pick it up?

A: I'll pay now, please.

B: Great, that comes to $12.50. Here's your receipt. Thank you for choosing us.

A：我要一份鸡肉三明治、一份薯条和一杯可乐。

B：好的，大约 10 分钟就好了。您是现在付款，还是取餐时付款？

A：我现在付款。

B：好的，一共 12.5 美元。这是您的收据。感谢您选择我们餐厅。

Scene 21　是否打包

A: Excuse me. Sorry, I'm in a hurry. Can I get my food to go?

B: Sure, would you like a to-go box?

A: Yeah, please.

B: No problem. I'll wrap that up for you. Oh, by the way, the box is 5 RMB.

A: 5 RMB? Actually, I'm not in that much of a hurry. I think I'll just eat here.

A: OK.

A：打扰一下。抱歉，我赶时间。我的食物可以打包带走吗？

B：当然可以。您需要打包盒吗？

A：需要。

B：没问题。我帮您装好。哦，顺便说一下，这个盒子 5 元。

A：5 元？事实上，我也没那么急。我想我还是在这里吃吧。

B：好的。

Scene 22　打包食物

A: Excuse me. Can I have a takeout box, please?

B: Sure, would you like me to box that up for you?

A: Yes, please.

B: Alright, I'll be right back with a takeout box for you.

A：打扰一下。我可以要一个打包盒吗？

B：当然可以。需要我帮您装起来吗？

A：需要，请打包。

B：好的，我马上给您拿个打包盒过来。

Scene 23　上错菜品

A: Excuse me. Wrong dish. Can you change it, please?

B: Sure. Which dish did you order?

A：打扰了，菜上错了。你能换一下吗？

B：当然。您点的是哪道菜？

□ receipt *n.* 收据

□ in a hurry 匆忙

□ wrap *v.* 包装

□ box up 打包

饮食生活

A: I ordered the steak, but this is chicken.

B: I apologize for the mistake. I'll have the steak prepared for you right away.

A：我点的是牛排，但这是鸡肉。

B：抱歉，我弄错了。我马上给您准备牛排。

Scene 24　质量问题

A: Excuse me. There's something wrong with this dish. Can I have it replaced?

B: I'm sorry to hear that. What seems to be the problem?

A: The food doesn't taste quite right. I think it might be spoiled.

B: I apologize for the inconvenience. We'll get you a new dish right away.

A: Thank you. I appreciate it.

A：打扰了，这道菜有点问题。我可以换一道吗？

B：非常抱歉。是什么问题呢？

A：这食物尝起来不太对劲。我觉得它可能变质了。

B：给您带来不便，我深表歉意。我们马上给您上新菜。

A：谢谢。非常感谢。

Scene 25　餐厅洗手间

A: Excuse me. Where is the restroom?

B: The restroom is just around the corner to the left.

A: Thanks. I appreciate it.

B: No problem. Let me know if you need anything else.

A：打扰了。请问洗手间在哪儿？

B：洗手间就在拐角处的左边。

A：谢谢。非常感谢。

B：不客气。如果您还有什么需要，请告诉我。

Scene 26　结账方式

A: Excuse me. Could we have the check, please?

B: Sure thing. I'll bring it over right away. Would you like to pay with cash or card?

A: I think we'll pay with cash. Could you please let us know the total amount?

B: Absolutely. Your total comes to $45.50.

A：打扰了。请问我们可以结账吗？

B：当然可以。我马上把账单给您拿过来。请问您想付现金还是刷卡？

A：我想我们还是付现金吧。请告诉我们总金额好吗？

B：当然可以。总共是 45.5 美元。

重点词汇
及表达

☐ apologize v. 道歉

☐ prepare v. 准备

☐ replace v. 替换

☐ spoil v. 破坏，变质

☐ inconvenience n. 不便

☐ restroom n. 洗手间

☐ around the corner 在拐角处

☐ check n. 账单

☐ the total amount 总金额

A: OK. Thanks. Here's $50. Keep the change.

A：好的。谢谢，这是 50 美元。不用找零了。

B: Thank you very much.

B：非常感谢。

Scene 27　西餐礼仪

A: Do you know anything about western dining etiquette?

A：你了解西方的用餐礼仪吗？

B: Not really. Why do you ask?

B：不完全了解。怎么问这个？

A: I have a business dinner coming up, and I don't want to embarrass myself.

A：我最近要参加一场商务晚宴。我不想让自己难堪。

B: Well, I know you're supposed to keep your hands on the table, not your lap.

B：哦，我知道你应该把手放在桌子上，而不是放在腿上。

A: Hmm, OK. Anything else?

A：嗯，好的。还有别的需要注意吗？

B: Oh, and the fork and knife have different positions. It depends on whether you're finished or not.

B：哦，刀叉需要放在不同的位置。这取决于你是否用完餐了。

A: That sounds complicated. I better look up more information before my dinner.

A：听起来很复杂。我最好在参加晚宴前多查一些资料。

Scene 28　使用筷子

A: Hey, do you know how to use chopsticks?

A：嘿，你知道怎么使用筷子吗？

B: No, I have no idea.

B：我不知道。

A: Let me show you. Hold one chopstick between your thumb and your index finger like this. And then, place the other one between your index and middle finger. Now move the top one up and down to pick up the food.

A：我示范给你看。像这样用拇指和食指夹住一根筷子。然后，把另一根筷子放在食指和中指之间。现在上下移动上面的那根筷子来夹食物。

B: OK. I think I got it. Thanks!

B：好的。我想我会使用了。谢谢！

073

饮食生活

- [ ] western dining etiquette 西餐礼仪
- [ ] embarrass *v.* 使难堪
- [ ] position *n.* 位置
- [ ] chopstick *n.* 筷子
- [ ] index finger 食指
- [ ] pick up 夹起

Scene 29　小费文化

A: Oh, I forgot to leave a tip.

B: Don't worry. You can leave it next time.

A: Is tipping necessary here?

B: Yes, it's part of the culture in this country.

A: How much should I leave?

B: Usually 15%–20% of the total bill.

A：哦，我忘了给小费了。

B：没事。下次记得给就好了。

A：这个地方必须给小费吗？

B：是的，给小费是这个国家文化的一部分。

A：我应该给多少钱？

B：通常是账单总额的 15%～20%。

Scene 30　自助餐

A: Excuse me. Where is the self-service buffet located?

B: The buffet is located on the other side of the restaurant.

A: Thank you. Is it all-you-can-eat?

B: Yes, it is. The price includes unlimited access to the buffet.

A: Sounds good. What kind of food is available?

B: We have a variety of options, including salads, soups, entrees, and desserts.

A: That all sounds delicious. Thank you for your help.

B: You're welcome. Enjoy your meal!

A：打扰一下。请问自助餐厅在哪儿？

B：自助餐在餐厅的另一侧。

A：谢谢。可以吃到饱吗？

B：是的。这个价钱包括无限制地享用自助餐。

A：听起来不错。有什么食物可以吃？

B：我们提供多种选择，包括沙拉、汤、主菜和甜点。

A：听起来都很好吃。谢谢你的帮助。

B：不客气。祝您用餐愉快！

Scene 31　抢着买单

A: Are you full?

B: Yes, I'm very full.

A: Did you enjoy the food?

B: Yes, it's delicious.

A: OK. I pay. My treat.

B: No, I wanna pay.

A：你吃饱了吗？

B：是的，我很饱。

A：你喜欢这些食物吗？

B：喜欢，很美味。

A：好的。我付钱。我请客。

B：不用了，我来付钱。

重点词汇
及表达

☐ leave a tip 留下小费

☐ culture *n.* 文化

☐ self-service buffet 自助餐厅

☐ unlimited *adj.* 没有限制的

☐ entree *n.* 主菜

☐ dessert *n.* 甜点

☐ treat *n.* 款待

A: No, you are in Shenzhen. And I'm the host. I pay.

B: Em...How about we split the bill?

A: No, no, no. You know, there's a saying in China. "When in Rome, do as the Romans do." If you treat me like a real friend, you should let me pay. I'm happy to pay for you.

B: OK. But next time when you come to the US, I'm paying.

A: OK. Let's go.

A：不行，你是在深圳。我是东道主。我来付钱。

B：嗯……我们 AA 怎么样？

A：不，不，不。你知道，中国有句谚语："入乡随俗。"如果你把我当成真正的朋友，就应该让我付钱。我很乐意为你买单。

B：好吧。但是下次你来美国时，我来付钱。

A：好的。我们走吧。

Unit 2 At a Bar 在酒吧

Scene 1 吧台点单

A: Hey, what can I get for you?

B: Just a beer. Thank you.

A: OK. Would you like draft or bottle?

B: Bottle, please.

A: OK. Here you go, Ma'am.

B: Thank you.

A: You're welcome. Enjoy your evening.

A：您好，请问您想要点什么？

B：啤酒就行了。谢谢!

A：好的。请问您要生啤还是瓶装啤酒？

B：瓶装啤酒。

A：好的。给您，女士。

B：谢谢。

A：不客气。祝您晚上过得愉快。

Scene 2 酒品推荐

A: Hey, what can I get for you?

B: I don't know. What do you recommend?

A: Well, we have whisky and soda. But you are too cute of a girl to drink such a manly drink. We also have some more girly drinks, like Margaritas, Martinis, and Mojitos.

A：嘿，要喝点什么？

B：我不知道。你有什么推荐的吗？

A：嗯，我们有威士忌和苏打水。但你太可爱了，不应该喝这么有男子气概的饮品。我们还有一些女孩喝的饮品，像玛格丽塔鸡尾酒、马丁尼鸡尾酒和莫吉托鸡尾酒。

075

☐ host *n.* 东道主，主人

☐ split the bill 分摊或平分账单（又叫"AA"）

☐ When in Rome, do as the Romans do. 入乡随俗。

☐ draft *n.* 生啤

☐ bottle *n.* 瓶装啤酒

☐ whisky *n.* 威士忌

☐ manly *adj.* 有男子气概的

B: Guess what? I'd like to try whisky. I may look cute. But I'm rough around the edges.

A: OK. Straight up, Ma'am?

B: Yes. Straight up. Absolutely. Certainly. You know, without ice. I don't like ice in my drink. It spoils the taste.

A: OK. Would you like to say "when", please?

B: Oh，when.

A: OK. There you go. Enjoy your evening.

B: You know what? You are the most handsome bartender I've ever seen.

A: Wow, thank you. Can I get you a drink on the house?

B: 你猜怎么着？我想尝尝威士忌。我可能看起来很可爱。但我不拘小节。

A: 好的。直饮吗，女士？

B: 是的，直饮。当然是这样。你知道的，不加冰。我不喜欢在酒里加冰，那样会破坏口感。

A: 好的。请你告诉我加到什么时候停下好吗？

B: 好，停。

A: 好的。给你。祝你晚上过得愉快。

B: 你知道吗？你是我见过的最帅气的酒保。

A: 哇，谢谢。我能请你喝一杯吗？

Scene 3 调制酒品

076

A: Hi, can I order a drink, please?

B: Of course. What would you like?

A: Can you make me something special? I like fruity drinks but not too sweet.

B: Sure, I can make you a custom drink based on your taste preferences. How about a berry margarita with less sugar?

A: That sounds perfect. Thank you.

A: 你好，我能点一杯饮品吗？

B: 当然可以。请问您想要什么？

A: 你能给我调制点特别的饮品吗？我喜欢水果味的饮品，但不要太甜。

B: 当然可以，我可以根据您的口味喜好定制饮品。来杯低糖的浆果玛格丽塔酒怎么样？

A: 听起来棒极了。谢谢!

Scene 4 特色酒品

A: Hi, do you have any local specialty drinks?

B: Yes, we have a few. The most popular one is the XYZ cocktail, made with local ingredients.

A: Oh, that sounds interesting. Can you tell me more about it?

A: 嗨，你们有什么当地特色饮品吗？

B: 有，我们有一些。最受欢迎的是 XYZ 鸡尾酒，是用当地的食材调制成的。

A: 哦，听起来很有趣。你能跟我说说更多细节吗？

重点词汇
及表达

☐ rough around the edges 不拘小节

☐ bartender *n.* 酒保

☐ get sb a drink on the house 请某人喝一杯

☐ fruity *adj.* 水果味的

☐ custom drink 定制饮品

☐ cocktail *n.* 鸡尾酒

☐ ingredient *n.* 成分

B: Sure, it's a mix of ABC liquor, fresh juice, and a splash of soda. Would you like to try one?

B: 当然可以。它是由 ABC 白酒、鲜榨果汁和少许苏打水混合而成的。您想尝尝吗？

Scene 5　比较酒品

A: Excuse me. Could you tell me the alcohol content of these two drinks?

A: 打扰一下。你能告诉我这两种饮品的酒精含量吗？

B: Sure, the first one is 15%, and the second one is 20%.

B: 当然可以，第一种是 15%，第二种是 20%。

A: Hmm, I think I'll go with the second one. That sounds more like what I'm looking for.

A: 嗯，我想我选第二种。它听起来更像是我想要的。

Scene 6　佐酒小食

A: Excuse me. What kind of snacks do you have to go with drinks?

A: 打扰一下。请问你们有什么小食搭配饮品吗？

B: We have nuts, chips, and chicken wings.

B: 我们有坚果、薯片和鸡翅。

A: How much are they?

A: 多少钱？

B: Nuts and chips are $5 each, and chicken wings are $10.

B: 坚果和薯片每包 5 美元，鸡翅 10 美元。

A: Alright! I'll have the chicken wings and a beer.

A: 好的，我要鸡翅和一杯啤酒。

B: Great, coming right up!

B: 没问题，马上送过来！

077

饮食生活

Unit 3　Ordering Fast Food 订快餐

Scene 1　麦当劳点餐

A: Hi, what can I get for you?

A: 您好，请问您要点什么？

B: I'd like a Number 1, please.

B: 我要 1 号套餐。

A: What kind of drink?

A: 您要什么饮料？

B: Coke without ice.

B: 不加冰的可乐。

□ liquor *n.* 液体　　　　　□ nut *n.* 坚果

□ alcohol *n.* 酒精　　　　□ chip *n.* 薯片

□ snack *n.* 零食

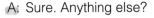

A: Sure. Anything else?

B: No, that's it.

A: Is that for here or to go?

B: For here.

A: Your total is gonna be $6.79.

B: OK.

A: Thank you. Have a nice day.

A：好的。还要别的东西吗？

B：不要了，就这些。

A：在这里吃还是带走？

B：在这里吃。

A：总共是 6.79 美元。

B：好的。

A：谢谢。祝您过得愉快。

Scene 2　巨无霸套餐

A: What would you like to order?

B: Can I get a Big Mac with fries, please?

A: Would you like a meal or just the burger?

B: A meal, please.

A: OK. A Big Mac meal. Alright. What drink would you like?

B: Chocolate milk.

A: Anything else for you?

B: That's all.

A: Would that be for here or to go?

B: To go, please.

A: $6.79. Thank you.

A：请问您想要点什么？

B：请给我一个巨无霸汉堡和薯条，好吗？

A：请问您要套餐还是只要汉堡？

B：套餐。

A：好的。一份巨无霸汉堡套餐。好了。请问您想喝点什么？

B：巧克力牛奶。

A：还要别的吗？

B：就这些。

A：在这里吃还是带走？

B：外带。

A：6.79 美元。谢谢！

Scene 3　麦乐鸡块套餐

A: Good morning. What can I get for you today?

B: Can I get a chicken McNuggets Meal with a large Sprite and a McFlurry?

A: What kind of sauce would you like for the McNuggets?

B: I'll have the honey mustard.

A：早上好。今天您要点什么？

B：我要一份麦乐鸡块套餐，外加一大杯雪碧和一份麦旋风。

A：麦乐鸡块要加什么酱？

B：我要蜂蜜芥末酱。

重点词汇
及表达

☐ Is that for here or to go?
　在这里吃还是带走？

☐ Big Mac 巨无霸

☐ burger *n.* 汉堡

☐ Sprite *n.* 雪碧

☐ mustard *n.* 芥末

078

A: Would that be it?

B: Can I also get an apple pie?

A: Sure. Would that complete your order?

B: Yes.

A: Is that for here or to go?

B: To go, please.

A: OK. Your total comes to $10.97.

B: Apple Pay.

A: Sure, go ahead.

A: 您就要这些吗?

B: 我可以再加一个苹果派吗?

A: 当然可以。这些就是您点的所有东西吗?

B: 是的。

A: 在这儿吃还是带走?

B: 外带。

A: 好的。总共 10.97 美元。

B: 我用苹果支付。

A: 当然可以,请便。

Scene 4 点外带快餐

A: Hey, what could I get for you today?

B: Can I get a Double Quarter Pounder Meal and an order of ten-piece McNuggets?

A: Sure. What kind of drink would you like for the meal?

B: A diet coke. Can I get the sweet and sour sauce, please?

A: Sure. Anything else for you?

B: That's all.

A: Would that be for here or to go?

B: For here, please.

A: OK. Your total comes to $11.88.

B: OK. Here is $12.

A: Thank you. And here is 12 cents change. Here is your receipt and your order number. Please wait on the side for your food. And your number will show up on the screen.

A: 您好,请问您今天想吃点什么?

B: 我想要一份双层四分之一磅汉堡套餐和一份十块装麦乐鸡,可以吗?

A: 当然可以。汉堡套餐想要什么饮料?

B: 无糖可乐。请给我一份酸甜酱,好吗?

A: 好的。还要别的吗?

B: 就这些。

A: 在这里吃还是带走?

B: 在这里吃。

A: 好的。总共 11.88 美元。

B: 好的。这是 12 美元。

A: 谢谢。这是 12 美分的找零。这是您的收据和订单号。请在旁边等候取餐。您的取餐号会出现在屏幕上。

079

饮食生活

☐ Apple Pay 苹果支付

☐ sweet and sour sauce 酸甜酱

☐ show up 出现

Scene 5　肯德基点餐

A: What would you like to order?

B: A grilled chicken fillet burger.

A: Would you like to make it a combo?

B: Sure. Just give me combo NO.1.

A: What would you like to have for the drink?

B: Coke, please, with ice.

A: Anything else?

B: Yes, I'd like to have a side of baked beans without gravy. Can you make it?

A: Sure.

B: OK. Do you accept Apple Pay?

A: Yes. Would you like it for here or to go?

B: To go. Thanks.

A: The total is $3.56.

B: Here you are.

A: Thank you.

A：请问您想要点什么?

B：烤鸡柳汉堡。

A：请问您想要一份套餐吗?

B：是的。就要 1 号套餐吧。

A：喝什么饮料?

B：请给我可乐，加冰。

A：您还要别的吗?

B：还要，小食我想要一份不加肉汁的焗豆。你们能做吗?

A：当然可以。

B：好的。你们接受苹果支付吗?

A：接受。您想在这里吃还是带走?

B：带走。谢谢。

A：总共 3.56 美元。

B：给你。

A：谢谢。

080

Scene 6　三件套套餐

A: What do you want to have?

B: Can I have a three-piece meal, please?

A: Sure. Would you like fries and a drink with that?

B: Yes, please. And can I get extra ketchup?

A: Sure thing. That'll be $7.50.

B: Here you go, and keep the change.

A：请问您想要点什么?

B：请给我一份三件套的套餐，好吗?

A：好的。您要薯条和饮料吗?

B：要。能多给我一份番茄酱吗?

A：当然可以。一共是 7.5 美元。

B：给你，不用找零了。

Scene 7　点快餐

A: Hi, what can I get for you today?

B: Can I have a Big Mac meal, please?

A: Sure, would you like fries and a drink with that?

A：您好，请问您今天想要点什么?

B：我可以要一份巨无霸套餐吗?

A：当然可以。请问您要薯条和饮料吗?

重点词汇及表达

☐ combo *n.* 套餐

☐ gravy *n.* 肉汁

☐ three-piece *n.* 三件套

☐ extra *adj.* 额外的

B: Yes, please. A medium size.

A: Alright, that will be $9.50.

B: Here you go.

A: Thank you. Your order will be ready shortly.

B：要。中号的。

A：好的，一共9.5美元。

B：给你。

A：谢谢。您点的餐很快就好了。

Scene 8　买面包

A: Hi, can I have two slices of toast, please?

B: Sure. White or wheat bread?

A: White bread, please.

B: Would you like butter or jam with that?

A: Just butter, please.

B: OK. That's two slices of white toast with butter. Anything else?

A: No, that's it. How much is it?

B: $2.50, please.

A：嗨，请给我两片吐司，好吗?

B：好的。您要白面包还是小麦面包?

A：请给我白面包。

B：请问您要加黄油还是果酱?

A：只加黄油。

B：好的。两片涂黄油的白吐司。您还要别的吗?

A：不要了，就这个。多少钱?

B：2.5美元。

Scene 9　垃圾食品

A: Oh, Mia. You look so pretty. And you're in perfect shape. What's your secret?

B: Well, you're what you eat. If you wanna be in shape, you have to eat healthy.

A: No wonder I'm so fat. I don't think preserved meat is a good idea. Preserved meat tastes awesome. But technically, it's junk food. It has a lot of fat in it.

B: But you eat it all the time.

A: Look at me. I eat a lot of junk food. That's why I'm so fat, and you're so slim.

B: OK. Maybe you're right. Preserved meat isn't a good idea.

A：哦，米娅。你看起来真漂亮。你的身材真好。你的秘诀是什么?

B：嗯，你吃的东西决定你的身材。如果你想保持身材，你必须吃得健康。

A：难怪我这么胖。我觉得吃腌肉不好。腌肉味道好极了。但严格来说，这是垃圾食品。它里面有很多脂肪。

B：但你总是吃啊。

A：看看我。我吃了很多垃圾食品。所以我这么胖，而你这么苗条。

B：好吧。也许你是对的。吃腌肉不好。

☐ medium *adj.* 中等的

☐ shortly *adv.* 很快地

☐ slice *n.* 片

☐ butter *n.* 黄油

☐ jam *n.* 果酱

☐ be in shape 保持身材

☐ preserved meat 腌肉

☐ slim *adj.* 苗条的

Unit 4 Ordering Takeout 点外卖

Scene 1 电话点外卖

A: Hello！ Do you offer delivery services?

B: Yes, we do. What's your location?

A: I'm in the downtown area.

B: Perfect, we can deliver to you. What would you like to order?

A: I'd like a large pepperoni pizza and some garlic bread.

B: Great, your order will be delivered in about 30 minutes.

A: Thank you so much. How do I pay?

B: You can pay with cash or card upon delivery.

A：你好! 你们提供送餐服务吗?

B：提供。请问您在什么位置?

A：我在市中心。

B：太好了，我们可以为您送餐。请问您想要点什么?

A：我要大份的意大利辣香肠比萨饼和一些蒜味面包。

B：好的，您点的餐大约 30 分钟后送到。

A：非常感谢。我怎么付款?

B：您可以选择在送餐时用现金或银行卡支付。

Scene 2 外卖在哪儿

A: Hi, I placed an order, but it hasn't arrived yet.

B: Sorry about that. What's your order number?

A: It's 12345.

B: Let me check. It seems like the driver is stuck in traffic.

A: When will it arrive?

B: It should be there in about 10 minutes.

A: OK. Thanks for letting me know.

A：你好，我下了订单，但是还没有送到。

B：抱歉。请问您的订单号是多少?

A：12345。

B：我查一下。送餐的司机好像被堵在路上了。

A：什么时候能送到?

B：大约 10 分钟后送到。

A：好的。谢谢你告诉我。

Scene 3 缺少东西

A: Hi, I ordered food, but something's missing.

A：嗨，我点了餐，但是送到时少了些东西。

□ delivery service 送货服务

□ deliver v. 递送

□ place an order 下订单

□ be stuck in traffic 被堵在路上

B: Oh no！ What's missing?

A: One of the drinks is missing.

B: Sorry about that. We'll send it ASAP.

A: Can you also add something extra for the inconvenience?

B: Sure, we'll add a dessert to your order.

A: Thank you so much. I appreciate it!

B：哦，不会吧! 请问少了什么?

A：少了一份饮料。

B：抱歉。我们会尽快送出的。

A：你能不能加一些额外的东西来弥补给我带来的不便?

B：当然可以，我们会在您的订单上加赠一份甜点。

A：非常感谢。我很感激!

Scene 4　取外卖

A: Hi, here's your food. That'll be $30.

B: Sure, here's $40.

A: Thank you. Would you like any change back?

B: No, you can keep it as a tip.

A: Thank you very much! Enjoy your meal!

B: Thank you! Have a good one!

A：您好，这是您的食物。一共30美元。

B：好的，这是40美元。

A：谢谢。我需要给您找零吗?

B：不用了，你可以留着当作小费。

A：非常感谢! 祝您用餐愉快!

B：谢谢! 祝你过得愉快!

Scene 5　订餐

A: How do you use UberEATS to order food?

B: Download the app. Select restaurant. Add items to cart.

A: How do I pay for the food?

B: You can use a credit card or PayPal.

A: How long will it take to deliver?

B: Depends on the restaurant and location.

A: Do they deliver 24/7?

B: Depends on the restaurant's hours of operation.

A：你是怎么用优食软件订餐的?

B：下载应用程序。选择餐厅。往购物车中添加商品。

A：我怎么支付餐费?

B：你可以用信用卡或贝宝。

A：要多久才能送到?

B：这要看餐厅和位置。

A：他们全天送餐吗?

B：这取决于餐厅的营业时间。

☐ ASAP(as soon as possible) 尽快

☐ tip *n.* 小费

☐ UberEATS *n.* 优食（一款订餐软件）

☐ select *v.* 选择

☐ cart *n.* 购物车

☐ credit card 信用卡

☐ hour of operation 营业时间

Unit 5 At a Cafe 在咖啡馆

Scene 1 在咖啡馆点餐

A: Hello, what can I get for you today?

B: Give me the cappuccino, please.

A: Cappuccino. With ice or without ice?

B: With ice, please.

A: What about milk?

B: 2% milk.

A: Which size would you like to have? We have tall, grande and venti.

B: Venti is OK.

A: Anything else?

B: Did I say to add two pumps of chai?

A: No, you didn't.

B: Oh, give me two pumps of chai.

A: Two pumps of chai. May I have your name?

B: Yes. James.

A: James. J-a-

B: J-a-m-e-s.

A: OK. So, your total is 5 bucks.

B: 5 bucks. OK.

A: Please wait on the side. Thank you. Have a nice day.

A：您好，今天您要点什么？

B：请给我一杯卡布奇诺。

A：卡布奇诺。加冰还是不加冰？

B：请加冰。

A：加牛奶吗？

B：加 2% 的牛奶。

A：您要哪种杯型的？我们有中杯、大杯和特大杯。

B：我要特大杯。

A：还要别的吗？

B：我说过加两泵茶吗？

A：没说过。

B：哦，给我两泵茶。

A：两泵茶。能告诉我您的名字吗？

B：好的。詹姆斯。

A：詹姆斯。J-a -

B：J-a-m-e-s。

A：好的。所以，总共 5 美元。

B：5 美元。好的。

A：请在旁边稍等片刻。谢谢您！祝您过得愉快。

Scene 2 推荐咖啡

A: Hi, what would you recommend for a coffee?

A：嗨，你能推荐点什么咖啡吗？

084

□ tall, grande and venti
  中杯、大杯和特大杯

B: Hi there. We have a few options depending on what you like. Do you prefer something strong or mild?

A: I prefer something mild. What do you suggest?

B: Our house blend is great.

A: I'll try that. Milk and sugar, please.

B: Sure thing. How much milk and sugar?

A: Just a little milk and one sugar.

B: Got it. Here's your house blend. Enjoy!

B：您好。我们有几种选择，取决于您喜欢什么。您喜欢喝浓一点的还是淡一点的？

A：我喜欢喝淡一点的。你有什么建议？

B：我们这儿的招牌拼配咖啡很不错。

A：我试试。请加牛奶和糖。

B：好的。加多少牛奶和糖？

A：只要一点点牛奶和一块糖。

B：好的。这是您的招牌拼配咖啡。请享用吧！

Scene 3   加糖与否

A: Hi, can I get a cappuccino, please?

B: Sure. Would you like any sugar with that?

A: Yes, please. How many sugars do you recommend?

B: It depends on how sweet you like it. Our standard is two sugars, but you can add more or less according to your preference.

A: I'll go with two sugars, then. Thank you.

B: You're welcome. Your cappuccino will be ready shortly.

A：嗨，请给我一杯卡布奇诺，好吗？

B：好的。请问您要加糖吗？

A：要。你建议加多少糖？

B：那要看您喜欢哪种甜度。我们的标准是两块糖，但您可以根据自己的喜好多加或少加。

A：那我要两块糖。谢谢你！

B：不客气。您的卡布奇诺马上就准备好了。

Scene 4   询问杯型

A: Hi, can you tell me what sizes of cups you have for Americano?

B: Sure! We have small, medium, and large.

A: OK. I'll have a medium Americano, please.

A：你好，你能告诉我美式咖啡有哪些杯型吗？

B：当然可以！我们有小杯、中杯和大杯的。

A：好的。请给我一杯中杯美式咖啡。

085

饮食生活

☐ depend on 取决于
☐ house blend 招牌拼配咖啡
☐ sugar *n.* 糖

☐ standard *n.* 标准
☐ small, medium, and large
　小杯、中杯和大杯

B: Got it. Would you like any milk or sugar?

A: No, thank you. Just black.

B: Alright, that'll be ready for you in a few minutes.

Scene 5 时令咖啡

A: Hi, what seasonal coffee drinks do you have available?

B: Right now, we have a pumpkin spice latte and a peppermint mocha.

A: Oh, those both sound good. Which one do you recommend?

B: If you like something sweet and spicy, the pumpkin spice latte is a great choice. If you prefer something minty and chocolaty, go for the peppermint mocha.

A: Hmm, I think I'll try the pumpkin spice latte. Can I get that in a medium size, please?

B: Of course! And would you like any sugar or cream in that?

A: Just a little bit of sugar, please.

B: Great! That will be ready for you in just a few minutes.

Scene 6 佐食甜点

A: Hi, do you have any special desserts to go with our coffee?

B: Yes, we have a few options. Would you like me to list them for you?

A: Sure. That would be great.

B：好的。请问加牛奶还是加糖？

A：不用了，谢谢。就要黑咖啡。

B：好的，几分钟后就好。

A：嗨，你们有什么时令咖啡饮品？

B：我们现在有辛香南瓜拿铁和薄荷摩卡。

A：哦，听起来都不错。你推荐哪种？

B：如果您喜欢又甜又辣的饮品，辛香南瓜拿铁是不错的选择。如果你偏爱薄荷味和巧克力味的饮品，可以选择薄荷摩卡。

A：嗯，我想试试辛香南瓜拿铁。请给我中杯的，好吗？

B：好的。请问您要加糖或奶油吗？

A：只用加一点点糖。

B：好的。再过几分钟就好了。

A：嗨，你们有什么特别的甜点来配我们的咖啡吗？

B：哦，我们有几种选择。要我把它们列出来吗？

A：当然。那太好了。

重点词汇
及表达

☐ seasonal *adj.* 应季的，时令的

☐ pumpkin spice latte 辛香南瓜拿铁

☐ peppermint mocha 薄荷摩卡

☐ go with 与……搭配

☐ list *v.* 列清单

B: We have a seasonal fruit tart, chocolate croissant, and a caramel macchiato cheesecake.

A: Oh, the cheesecake sounds amazing! How much is it?

B: It's $5.50. Would you like me to add it to your order?

A: Yes, please!

B：我们有时令水果挞、巧克力牛角包和焦糖玛奇朵芝士蛋糕。

A：哦，芝士蛋糕听起来很棒! 多少钱?

B：5.5 美元。要我把它加到您的订单里吗?

A：要，加上吧!

Part 6
Choosing a Hotel
选择酒店

Unit 1 Make a Reservation 预订房间

Scene 1 预订房间

A: Hi, I'd like to check if you have any available rooms for tomorrow night.

B: Sure, let me check for you. How many people will be staying?

A: It's just me.

B: OK. We have a few rooms available. Would you like to make a reservation?

A: Yes, please. How much is the room per night?

B: It's $100 per night.

A: Great. I'll go ahead and make the reservation then.

B: Wonderful! We look forward to seeing you tomorrow night.

A：嗨，我想看看你们明天晚上是否还有空房。

B：好的，我帮您查一下。有多少人入住？

A：只有我。

B：好的。我们还有几间空房。您要预订吗？

A：要。一间房每晚多少钱？

B：每晚 100 美元。

A：好的，那我去预订了。

B：太棒了! 我们期待您明晚的入住。

090

Scene 2 预订单人间

A: Hi, I'd like to book a room, please.

B: Sure, what type of room do you need?

A: A single room for two nights.

B: That will be $200. Will you pay now or later?

A: Later, please.

A：你好，我想订一个房间。

B：好的，您需要什么样的房间？

A：一个单人间，住两晚。

B：一共 200 美元。您是现在付款还是稍后付款？

A：稍后付款。

Scene 3 预订套房

A: Hi, I'm interested in booking a suite.

B: Sure. How many people will be staying?

A: Two adults and one child.

B: Alright. That will be $300 per night.

A: Sounds good. Can I pay in cash?

A：你好，我想订一间套房。

B：好的。有多少人入住呢？

A：两个大人和一个孩子。

B：好的。那就是每晚 300 美元。

A：听起来不错。我可以付现金吗？

重点词汇
及表达

☐ make a reservation 预订
☐ book a room 预订房间
☐ single room 单人间

☐ suite *n.* 套房
☐ pay in cash 现金支付

Scene 4　现场订房

A: Hi, do you have any rooms available tonight?

B: Yes, we do. What kind of room are you interested in?

A: What options do you have, and what are the prices?

B: We have standard rooms, double rooms, deluxe rooms, and suites. Prices start at $100 per night.

A: And how can I pay for the room?

B: We accept cash and all major credit cards.

A：嗨，今晚你们还有空房吗？

B：有。请问您想要什么样的房间？

A：有哪些可选的？价格是多少？

B：我们有标准间、双人大床房、豪华房和套房。起价为每晚100美元。

A：我怎么付房费呢？

B：我们接受现金和所有主流信用卡支付。

Scene 5　预订钟点房

A: Excuse me. Do you have an hourly room here?

B: Yes, we do. May I know your check-in and check-out times, please?

A: I would like to check in at 1:00 pm and check out at 6:00 pm.

B: OK. We can offer you our hourly rate, which is $8 per hour.

A: Great. How do I make a reservation for the hourly room?

B: You can either call us to reserve or book directly on our website.

A：打扰一下，你们这里有钟点房吗？

B：有。请问您什么时候入住和退房呢？

A：我想在下午1点入住，6点退房。

B：好的。我们可以按小时收费，每小时8美元。

A：好的，我该如何预订钟点房呢？

B：您可以打电话预订，也可以直接在我们的网站上预订。

091

Scene 6　更改预订

A: Hi, can I help you with anything?

B: Yes, I would like to change my room type.

A: Sure, what type of room would you like?

B: I want a room with a king-size bed.

A：您好，请问我能帮您什么忙吗？

B：哦，我想换个房型。

A：好的，您想要什么样的房间？

B：我想要一个有特大号床的房间。

选择酒店

☐ standard room 标准间

☐ double room 双人大床房

☐ deluxe room 豪华房

☐ hourly *adj.* 每小时的

☐ check in 入住

☐ king-size *adj.* 特大的

A: Let me check if we have any available. Yes, we do. Would you like me to make the switch for you?

B: Yes, please.

A: Alright, I have updated your reservation.

A：我查一下是否还有空房间。嗯，有空房间。需要我帮您换吗？

B：需要，换吧。

A：好的，我已经更新了您的预订。

Unit 2 Check-in 入住酒店

Scene 1 入住酒店

A: Hi, I have a reservation under the name Smith.

B: Great. Can I see your ID and credit card, please?

A: Sure, here they are.

B: Thank you. Would you like a room with a view?

A: Yes, please. Is that available?

B: Yes, it is. Here's your key card. Enjoy your stay!

A：你好，我以史密斯的名字预订了房间。

B：好的。我能看一下您的身份证和信用卡吗？

A：当然可以，给你。

B：谢谢。您想要能看到风景的房间吗？

A：是的，想要。有空房吗？

B：有。这是您的钥匙卡。祝您入住愉快！

092

Scene 2 办理入住手续

A: Good evening, Ma'am. What can I do for you?

B: I made a reservation under the name of Lily for 1 single room.

A: Just a minute, please. Let me check the reservation records. OK, I see. One single room from Friday to Sunday, right?

B: Yes, exactly.

A: Can I have your passport, please?

B: Certainly, here you are.

A：晚上好，女士。请问我能为您做些什么？

B：我以莉莉的名义预订了一个单人间。

A：请稍等。我查一下预订记录。嗯，看到了。周五到周日，一个单人间，对吗？

B：是的，没错。

A：请问我能看一下您的护照吗？

B：当然可以，给你。

重点词汇及表达

□ make the switch 做出改变

□ view *n.* 风景

□ key card 钥匙卡；磁卡

□ reservation record 预订记录

B: Thank you. And please fill in the registration form.

A: All right.

B: How would you like to pay, cash or credit?

A: Credit, please.

B: Here are the keys to your room. Please make sure you have them with you all the time. You need to show them when you sign up for your meals and when you order drinks in restaurants and bars.The bellman will show you up to your room.

B: 谢谢。请填写一下登记表。

A: 好的。

B: 您怎么付款，现金还是信用卡？

A: 信用卡。

B: 这是您房间的钥匙。请确保一直把它们带在身上。当您在餐厅和酒吧登记用餐和点饮料时，您需要向他们出示。行李员会带您去您的房间。

Scene 3   团体入住

A: Good afternoon. May I help you?

B: Good afternoon. I'm Lily, the tour leader from the Lily Travel Agency.

A: Welcome to our hotel.

B: Thanks.

A: You made a reservation for 12 twin rooms for today, September 18th. Is this correct?

B: Yes. I'm afraid we have some last-minute changes. I need a connecting room for a family of five.

A: I'm sorry we don't have any more connecting rooms. Can I suggest a suite instead?

B: How much is it?

A: It costs twice as much as the connecting room.

B: It's reasonable. I'll take it.

A: Your check-out time is at 8:00 am tomorrow. Are there any other changes in your schedule?

B: Yes, I'd like to check out at 8:30 am.

A: 下午好。我能为您效劳吗？

B: 下午好。我是莉莉，莉莉旅行社的领队。

A: 欢迎光临我们酒店。

B: 谢谢。

A: 您预订了今天，9月18日的12间双人房。对吗？

B: 对。抱歉我们临时有些变动。我需要一间连通房给一个五口之家住。

A: 抱歉，我们没有更多的连通房了。我推荐您订一间套房，可以吗？

B: 多少钱？

A: 它的费用是连通房的两倍。

B: 很合理。我订一间吧。

A: 您的退房时间是明天上午8点。请问您的日程安排还有其他变动吗？

B: 有，我想在上午8点半退房。

□ registration form 登记表

□ sign up for 登记

□ travel agency 旅行社

□ twin room 双人间

□ check-out n. 退房

A: 8:30. Noted. Anything else?

A：8点半退房。给您记下来了。请问您还有别的事吗？

B: Please give us a **wake-up call** at 6:45 am.

B：请在早晨6点45分叫醒我们。

A: Sure, wake-up call at 6:45 tomorrow morning. And your luggage will be collected at 7:45. Is it OK?

A：好的，明早6点45分提供叫醒服务。您的行李在7点45分收取。可以吗？

B: Yes.

B：可以。

A: Here are the registration cards. Please help your guests fill them in. Thank you very much.

A：这些是登记卡。请帮您的客人填写好。非常感谢。

B: Done. Here you are.

B：填好了。给您。

A: Thank you. Would you please sign your name here, Ma'am?

A：谢谢。女士，请您在这里签名，好吗？

B: Oh, yeah.

B：哦，好的。

B: Here are your keys. Is there anything else I can do for you?

B：这是您的钥匙。我还能为您做些什么吗？

A: No, that's all. Thank you.

A：没事了，就这些！谢谢！

B: Thank you. I hope you enjoy your stay in the hotel.

B：也谢谢您。希望您在酒店过得愉快。

 Hotel Breakfast 酒店早餐

Scene 1 早餐式样

A: Good morning, Sir. What would you like to have for your breakfast?

A：早上好，先生。请问您早餐想吃点什么？

B: What do you **serve** here?

B：你们这儿供应什么？

A: We serve continental breakfast and American breakfast.

A：我们供应欧式早餐和美式早餐。

B: What do you serve for continental breakfast?

B：你们供应什么样的欧式早餐？

A: We serve rolls with butter and coffee.

A：我们供应黄油面包卷和咖啡。

B: How about American breakfast?

B：美式早餐有什么？

重点词汇
及表达

- □ wake-up call 叫醒服务
- □ serve v. 供应
- □ continental breakfast 欧式早餐
- □ American breakfast 美式早餐

A: Apple juice or orange juice, tea or coffee, toast with butter or jam, eggs with bacon.

B: I will have orange juice, toast, and 2 eggs. Can I have ham instead of bacon?

A: Certainly, Sir. How would you like the eggs?

B: Sunny-side up, please.

A: OK.

A：苹果汁、橙汁、茶、咖啡、加黄油或果酱的面包、鸡蛋培根。

B：我要橙汁、烤面包和两个鸡蛋。我可以把培根换成火腿吗?

A：当然可以，先生。鸡蛋要怎么做?

B：太阳蛋。

A：好的。

Scene 2 早餐选择

A: Good morning! What would you like for breakfast?

B: I'm in the mood for a ham and cheese omelet.

A: Great choice. How would you like your eggs cooked?

B: Can I get it with scrambled eggs?

A: Sure thing. I'll put in your order right away.

A：早上好! 请问您早餐想吃什么?

B：我想吃火腿芝士煎蛋卷。

A：不错的选择。您的鸡蛋要怎么做?

B：我想要炒鸡蛋，可以吗?

A：当然可以。我马上给您下单。

Scene 3 素食早餐

A: Good morning! What can I get for you?

B: Do you have any vegetarian breakfast options?

A: Yes, we have an omelet with peppers, onions, and mushrooms.

B: That sounds perfect. Can you make it with egg whites only?

A: Of course. We can do that for you. Anything else?

B: No, that's it. Thank you.

A：早上好! 请问您想吃点什么?

B：你们有素食早餐可选吗?

A：有，我们有煎蛋卷配辣椒、洋葱和蘑菇。

B：听起来很不错。你能只用蛋白做吗?

A：当然可以。我们可以为您烹制。请问您还要别的吗?

B：不用了，就要这个。谢谢。

Scene 4 做错鸡蛋

A: Hey, what would you like for your breakfast?

B: I'd like fried eggs and ham. Over easy.

A：嘿，请问您早餐想吃点什么?

B：我要煎蛋和火腿。鸡蛋煎两面。

☐ ham and cheese omelet 火腿芝士煎蛋卷

☐ scrambled egg 炒鸡蛋

☐ pepper *n.* 辣椒

☐ onion *n.* 洋葱

☐ mushroom *n.* 蘑菇

☐ over easy 两面都煎熟，但是蛋黄还有点稀的煎鸡蛋

A: OK. Fried eggs and ham. Easy?

B: Yeah, over easy.

A: Easy. OK. Easy. Here is your egg. Easy.

(The server came with a raw egg. He interpreted "easy" as meaning "not cooked at all".)

B: Oh, this is not what I ordered.

A: Easy.

B: No. In America, when we talk about fried eggs, we usually use 4 types—sunny-side up, over easy, over medium, and over hard. Sunny-side up is when just one side of the egg is cooked a lot. The other side, the side that's up, is very runny.

A: Oh, so it looks like sunshine.

B: Exactly. Looks like sunshine on a plate. Over easy is when both sides are cooked, but the yolk is still a bit runny. Over medium, the yolk is just in between medium. And over hard is when the yolk is at its hardest point.

A: Oh, I understand. So when you say over easy, I actually need to fry the eggs and fry both sides. But the yolk is runny.

B: Exactly.

A: I'm so sorry for this. I'm going to make you a new one.

A：好的。煎鸡蛋和火腿。简单？

B：哦，两面煎的。

A：简单。好的。简单。这是您的鸡蛋。简单鸡蛋。

（服务员拿着生鸡蛋来了。他认为"easy"的意思是"完全不用煎"。）

B：哦，我点的不是这个。

A：但你说的是"简单鸡蛋"。

B：不是。在美国，当我们谈论煎鸡蛋时，通常有4种类型：一面煎的太阳蛋，两面煎的流心蛋，两面煎的半熟鸡蛋以及两面煎的全熟鸡蛋。sunny-side up（一面煎的太阳蛋）指只煎鸡蛋的一面。另一面，就是向上的那一面，蛋黄是很稀的。

A：哦，所以看起来像太阳。

B：没错。看起来像放在盘子里的太阳。over easy（两面煎的流心蛋）指两面都煎熟，但是蛋黄还有点稀的煎鸡蛋。over medium（两面煎的半熟鸡蛋）指蛋黄火候正好的煎鸡蛋。over hard（两面煎的全熟鸡蛋）就是把蛋黄煎至全熟。

A：哦，明白了。所以当你说over easy时，实际上我需要煎鸡蛋，两面都煎，而蛋黄是稀的。

B：没错。

A：对此我很抱歉。我给您重新做一份。

重点词汇口表达

☐ sunny-side up 一面煎得很熟的鸡蛋

☐ over medium 蛋黄火候正好的煎鸡蛋

☐ over hard 蛋黄最硬的煎鸡蛋

Unit 4 Hotel Facilities 酒店设施

Scene 1   配套设施

A: Excuse me. Do you have any fitness facilities or laundry rooms in the hotel?

B: Yes, we have a fitness center on the third floor and a laundry room on each floor.

A: Great, thank you. What are the opening hours for the fitness center?

B: The fitness center is open 24 hours a day.

A：打扰了。请问酒店里有健身设施或洗衣房吗？

B：有，三楼有健身中心，每层都有洗衣房。

A：太好了，谢谢。请问健身中心什么时候开放？

B：健身中心 24 小时开放。

Scene 2   无线网络密码

A: Hi, could you please tell me the Wi-Fi password for the hotel?

B: Yes, sure. The Wi-Fi password is "hotelguests123".

A: OK. Got it. Thank you so much.

B: Is there anything else I can assist you with?

A: No, that's all. Thanks again!

B: You're welcome. Have a nice day!

A：你好，你能告诉我酒店的无线网络密码吗？

B：当然可以。无线网络密码是"hotelguests123"。

A：好的。明白了。非常感谢。

B：还有什么需要我帮忙吗？

A：不需要了，就这些。再次感谢！

B：不客气。祝您过得愉快！

Scene 3   缺漏物品

A: Excuse me. There are no slippers or hangers in my room.

B: I'm sorry about that. I'll bring them up for you.

A: Thanks. I appreciate it.

B: Here you are. Is there anything else you need?

A: No, that's all. Thank you.

A：打扰了。我的房间里没有拖鞋和衣架。

B：抱歉。我帮您拿上来。

A：谢谢。非常感谢。

B：给您。请问您还需要什么吗？

A：不用了，就这些。谢谢你！

選擇酒店

097

- fitness facilities 健身设施
- laundry room 洗衣房
- fitness center 健身中心
- password n. 密码
- assist v. 帮助
- slipper n. 拖鞋
- hanger n. 衣架

Scene 4　找吹风机

A: Excuse me. Do you know where the hair dryer is in the room?

B: It should be in the top drawer.

A: I looked, but it's not there.

B: Let me check for you. Ah, it's in the bathroom.

A: Thanks so much!

A：打扰一下，你知道吹风机在房间里的什么地方吗？

B：应该在最上层的抽屉里。

A：我找过了，但里面没有。

B：我帮你找找。啊，在浴室里。

A：非常感谢!

Scene 5　租充电器

A: Excuse me. Do you have a charger and a Type-C cable I can borrow?

B: Yes, we do. I can bring them to your room.

A: That would be great. Thank you so much!

B: No problem. Just give me your room number.

A: It's 1206.

B: OK, I'll be there in a minute.

A：打扰一下。你们有充电器和 Type-C（注：一种连接口型号）连接线吗？我想借用一下。

B：有。我可以把它们送到您的房间。

A：那太好了。非常感谢!

B：不客气。请告诉我您的房间号。

A：1206。

B：好的，我马上就到。

Scene 6　找电源适配器

A: I need to rent an adaptor. How much is it?

B: It's $5 per day. And the deposit is $20.

A: That's fine. Can I pay the deposit with my credit card?

B: No, we only accept cash for the deposit.

A: Alright, I'll go find an ATM.

A：我需要租一个电源适配器。多少钱?

B：每天 5 美元。押金是 20 美元。

A：好的。我可以用信用卡支付押金吗?

B：不行，我们只接受现金支付押金。

A：好的，我去找一台自动取款机。

Scene 7　租电源适配器

A: Do you have an adaptor to rent?

B: Yes, we do. It's $5 per day.

A：你们有电源适配器出租吗?

B：有。每天 5 美元。

重点词汇
又表达

□ hair dryer 吹风机
□ drawer n. 抽屉
□ bathroom n. 浴室
□ in a minute 马上，立刻

□ adaptor n. 适配器
□ deposit n. 押金

A: OK. I'll take one. How much is the deposit?

B: $20. You'll get it back when you return the adaptor.

A: Sounds good.

A：好的。我要一个。押金是多少?

B：20 美元。您归还电源适配器的时候，押金会退给您。

A：听起来不错。

Scene 8 插座不匹配

A: Room service. What can I do for you?

B: This is Ms. Zheng's room 336. Do you have any adaptors? The socket doesn't work for me.

A: Yes. We'll send it to you right away. We don't charge for the adaptor. But we need $100 for the deposit. Is it OK?

B: No problem. Thanks.

A：客房服务。我能为您做些什么吗?

B：我是 336 房间的郑女士。你们有电源适配器吗? 这个插座用不了。

A：有。我们马上给您送过去。电源适配器不收费。但是我们要收 100 美元的押金，可以吗?

B：没问题。谢谢。

Unit 5 Hotel Room Service 酒店客房服务

Scene 1 帮搬行李

A: Excuse me. Could you help me with my luggage to the room, please?

B: Of course, Sir. I'd be happy to assist you.

A: Thank you. How much would be an appropriate tip for you?

B: It's entirely up to you, Sir. Any amount is appreciated.

A：打扰一下，你能帮我把行李搬到房间吗?

B：当然可以，先生。我很乐意为您服务。

A：谢谢。给你多少小费比较合适?

B：这完全由您决定，先生。给多少我都很感谢。

Scene 2 叫醒服务

A: Hello, could I please schedule a wake-up call for tomorrow morning?

B: Sure. What time would you like to be woken up?

A：你好，可以为我安排明天早晨的叫醒服务吗?

B：当然可以。您希望在什么时候叫醒您?

☐ room service 客房服务

☐ charge *v.* 收费

☐ luggage *n.* 行李

☐ appropriate *adj.* 合适的

☐ wake up 叫醒

A: Could you please set it for 7:00 am?

B: Of course, I'll make sure to set it for 7:00 am. Is there anything else I can help you with?

A: No, that's it. Thank you very much.

B: You're welcome. Have a good night's sleep!

A：你能把时间定在早晨 7 点吗？

B：当然可以，我保证早晨 7 点叫醒您。请问还有什么需要我帮忙的吗？

A：没有了，就这个。非常感谢。

B：不客气。祝您睡个好觉！

Scene 3 询问洗衣服务

A: Excuse me. Can I drop off my laundry here?

B: Sure. Do you have a laundry bag?

A: No, I don't. Do you have one?

B: Yes, here you go. What time would you like it back?

A: Tomorrow morning, please.

B: OK. We'll have it ready for you. What's your room number?

A: Room 212. Thank you!

A：打扰一下，我可以把待洗衣物放在这里吗？

B：当然可以。请问您有洗衣袋吗？

A：我没有。你有吗？

B：有，给您。您希望什么时候取回这些衣服？

A：明天早晨。

B：好的。我们会为您准备好的。您的房间号是多少？

A：212 房间。谢谢你！

Scene 4 酒店洗衣服务

A: Hi, do you know if the hotel has laundry service?

B: Yes, they do. It's on the second floor.

A: Great, thanks. Do you know how much it costs?

B: I think it's $5 per load.

A: Perfect, I'll need to wash some clothes later.

B: You can also buy detergent at the front desk.

A：嗨，你知道酒店提供洗衣服务吗？

B：知道，他们提供。在二楼。

A：太好了，谢谢。你知道费用是多少吗？

B：我记得是每次 5 美元。

A：太好了，我一会儿要洗衣服。

B：您也可以在前台购买洗衣液。

Scene 5 提供洗衣服务

A: Housekeeping. What can I do for you?

B: I have some laundry to be done.

A：保洁。我能为您做些什么？

B：我有一些衣服要洗。

重点词汇
及表达

☐ make sure 确保

☐ laundry *n.* 待洗衣物

☐ laundry bag 洗衣袋

☐ laundry service 洗衣服务

☐ detergent *n.* 洗衣液

☐ housekeeping *n.* 保洁

A: Well, would you fill out the laundry form, please? The laundry bags and laundry forms are in the drawer of the writing desk.

B: Would you send someone to pick up my laundry?

A: Yes, Ma'am. I will send someone immediately. Just put your laundry in the laundry bag.

(A few minutes later)

A: Housekeeping. May I come in?

B: Yes, come in, please.

A: Good morning, Ma'am. I'm here to collect your laundry.

B: Here you are. When can I have it back?

A: Usually in a day. If you need it urgently, we'll charge extra.

B: There is no need to hurry. Thank you.

A：哦，请您填写一下洗衣单好吗？洗衣袋和洗衣单在写字台的抽屉里。

B：你能派人来取我要洗的衣服吗？

A：好的，女士。我马上派人去。您只需要把待洗衣物放在洗衣袋里就可以了。

（几分钟后）

A：保洁。我可以进来吗？

B：可以，请进。

A：早上好，女士。我过来取您的待洗衣物。

B：给你。我什么时候能拿回来？

A：通常在一天之内。如果您要加急，我们会另外收费。

B：不着急。谢谢你！

Scene 6 维修电器

A: Hello, the TV in my room is not working. Can you please send someone to fix it?

B: I'm sorry to hear that. What is your room number?

A: My room number is 203.

B: OK. I will send someone to your room to fix the TV.

A: Thank you. How long will it take?

B: It should take around 10–15 minutes. We'll try to fix it as soon as possible.

A: Alright, thank you for your help.

B: You're welcome. Please let us know if you need anything else.

A：你好，我房间里的电视坏了。你能派人来修一下吗？

B：听到这个消息我很抱歉。您的房间号是多少？

A：我的房间号是203。

B：好的。我会派人去您的房间修电视。

A：谢谢。要花多长时间？

B：大约需要10~15分钟。我们会尽快修好的。

A：好的，谢谢你的帮助。

B：不客气。如果您还需要什么，请告诉我们。

□ fill out 填写

□ laundry form 洗衣单

□ urgently *adv.* 紧急地

□ fix *v.* 修理

Scene 7 清理房间

A: Hi, I won't be in the room this morning. Can the housekeeping come and clean the room, please?

B: Sure. What time will you be out?

A: Probably until noon. Can they come before that?

B: Yes, they will come and change the sheets and towels. Is there anything else you need?

A: No, that's all. Thank you!

B: You're welcome. Have a nice day!

A：嗨，今天上午我不在房间里。客房服务员能来打扫一下房间吗？

B：当然可以。请问您什么时候不在？

A：我可能要到正午才回来。他们可以在那之前来吗？

B：可以，他们会来换床单和毛巾。请问您还需要什么？

A：没有了，就这些。谢谢你！

B：不客气。祝您过得愉快！

Unit 6 Check-out 退房结账

Scene 1 结清费用

A: Excuse me. How can I settle the bill for the room amenities before checking out?

B: Sure, you can either pay with cash or a credit card at the front desk. Do you need me to print the itemized bill for you?

A: No, that's OK. I'll pay with my credit card. Can you tell me the total amount?

B: Certainly, the total is $120.

A: OK. Thank you. Here's my credit card.

B: Thank you. Please insert your card here and enter your PIN number.

A：打扰了。请问退房前我怎样结算房间里的额外消费？

B：哦，您可以在前台用现金或信用卡付款。需要我帮您打印账单明细吗？

A：不用了。我用信用卡支付。你能告诉我总金额吗？

B：当然可以，总共 120 美元。

A：好的。谢谢你！这是我的信用卡。

B：谢谢，请在这里插卡并输入密码。

重点词汇及表达

☐ change the sheet 换床单
☐ towel *n.* 毛巾
☐ settle the bill 结账
☐ amenity *n.* 便利设施

☐ print the itemized bill 打印账单明细
☐ insert *v.* 插入

Scene 2 退房结账

A: Hi, I need to check out now.

B: Sure. Can I have your room number?

A: It's Room 205.

B: Alright, let me check. Looks like everything is in order. Would you like a receipt?

A: Yes, please.

B: Here you go. Thank you for staying with us.

A：你好，我现在需要退房。

B：好的。能告诉我您的房间号吗？

A：205 房间。

B：好的，我查一下。看起来一切井然有序。请问您要收据吗？

A：要。

B：给您。感谢您入住我们酒店。

Scene 3 续住费用

A: Excuse me. I'd like to extend my stay. How can I do that?

B: Sure, you can come to the front desk. And we can help you with that.

A: Do I need to check out and then check back in again?

B: No, you can just let us know the dates you want to extend. And we'll update your reservation.

A: Is there any extra paperwork or payment needed?

B: We'll just need to update your information, and you'll need to pay for the additional nights.

A: OK. Thank you for letting me know.

B: You're welcome. If you have any other questions, feel free to ask.

A：打扰了，我想延长我的住宿时间。我该怎么做呢？

B：好的，您可以来前台。我们可以帮您办理。

A：我需要退房后再重新入住吗？

B：不用，您只需要告诉我们您想延长的日期。我们会更新您的预订信息。

A：还需要额外的文书工作或付款吗？

B：我们只需要更新您的信息。此外，您需要支付额外的住宿费用。

A：好的。谢谢你告诉我这些。

B：不客气。如果您还有什么疑问，随时问我。

103

选择酒店

☐ in order 井然有序

☐ extend one's stay 延长住宿时间

☐ the front desk 前台

☐ additional *adj.* 额外的

Part 7　Transportation

交通出行

Unit 1 Ordering a Taxi 叫出租车

Scene 1   预订出租车

A: Hi, can you help me book a taxi?

B: Sure. Where would you like to go?

A: To the airport, please.

B: What time do you need the taxi?

A: I need it at 3:00 pm.

B: OK, the taxi will arrive at your location at 2:45 pm. Can I have your name and phone number, please?

A: My name is John, and my phone number is 123-456-7890.

A：你好，你能帮我订一辆出租车吗？

B：当然可以。您想去哪里？

A：去机场。

B：您什么时候需要出租车？

A：下午 3 点。

B：好的，出租车将在下午 2 点 45 分到达您所在位置。能告诉我您的姓名和电话号码吗？

A：我叫约翰。我的电话号码是 123-456-7890。

Scene 2   软件叫车

A: Excuse me. Can you tell me how to use the app to call a taxi?

B: Sure. First, you need to download the taxi app and create an account.

A: OK, then what should I do next?

B: After that, open the app and enter your pick-up location and destination.

A: Got it. How do I pay for the ride through the app?

B: You can link your bank card to the app and pay for the ride automatically.

A: Thank you so much for your help!

B: No problem. Have a safe and comfortable trip!

A：打扰一下，你能告诉我怎样用软件叫出租车吗？

B：当然可以。首先，您需要下载出租车软件并创建一个账户。

A：好的，接下来我该做什么？

B：然后打开应用程序，输入您的上车地点和目的地。

A：明白了。我怎样通过软件支付车费呢？

B：您可以把您的银行卡绑定在这个软件上，然后就可以自动支付车费了。

A：非常感谢你的帮助！

B：不客气。祝您旅途平安舒适！

□ taxi *n.* 出租车
□ airport *n.* 机场
□ create an account 创建账户
□ automatically *adv.* 自动地

□ comfortable *adj.* 舒适的

Scene 3　路线选择

A: Hi, can you take me to the airport, please?

B: Sure. Which terminal do you need?

A: Terminal 2, please.

B: OK. Do you have a preferred route, or should I take the fastest one?

A: Please take the fastest one.

B: Got it. We'll take the highway then.

A: Thank you.

B: No problem. We should arrive in about 20 minutes.

A: Great, thanks for your help.

B: You're welcome. Have a safe flight!

A：你好，你能送我去机场吗？

B：当然可以。您要去哪个航站楼？

A：2 号航站楼。

B：好的。您有首选的路线吗？或者我就选择时间最短的路线？

A：请选择时间最短的路线。

B：明白了。那我们走高速公路吧。

A：谢谢。

B：不客气。我们大约20分钟后到达。

A：太好了，谢谢你的帮助。

B：不客气。祝您一路平安!

Scene 4　使用导航

A: Excuse me. Do you know how to get to the Museum of Art?

B: I'm sorry. I'm not familiar with that location. Do you know the address?

A: Yes, it's 123 Main Street.

B: Let me input that into my GPS. Oh, I see. It's about 20 minutes away. Would you like me to follow the GPS?

A: Yes, please. Thank you!

B: No problem. We should arrive at the destination soon.

A：打扰一下，你知道怎么去艺术博物馆吗？

B：抱歉，我对那个地方不熟悉。您知道地址吗？

A：知道，主街123 号。

B：我把它输入我的 GPS 导航。哦，我知道了。大约20分钟的路程。我跟着 GPS 导航走，好吗？

A：好的。谢谢你!

B：不客气。我们很快就会到达目的地。

Scene 5　支付方式

A: How much is the fare to the airport?

B: It's $30.

A: Is that the fixed price, or can we negotiate?

A：去机场多少钱？

B：30 美元。

A：这是固定价格吗？还可以协商吗？

☐ terminal *n.* 航站楼

☐ highway *n.* 高速公路

☐ input *v.* 输入

☐ destination *n.* 目的地

☐ fare *n.* 费用

☐ fixed price 固定价格

B: It's a fixed price. I can't negotiate, sorry.

A: OK, and what payment methods do you accept?

B: We accept cash and card payments.

A: Great, I'll pay with my card then.

B: Sure, just let me know when you're ready to pay.

B：这是固定价格。抱歉，不能讨价还价。

A：好的，你们接受什么付款方式？

B：我们接受现金和刷卡支付。

A：好的，那我刷卡支付。

B：好的，您准备付款时告诉我一声。

Scene 6 晕车开窗

A: Excuse me. Could you please drive a bit slower? I feel a bit sick.

B: Sure, I'll slow down. Is there anything else I can do to help?

A: Could you also roll down a window for some fresh air?

B: Of course, no problem. I hope this helps.

A: Thank you. I appreciate it. I'm not used to riding in cars for too long.

B: No worries. Take your time. We'll get there safely.

A：抱歉，你能开慢一点吗？我觉得有点不舒服。

B：当然可以，我会开慢点。请问还需要我做点什么吗？

A：你能把车窗摇下来让新鲜空气进来吗？

B：当然可以，没问题。我希望这对您有帮助。

A：谢谢，我很感激。我不习惯长时间坐车。

B：别担心，慢慢来。我们会安全到达的。

Scene 7 搭乘出租车

A: Ma'am, I know you are in a hurry. But no smoking is allowed in this car. Please understand.

B: Oh, I'm sorry. Just drop me off here, and I'll walk to the airport.

A: I'm sorry. I can't stop here. It's not allowed. Here we are. The airport is over there.

B: How much is it?

A: $38.

B: OK. Here is forty and keep the change.

A：女士，我知道您很着急。但是车内禁止吸烟。请您理解。

B：哦，抱歉。让我在这里下车，我步行去机场。

A：抱歉，我不能在这里停车。这是不允许的。我们到了。机场在那边。

B：多少钱？

A：38 美元。

B：好的。这是 40 美元，不用找零了。

重点词汇
及表达

☐ negotiate *v.* 协商

☐ sick *adj.* 难受的

☐ fresh air 新鲜空气

☐ safely *adv.* 安全地

108

A: Let me open the trunk for you.

B: OK. Thank you.

A: Oh, your suitcase is pretty heavy. OK. Have a good trip.

B: Thank you.

A: Bye.

A：我来帮您打开后备厢。

B：好的。谢谢你!

A：哦，您的行李箱真重。好了。祝您旅途愉快!

B：谢谢。

A：再见。

Unit 2 Taking the Subway 乘坐地铁

Scene 1 运营时间

A: Excuse me. what time does the subway start running?

B: The first train starts at 6:00 am, and the last train departs at 11:00 pm.

A: What about on weekends?

B: On weekends, the subway starts running at 7:00 am, and the last train departs at midnight.

A: How often do the trains come?

B: During peak hours, trains come every 2–3 minutes. Off-peak, they come every 5–10 minutes.

A: Thank you for the information.

A：打扰了，请问地铁什么时候开始运营?

B：首班车早晨6点发车，末班车晚上11点发车。

A：在周末呢?

B：周末地铁早晨7点开始运营，末班车午夜发车。

A：列车多久来一次?

B：在高峰时段，每2~3分钟一班地铁。在非高峰时段，每5~10分钟一班。

A：谢谢你提供的信息。

109

Scene 2 支付方式

A: Excuse me. Where can I buy a subway ticket?

B: You can buy a ticket at the ticket vending machines or the ticket counter.

A: Do you accept credit cards or only cash?

A：打扰了。请问我在哪儿可以购买地铁票?

B：您可以在自动售票机或售票处买票。

A：你们接受信用卡支付吗? 还是只接受现金?

☐ trunk *n.* 后备厢

☐ suitcase *n.* 行李箱

☐ subway *n.* 地铁

☐ depart *v.* 出发

☐ at midnight 在午夜

☐ ticket vending machine 自动售票机

☐ ticket counter 售票处

B: We accept both credit cards and cash. You can use **contactless payment methods** as well.

A: That's great. Any **price differences**?

B: No, the price is the same. But you can get some discounts if you use a **transit card** or a mobile app.

A: Got it. Thank you for your help.

B: 我们接受信用卡和现金。您也可以使用非接触支付方式。

A: 太棒了。价格有差异吗？

B: 没有，价格是一样的。但如果您使用交通卡或移动应用程序，可以获得一些折扣。

A: 明白了。谢谢你的帮助。

Scene 3 地铁停运

A: Why is the subway not running?

B: There is a **technical issue**.

A: Do you know when it'll **be back in service**?

B: I'm not sure, but they're working on it.

A: Is there any other way to get to my destination?

B: You can take a bus or a taxi.

A: 地铁怎么停运了？

B: 出现了技术故障。

A: 你知道什么时候能恢复运营吗？

B: 我不确定，但他们正在抢修。

A: 我还可以通过别的方式到达目的地吗？

B: 您可以乘坐公交车或出租车。

110

Scene 4 遗失物品

A: Excuse me. Can you help me?

B: Sure, what's the matter?

A: I **accidentally** dropped my phone on the subway. Is there anything I can do?

B: Let me check with **the lost and found** department. What subway line were you on?

A: I was on the blue line heading south.

B: OK, I'll call them and see if they have your phone. What's the model and color?

A: It's an iPhone 14, black.

B: Got it. Please give me your contact information, and I'll let you know if we find it.

A: 打扰了，你能帮我一下吗？

B: 当然可以。怎么了？

A: 我不小心把手机落在地铁上了。有什么办法找回来吗？

B: 我去问问失物招领处。请问您乘坐的是哪条地铁线路？

A: 我当时在往南行驶的蓝色线路上。

B: 好的，我会给他们打电话，问问他们是否看到了您的手机。您的手机是什么型号、什么颜色的？

A: 我的手机是黑色的苹果14。

B: 知道了。请留下您的联系方式。如果找到了，我们会通知您的。

重点词汇
及表达

☐ contactless payment method 非接触支付方式

☐ price difference 价格差异

☐ transit card 交通卡

☐ technical issue 技术故障

☐ be back in service 恢复运营

☐ accidentally *adv.* 意外地

☐ the lost and found 失物招领

A: Thank you so much. Here's my number and email.

A：非常感谢。这是我的电话号码和电子邮箱。

Scene 5　地铁换乘

A: Excuse me. Do you know how to transfer to Line 2 from here?

B: Yes, you can take this Line 1 to the next station, and then transfer to Line 2.

A: Thank you. Is it easy to find the transfer station?

B: Yes, it's very straightforward. Just follow the signs to the transfer corridor.

A: OK, got it. How long does the transfer usually take?

B: It depends on the time of day, but usually it takes about 5 to 10 minutes.

A: Thank you so much for your help!

B: You're welcome. Have a safe trip!

A：打扰一下。你知道从这里怎么换乘2号线吗？

B：知道，你可以乘坐1号线到下一站，然后换乘2号线。

A：谢谢。换乘站容易找吗？

B：容易，很简单直接。跟着指示牌就可以走到换乘通道。

A：好的，知道了。换乘通常需要多长时间？

B：这取决于一天中的不同时段，但通常需要大约5~10分钟。

A：非常感谢你的帮助！

B：不客气。一路平安！

Scene 6　地铁广播

A: Attention all passengers, please mind the gap between the train and the platform. This is the last train of the night. Please ensure that you have all of your belongings with you as you exit the train. Thank you for riding with us, and have a safe journey home.

B: Dear passengers, your attention, please. The train bound for Dayun Station is arriving soon. Please do not cross the yellow safety lines on the platform, and mind the gap between the train and the platform. We wish you a safe and pleasant journey.

A：各位乘客请注意，请小心列车与站台之间的空隙。这是今晚的最后一班列车。离开车厢时，请确保带好您所有的随身物品。感谢您乘坐此次地铁，回家路上一路平安。

B：亲爱的乘客们，请注意。开往大运站的列车就要到站了。请不要越过站台上的黄色安全线。注意列车与站台之间的空隙。祝您旅途平安愉快。

交通出行

□ transfer v. 换乘

□ sign n. 标识

□ transfer corridor 换乘通道

□ gap n. 空隙

□ platform n. 站台

□ ensure v. 确保

□ belongings n. 财物

□ exit v. 离开

C: Ladies and gentlemen, we have now arrived at Dayun Station. The doors will open on the left. Please take all your belongings with you and mind the gap between the train and the platform as you exit. We hope you had a comfortable journey with us, and thank you for choosing our service. Please note that the next station is Ailian Station.

C：女士们，先生们，我们现在已经到达大运站。列车将会开启左侧车门。下车时请带好您的随身物品，并注意列车与站台之间的空隙。希望您旅途愉快，感谢您选择我们的服务。请注意，下一站是爱联站。

Unit 3 Taking a Bus 乘坐公交车

Scene 1 公交出行

A: Excuse me. Do you know how to get to the museum by bus?

B: Sure. Which museum are you looking for?

A: The City Museum.

B: OK, you can take Bus 23 from this stop and **get off** at the third stop after the bridge. Then walk straight for 5 minutes, and you'll see the museum on your left.

A: Thank you so much! Is the bus stop clearly marked?

B: Yes, it is. You can also check the bus route and schedule on the **public transportation** app if you have one.

A: Great, thanks again for your help!

B: No problem. Have a nice visit to the museum!

A：打扰了。你知道怎么坐公交车去博物馆吗？

B：知道。你要去哪个博物馆？

A：城市博物馆。

B：好的，你可以从这一站乘坐23路公交车，在过桥之后的第三站下车。然后直行5分钟，你会看到博物馆就在你的左边。

A：太谢谢你了！公交车站有明显的标识吗？

B：有。如果你安装了公交软件，你也可以在上面查看公交车路线和时刻表。

A：太好了，再次感谢你的帮助！

B：不客气，祝你参观博物馆时玩得开心！

□ get off 下车

□ public transportation 公共交通

Scene 2　信息咨询

A: Excuse me. Where can I get on Bus No. 4?

B: Just around the corner. There is a bus stop there.

A: Do you know how often Bus No. 4 comes?

B: The bus runs about every 10 minutes.

A: Thanks.

A：打扰一下。我在哪儿可以乘坐 4 路公交车？

B：就在拐角处。那里有一个公交车站。

A：你知道 4 路公交车多久来一次吗？

B：公交车大约每 10 分钟一班。

A：谢谢。

Scene 3　运营时间

A: Excuse me. Do you know what time Bus 123 starts running in the morning?

B: I'm not sure, but I think it starts at 6:00 am.

A: And what time does it stop running at night?

B: I think the last bus runs around 11:00 pm.

A: OK, thanks for the information.

B: No problem. Have a good day!

A：打扰一下。你知道 123 路公交车早晨几点开始发车吗？

B：我不确定，但我想是早晨 6 点开始。

A：晚上什么时候停运呢？

B：我记得最后一班公交车是晚上 11 点左右停运。

A：好的，谢谢你提供的信息。

B：不客气。祝您过得愉快！

Scene 4　买票

A: Fares, please. Any more fares?

B: Yes, to the railway station, one ticket.

A: You're on the wrong bus. You're supposed to take the No. 4 bus at the opposite bus stop.

B: That's too bad. What should I do?

A: Just get off at the next stop. Then take the No. 4 bus at the opposite bus stop.

A：请买票。还有谁买票吗？

B：我买票，去火车站，一张票。

A：您坐错车了。您应该在对面的公交车站乘坐 4 路公交车。

B：太糟糕了。我该怎么办？

A：在下一站下车就行了。然后在对面的公交车站乘坐 4 路公交车。

☐ run v. 运行

☐ stop running 停运

☐ be supposed to 应该

☐ opposite adj. 对面的

Scene 5　购买月票

A: Hi, I'd like to purchase a bus pass, please.

B: Sure. What type of pass would you like?

A: I need a monthly pass.

B: OK, that'll be $70. Do you have the exact change?

A: Yes, here you go.

B: Thank you. Here's your pass. It's valid for unlimited rides for the next 30 days.

A: Great, thank you for your help.

B: You're welcome. Have a good day!

A：你好，我想购买一张公交通票。

B：好的。您想要哪种通票？

A：我需要一张月票。

B：好的，一共70美元。您正好有这么多零钱吗？

A：有，给你。

B：谢谢。这是您的通票。在接下来的30天内可以无限次乘坐。

A：太好了，谢谢你的帮助。

B：不客气。祝您过得愉快！

Scene 6　没有零钱

A: Excuse me. I'd like to buy a bus ticket, but I don't have any change.

B: That's OK. You can use a card to pay or buy a ticket from the driver.

A: I don't have a card either.

B: No problem. You can buy a ticket from the driver when you board the bus. He accepts Apple Pay or Alipay.

A: Thank you. Apply Pay works for me.

B: You're welcome. Enjoy your ride!

A：打扰了，我想买一张公交车票，但是我没有零钱。

B：没关系。您可以用卡向司机付款或买票。

A：我也没有卡。

B：没问题。您上车时可以找司机买票。他接受苹果支付和支付宝。

A：谢谢。我用苹果支付。

B：不客气。旅途愉快！

Scene 7　坐错车

A: Excuse me. Did I get on the wrong bus? I need to go to the train station.

B: Yes, this bus doesn't go to the train station. You can get off at the next stop and transfer to the correct bus.

A：打扰一下。请问我上错车了吗？我要去火车站。

B：是的，这趟公交车不去火车站。你可以在下一站下车，然后换乘正确的公交车。

114

重点词汇
及表达

☐ purchase v. 购买

☐ pass n. 通票

☐ monthly pass 月票

☐ unlimited ride 无限次乘坐

☐ bus ticket 公交车票

☐ board v. 上（车、船等）

A: Oh no, I'm going to be late. Can you please help me plan a new route?

B: Sure, let me check on my phone. You can take this bus to the next stop, and then transfer to the No. 123 bus.

A: OK, got it. Thanks for your help!

B: No problem. Have a safe trip!

Scene 8　交通堵塞

A: Do you know how long it takes to get to the railway station?

B: Usually 30 minutes. But this is the peak hour, so it may take 50 minutes.

A: Oh my god. My train is leaving in 40 minutes.

B: Take the subway, then. It only takes 15 minutes. No traffic jams. The subway station is right near the bus stop.

A: Thanks so much.

Scene 9　公交广播

A: Attention all passengers! This is your driver speaking. We will be arriving at the next stop in approximately 5 minutes. Please remember to take all of your belongings with you as you exit the bus. We hope you have a pleasant day, and thank you for riding with us.

A：哦，天哪，我要迟到了。您能帮我规划一条新路线吗？

B：当然可以，我在手机上查一下。你可以坐这趟车到下一站，然后换乘123路公交车。

A：好的，知道了。感谢您的帮助！

B：不客气。一路平安！

A：你知道去火车站需要多长时间吗？

B：通常是30分钟。但是现在是高峰时段，所以可能需要50分钟。

A：哦，天哪。我要乘坐的火车40分钟后发车。

B：那就乘坐地铁吧。只需要15分钟。没有交通堵塞。地铁站就在公交车站附近。

A：非常感谢。

A：各位乘客请注意，我是司机。我们将在大约5分钟后到达下一站。下车时，请记得带上您所有的随身物品。我们希望您拥有愉快的一天，感谢您乘坐这班公交车。

115

☐ route *n.* 路线

☐ Have a safe trip! 一路平安!

☐ railway station 火车站

☐ peak hour 高峰时段

☐ passenger *n.* 乘客

☐ approximately *adv.* 大约

Unit 4 Taking a Train 乘坐火车

Scene 1　购票方式

A: Excuse me. Can you help me? How can I buy a train ticket to get to Dallas?

B: Sure, there are a few ways you can buy a ticket. You can buy it online or at the train station.

A: Which way is better?

B: If you have access to the Internet, buying it online is convenient. You can also avoid long lines at the station.

A: That sounds good. How do I buy it online?

B: You can go to the train company's website and follow the instructions to buy a ticket. It's easy.

A: Thanks for your help.

A：打扰一下，你能帮我一下吗？我怎样才能买到去达拉斯的火车票？

B：嗯，有几种购票方式。您可以在网上或火车站买票。

A：哪种方式比较好？

B：如果您能上网，在网上买票很方便。您也可以避免在车站排长队。

A：听起来不错。我怎样在网上买呢？

B：您可以登录火车公司的网站，按照说明买票。操作很简单。

A：谢谢你的帮助。

116

Scene 2　购买火车票

A: Good morning. Could you tell me the times of the trains to London, please?

B: Yes. There are trains at 7:59, 9:18, and 10:32.

A: Is the 7:59 train an express train?

B: It's a local train. If you want to take the express train, take the one at 9:18.

A: OK. What about coming back? I'd like to come back at about 7:00 pm.

B: You still want an express train, right? There is one at 7:20.

A: Oh no, no need to hurry to come back. Just the stopping one.

B: OK. There's one at 7:10 pm.

A：早上好。请告诉我去伦敦的火车时刻表好吗？

B：好的。列车在7点59分、9点18分和10点32分发车。

A：7点59分的火车是特快列车吗？

B：是慢车。如果您想乘坐特快列车，就乘坐9点18分的那班车。

A：好的。那返程呢？我想在晚上7点左右回来。

B：您还是想乘坐特快列车，对吗？7点20分有一班。

A：哦，不，我不急着回来。慢车就可以了。

B：好的。晚上7点10分有一班。

□ have access to 可以利用

□ online *adv.* 在线上

□ instruction *n.* 说明

□ express train 特快列车

□ local train 普通列车，慢车

A: OK. How much is it for the return ticket?

B: 33 pounds.

A: Thanks.

A：好的。往返票多少钱？

B：33 英镑。

A：谢谢。

Scene 3　确认车次

A: Excuse me. Can you help me check my train number and seat?

B: Sure. May I see your ticket?

A: Here you are.

B: OK, you're on Train K53, and your seat is in Carriage 5, Seat 23.

A: Great, thank you. One more question, what time does the train leave?

B: The departure time is 9:45 am.

A：打扰一下。你能帮我查一下我的车次和座位吗？

B：当然可以。我可以看一下您的车票吗？

A：给你。

B：好的，您乘坐的是 K53 次列车，您的座位在 5 号车厢，座位号是 23 号。

A：好的，谢谢。还有一个问题，火车什么时候出发？

B：出发时间是上午 9 点 45 分。

Scene 4　改签火车票

A: Can I change my train ticket to a later time?

B: Sure, let me check for you. There's availability tomorrow at 10:00 am.

A: That works. Can you change it for me?

B: Of course. What's your reservation number?

A: It's 123456789. Thank you so much!

A：我可以把火车票换成晚一点的吗？

B：当然可以，我帮你查一下。明天上午 10 点有票。

A：时间合适。你能帮我换一下吗？

B：当然可以。您的订单号是多少？

A：123456789。非常感谢！

Scene 5　取消预订

A: Hi, I need to cancel my train ticket.

B: Sure. Do you have the booking reference?

A: Yes, here it is.

B: OK, your ticket is canceled, and the refund will be processed in a few days.

A: Thank you very much.

A：你好，我要取消我的火车票。

B：好的。您有订单凭证吗？

A：有，给你。

B：好的，您的车票已取消，退款将在几天内处理完成。

A：非常感谢。

交通出行

□ return ticket 往返票，双程票

□ train *n.* 列车

□ carriage *n.* 车厢

□ departure time 出发时间

□ availability *n.* 可利用性，有效性

□ reservation number 订单号

□ cancel *v.* 取消

□ booking reference 订单凭证

□ refund *n.* 退款

B: You're welcome. Is there anything else I can help you with?

B：不客气。请问还有什么需要我帮忙的吗？

Scene 6　安全检查

A: Excuse me. I think I have a problem. I have something in my bag that may not be allowed on the train.

A：抱歉，我想我遇到麻烦了。我包里有些东西是不允许带上火车的。

B: What is it, Sir?

B：是什么呢，先生？

A: It's a bottle of hairspray. I didn't know it was not allowed.

A：一瓶发胶。我之前不知道这是不允许带上火车的。

B: I'm sorry, Sir. We cannot allow flammable items like hairspray on board. You can either throw it away or leave it with me for safekeeping until you return.

B：抱歉，先生。发胶之类的易燃物品不能带上火车。您可以把它扔掉，也可以把它交给我保管到您返回。

A: Can I come back and collect it after my trip?

A：旅行结束后我可以回来取吗？

B: Of course, Sir. We will keep it safe for you. Please be sure to retrieve it within 30 days.

B：当然可以，先生。我们会为您妥善保管。请务必在 30 天内取走。

A: Thank you for your help. I'll leave it with you for safekeeping.

A：谢谢你的帮助。安全起见，我把它交给你保管吧。

B: You're welcome, Sir. Thank you for your cooperation.

B：不客气，先生。谢谢您的合作。

Scene 7　行李过重

A: Excuse me. I need some help with my luggage.

A：打扰一下。我需要有人帮忙拿行李。

B: Sure, what can I do for you?

B：没问题，我能为您做些什么？

A: I can't lift this heavy suitcase. Could you please help me carry it?

A：我提不动这个重箱子。你能帮我提一下吗？

B: Of course, let me take it for you. Where do you want it to go?

B：当然可以，我来帮您拿。您想把它放在哪儿？

A: Thank you. I need to put it on the train. Could you show me where I should go?

A：谢谢。我要把它放在火车上。你能告诉我该怎么走吗？

118

重点词汇
及表达

☐ hairspray *n.* 发胶

☐ flammable item 易燃物品

☐ on board 在车上

☐ safekeeping *n.* 妥善保管

☐ retrieve *v.* 取走

B: Sure, let me escort you to the platform and help you put it on the train.

B：当然可以。我送您去站台，帮您把它放在火车上。

Scene 8　火车餐车

A: Excuse me. Does this train have a dining car?

B: Yes, we do have a dining car. It's located at the end of the train.

A: What kind of food do you serve?

B: We offer a variety of options, such as sandwiches, burgers, salads, and snacks. We also have hot and cold drinks.

A: What are the hours of the dining car?

B: We're open from 7:00 am to 8:00 pm. However, we may adjust the hours based on the train schedule.

A: Thank you. I appreciate the information.

A：打扰一下。这列火车上有餐车吗？

B：有，我们有餐车。餐车位于火车的尾部。

A：你们供应什么样的食物？

B：我们提供多种选择，比如三明治、汉堡、沙拉和零食。我们也有热饮和冷饮。

A：餐车的营业时间是几点？

B：我们从早晨 7 点开到晚上 8 点。不过，我们可能会根据列车时刻表调整时间。

A：谢谢，感谢你提供的信息。

Scene 9　停靠站点

A: Excuse me. Can you tell me the stops for this train to Los Angeles?

B: Sure, the train will make stops in Chicago, Denver, and Las Vegas before arriving in Los Angeles.

A: Is that all the stops?

B: Yes, those are the major stops for this route.

A: Great, thanks for the information.

B: You're welcome. Enjoy your trip!

A：打扰一下，你能告诉我这趟开往洛杉矶的火车一路上有哪些站吗？

B：当然可以，火车到达洛杉矶之前会在芝加哥、丹佛和拉斯维加斯停留。

A：这就是全部的站点了吗？

B：是的，这些是这条线路上的主要站点。

A：好的，谢谢你提供的信息。

B：不客气。祝您旅途愉快！

Scene 10　火车晚点

A: Excuse me. Do you know why the train is delayed?

A：打扰了，请问你知道火车为什么晚点吗？

119

交通出行

☐ escort v. 护送

☐ dining car 餐车

☐ a variety of options 多种选择

☐ adjust v. 调整

☐ major stops 主要站点

☐ delay v. 延迟

B: There was an accident on the tracks. They're clearing it now.

A: How long do you think it will be delayed?

B: They haven't said, but it might be a while.

A: OK, thanks for the information.

B: 铁轨上发生了事故。他们正在清理。

A: 你认为列车会延误多久?

B: 他们还没说,但可能要等一段时间。

A: 好的,谢谢你提供的信息。

Scene 11　遗失行李

A: Excuse me. I think I left my luggage on the train. What should I do to get it back?

B: You can try calling the lost and found office at the station. They might have received your luggage.

A: Do you have their phone number?

B: Yes, it's 1234567890.

A: Thank you very much.

B: No problem. Good luck!

A: 打扰了,我想我把行李落在火车上了。我该怎么做才能拿回来呢?

B: 您可以试着打电话给车站失物招领处。他们可能已经拿到您的行李了。

A: 你有他们的电话号码吗?

B: 有,电话号码是 1234567890。

A: 非常感谢。

B: 不客气。祝您好运!

120

Scene 12　火车换乘

A: Excuse me. Could you tell me how to transfer to the next train?

B: Sure. Which train are you transferring to?

A: I need to transfer to the express train to Shanghai.

B: OK, you need to take the escalator up to the platform, and then follow the signs to the Shanghai train. It's on Platform 3.

A: Thank you so much! Is it easy to find the platform?

B: Yes, there are signs everywhere, and staff members to assist you if you need help.

A: 打扰一下,你能告诉我如何换乘下一班火车吗?

B: 当然可以。你要换乘哪一班火车?

A: 我需要换乘去上海的特快列车。

B: 哦,你需要乘坐自动扶梯到站台,然后按照指示牌找到开往上海的火车。火车在 3 号站台。

A: 太谢谢你了!站台容易找到吗?

B: 很容易,到处都有标识。如果你需要帮助,工作人员会帮你的。

重点词汇&表达

☐ accident *n.* 事故

☐ clear *v.* 清理

☐ get back 取回

☐ take the escalator 乘坐电梯

☐ staff member 工作人员

Scene 13　火车广播

A: Attention all passengers. This is a reminder that the train to London will be departing from Platform 2 in 10 minutes. Please ensure that you have all of your luggage with you and are seated in the correct carriage. We wish you a pleasant journey and thank you for choosing to travel with us.

A：各位乘客请注意，提醒大家开往伦敦的列车将于 10 分钟后从 2 号站台出发。请确保您携带了所有行李，并坐在正确的车厢里。我们祝您旅途愉快，并感谢您选择与我们一起出行。

Unit 5　Taking a Flight 搭乘飞机

Scene 1　信息咨询

A: Good morning. How may I help you?

A：早上好。我能为您效劳吗？

B: Good morning. Is there a flight to New York?

B：早上好。有飞往纽约的航班吗？

A: Yes, there is. Flight 226 departs at 10:30 am and arrives in New York at 12:30 pm.

A：有。226 号航班上午 10 点 30 分起飞，下午 12 点 30 分抵达纽约。

B: How many flights are there to New York per week?

B：去纽约的航班每周有几趟？

A: We have 2 flights, one on Tuesday and one on Friday.

A：我们有两趟航班，一趟在周二，一趟在周五。

B: I see. Thank you very much.

B：知道了。非常感谢。

A: You're welcome. My pleasure.

A：不客气。我很乐意帮忙。

Scene 2　咨询航班

A: Hi. How can I help you today?

A：嗨。今天我能为您做些什么？

B: Hi. Is there a flight to London?

B：嗨，有飞往伦敦的航班吗？

A: Yes, there is. Flight 113 departs at 9:00 am. And arrives in London at 2:00 pm.

A：有。113 号航班上午 9 点起飞。下午两点到达伦敦。

B: How many flights are there to London per week?

B：每周有几趟飞往伦敦的航班？

交通出行

- □ reminder *n.* 提醒
- □ pleasant journey 愉快的旅程
- □ flight *n.* 航班
- □ My pleasure. 乐意效劳。
- □ depart *v.* 出发
- □ arrive *v.* 到达

A: There are 3 flights every week, Monday, Friday and Saturday.

B: I see. Thank you.

A: You're welcome.

A: 每周有三趟航班，分别在周一、周五和周六。

B: 知道了。谢谢你!

A: 不客气。

Scene 3　购买机票

A: I need a flight to New York next Friday.

B: 8:00 am flight. Return Monday at 5:00 pm for $350.

A: I'll take it.

B: Name and credit card number, please.

A: James Smith. Here's my card.

B: Reservation made. Have a nice trip!

A: 我需要一张下周五去纽约的机票。

B: 早晨 8 点的航班。周一下午 5 点返回，350 美元。

A: 我买一张。

B: 请告诉我您的姓名和信用卡号码。

A: 詹姆斯·史密斯。这是我的信用卡。

B: 已预订。祝您旅途愉快!

Scene 4　选择座位

A: Excuse me. Can I change my seat to a window seat?

B: I'm sorry. All window seats are taken.

A: How about an aisle seat?

B: Sure. Which row do you prefer?

A: Anywhere is fine. Thank you.

B: No problem. I've changed your seat to 15D.

A: 打扰了，我能把座位换成靠窗的吗?

B: 抱歉。所有靠窗的座位都坐满了。

A: 挨着过道的座位呢?

B: 当然可以换。您想坐在哪一排?

A: 哪儿都可以。谢谢你!

B: 不客气。我已经把您的座位改为 15D 了。

Scene 5　取机票

A: Hi, I'm here to pick up my flight ticket.

B: Sure. What's your name and departure date?

A: My name is John Lee, and my departure date is next Friday.

B: OK, here's your ticket. Your flight leaves at 8:00 am from Gate 14.

A: 你好，我是来取机票的。

B: 好的。您的姓名和出发日期?

A: 我是约翰·李，出发日期是下周五。

B: 好的，这是您的机票。您的航班早晨 8 点在 14 号登机口出发。

重点词汇
及表达

☐ return v. 返回

☐ window seat 靠窗的座位

☐ aisle seat 挨着过道的座位

☐ row n. 排

☐ pick up 取回

122

A: Thank you. Can you tell me what terminal I need to go to?

B: Yes, you need to go to Terminal 2.

A: Great! Thank you for your help.

B: No problem. Have a safe trip!

Scene 6　退机票

A: Hi, I'm hoping to cancel my reservation.

B: Sure thing. Can I have your name and reservation number, please?

A: My name is Sarah Lee, and my reservation number is 15203410.

B: Alright, Sarah. Just to let you know, there will be a $50 cancellation fee. Are you OK with that?

A: Yes, that's fine. Thank you. Could you please confirm the refund?

B: Absolutely. You should see the refund in your account within 3–5 business days. Is there anything else I can help you with?

A: No, that's it. Thank you for your help.

B: Of course, Sarah. Let us know if you need any further assistance.

Scene 7　预订机场班车

A: How can I book a shuttle bus to the airport?

B: You can book online or at the bus station.

A: How much does it cost, and how long does it take?

B: It costs $20 and takes about 1 hour.

A: Can I pay with a credit card?

A：谢谢。你能告诉我该去哪个航站楼吗？

B：可以，您需要去 2 号航站楼。

A：太好了！谢谢你的帮助。

B：不客气。一路平安！

A：你好，我想取消我预订的机票。

B：没问题。请告诉我您的姓名和预订编号，好吗？

A：我叫萨拉·李，我的预订编号是 15203410。

B：好的，萨拉。提醒您一下，取消预订将会产生 50 美元的取消费用，您可以接受吗？

A：可以，没问题。谢谢你！你能确认一下退款情况吗？

B：当然可以。您应该能在 3~5 个工作日内看到退款到账。还有什么需要我帮忙的吗？

A：没有了，就这些。谢谢你的帮助。

B：不客气，萨拉。如果您需要更多帮助，请告诉我们。

A：我怎样才能预订去机场的班车呢？

B：您可以在网上或汽车站预订。

A：要花多少钱？需要多长时间？

B：20 美元，大约需要 1 小时。

A：我可以用信用卡支付吗？

交通出行

123

▫ cancellation fee 取消订单费

▫ confirm v. 确认

▫ assistance n. 帮忙

▫ shuttle bus 班车

B: Yes, you can pay with a credit card or cash.

A: Great, thanks for the information.

B: You're welcome. Have a safe trip!

B：可以，您可以用信用卡或现金支付。

A：太好了，谢谢你提供的信息。

B：不客气。一路平安!

Scene 8　办理登机手续

A: Hi. How may I help you?

B: Could you tell me where I can check in for Flight GA103 to London?

A: Yes. Go down the escalator, turn left, and you will see the counter.

B: Thank you. When do they begin to check in?

A: What time does your flight leave?

B: 11:00 am.

A: OK. It's 7:00 am now. So they will start check-in in about an hour.

B: Thanks very much.

A: You're welcome.

A：嗨。我能为您效劳吗?

B：你能告诉我飞往伦敦的 GA103 航班在哪儿办理登机手续吗?

A：可以。下了自动扶梯，向左拐，你就会看到服务台。

B：谢谢。他们什么时候开始办理登机手续?

A：您的航班什么时候出发?

B：上午 11 点。

A：好的。现在是早晨 7 点。他们大约一小时后开始办理登机手续。

B：非常感谢。

A：不客气。

124

Scene 9　领取登机牌

A: Check-in for my flight to Paris, please.

B: Passport and itinerary, please. How many bags?

A: One bag.

B: Boarding pass and Gate C12. Boarding in 30 minutes.

A: Thank you.

B: Have a safe flight!

A：请帮我办理去巴黎的登机手续。

B：请出示护照和行程表。您有几个包?

A：一个包。

B：这是您的登机牌。请前往 C12 登机口。30 分钟后登机。

A：谢谢。

B：祝您一路平安!

Scene 10　托运行李

A: Hey, I'm here to check in to New York by Flight GA123.

A：嘿，我是来办理飞往纽约的 GA123 航班登机手续的。

□ check in 办理登机手续

□ counter *n.* 柜台，服务台

□ boarding pass 登机牌

重点词汇及表达

B: OK. May I have your ticket and passport, please?

A: Yeah. Here is my ticket, and here is my passport.

B: Thank you. How many pieces of luggage would you like to check in?

A: 1 check-in and 1 carry-on.

B: OK. Here is your ticket, passport, and boarding pass.

A: Thank you very much.

B：好的。请出示您的机票和护照，好吗？

A：好的。这是我的机票和护照。

B：谢谢。您有几件行李要托运？

A：一件托运行李和一件随身行李。

B：好的。这是您的机票、护照和登机牌。

A：非常感谢。

Scene 11   行李称重

A: Excuse me, Miss. I'm here to check in for flight BC407 to New York.

B: Your ticket and passport, please?

A: Here they are. Can I get an aisle seat because I don't want to have to jump over people's legs to go pee?

B: Yes, of course. I do the same thing on long flights, sweetie. Do you have any luggage to check in?

A: Yes, 1 suitcase.

B: Could you please put it on the scale?

A: OK. Please tell me it's not overweight, is it?

B: I'm sorry. Your suitcase is 5 kg overweight.

A: What should I do?

B: Well, you don't have a carry-on suitcase with you. So you can take some of the stuff in this suitcase onto the plane with you.

A: OK, I'll do that.

B: Here is your passport, ticket, boarding pass, and baggage claim tag.

A：打扰一下，女士。我来办理飞往纽约的 BC407 航班登机手续。

B：请出示您的机票和护照。

A：给你。能为我安排一个挨着过道的座位吗？因为我不想去卫生间时还要跳过别人的腿。

B：当然可以。亲爱的，我在长途飞行中也会这么做。您有需要托运的行李吗？

A：有，一个行李箱。

B：请把它放在称重台上好吗？

A：好的。应该没超重，对吧？

B：抱歉，您的行李超重了 5 千克。

A：那我该怎么办？

B：哦，你没有随身行李，你可以把这个行李箱里的部分东西带上飞机。

A：好的，我就这么干。

B：这是您的护照、机票、登机牌和行李认领标签。

125

□ carry-on *n.* 随身携带的行李

□ check in 托运

□ overweight *adj.* 超重的

□ stuff *n.* 物品

□ baggage claim tag 行李认领标签

Scene 12　升级舱位

A: How can I upgrade my seat?

B: You can ask at the check-in counter or at the gate. It depends on whether it's available or not.

A: How much does it cost to upgrade?

B: The cost depends on the airline and the availability of seats. You can check with the airline for more information.

A: Can I use my frequent flyer miles to upgrade?

B: Yes, you can use your miles to upgrade if the airline offers that option.

A: OK! Thank you for the information.

B: You're welcome. Have a pleasant flight!

A：我怎样才能升级舱位呢?

B：您可以在登机服务台或登机口询问。这取决于是否有空位。

A：升级舱位需要多少钱?

B：价格取决于航空公司和是否有空位。您可以向航空公司查询更多信息。

A：我可以用我的飞行里程来升级舱位吗?

B：可以，如果航空公司提供这项服务，您可以用累计里程升级舱位。

A：好的! 谢谢你提供的信息。

B：不客气。祝您旅途愉快!

Scene 13　飞机延误

A: When will the flight depart since it's delayed?

B: We are waiting for clearance from air traffic control. We will update you as soon as possible.

A: Do you have an estimated time of departure?

B: I'm sorry. I don't have that information now. We will announce it when we know more.

A: How long do we have to wait here?

B: We expect the delay to be no more than 2 hours. We apologize for the inconvenience.

A: OK, thank you for letting me know.

B: You're welcome. We appreciate your patience.

A：航班延误了。什么时候起飞?

B：我们正在等待空中交通管制的许可。我们会尽快通知您。

A：你预计什么时间出发?

B：抱歉。我现在还没有这方面的信息。当我们了解更多情况时，我们会公布的。

A：我们要在这里等多久?

B：我们预计延误不超过 2 小时。给您带来不便，我们深表歉意。

A：好的，谢谢你告诉我。

B：不客气。感谢您的耐心。

重点词汇
及表达

☐ upgrade v. 升级

☐ airline n. 航空公司

☐ flyer mile 飞行里程

☐ clearance n. 许可

☐ air traffic control 空中交通管制

☐ estimated time 预估时间

☐ patience n. 耐心

Scene 14　机场安检

A: Is this the line for security?

B: Yes, it is. Do you have any liquids or gels in your carry-on?

A: No, just my laptop and some books.

B: OK, please put them in the bin and step through the scanner.

A: Do I need to take my shoes off?

B: No, that's not necessary unless they set off the alarm.

A：这是安检队伍吗？

B：是的。您的随身行李中有液体或凝胶吗？

A：没有，只有我的笔记本电脑和一些书。

B：好的，请把它们放进箱子里，然后通过扫描仪。

A：我需要脱鞋吗？

B：不用，没必要脱鞋，除非鞋子触发了警报。

Scene 15　转运行李

A: I have a connecting flight. Do I need to re-check my luggage?

B: No, your luggage will be transferred to your next flight.

A: Great, thank you for letting me know.

B: You're welcome. Have a good trip!

A：我要转机。我需要重新托运行李吗？

B：不需要，您的行李将被转移到您的下一趟航班。

A：太好了，谢谢你告诉我。

B：不客气。祝您旅途愉快!

Scene 16　帮忙拿行李

A: Excuse me. Can you help me with my luggage?

B: Sure. How many bags do you have?

A: Three bags. Two suitcases and one carry-on.

B: OK! I'll tag them for you. Have a nice flight.

A: Thank you!

A：打扰一下。你能帮我处理行李吗？

B：当然可以。您有几件行李？

A：三件。两个行李箱和一件随身行李。

B：好的。我给您贴上标签。祝您旅途愉快。

A：谢谢!

交通出行

127

- [ ] security *n.* 安检
- [ ] scanner *n.* 扫描仪
- [ ] set off the alarm 触发警报
- [ ] connecting flight 转机
- [ ] tag *v.* 贴标签

Scene 17　行李超重

A: My baggage is overweight. What should I do?

B: You can pay for the excess baggage fee or remove some items to make it within the weight limit.

A: How much is the excess baggage fee?

B: The fee varies depending on the airline and weight. You can check with the airline for more information.

A: Can I transfer some items to my carry-on baggage?

B: Yes, you can do that as long as it meets the carry-on baggage size and weight limit.

A: OK. I'll remove some items to make it within the weight limit.

B: Great. Let me know if you need any assistance.

A：我的行李超重了。我该怎么办?

B：您可以支付超重行李费，或者拿走一些东西让重量降到规定的范围内。

A：超重行李费是多少?

B：费用取决于航空公司和重量。您可以向航空公司查询更多信息。

A：我可以把一些物品转移到随身携带的行李中吗?

B：可以，只要随身行李的尺寸和重量符合规定就行。

A：好的。我去取出一些物品，使其在重量限制内。

B：好的。如果您需要帮助，请告诉我。

128

Scene 18　领取行李

A: Hi, excuse me. Where do I go to pick up my luggage?

B: You'll need to head to the baggage claim area. Just follow the signs, and you'll find it easily.

A: Got it. Is there anything else I need to know or bring with me?

B: Nope, you're all set. Just wait for your luggage to arrive on the conveyor belt, and you'll be good to go.

A: Great, thanks for your help.

B: No problem at all. Have a good day, and enjoy your trip!

A：嗨，打扰一下。我应该去哪里领取行李?

B：您需要去行李认领处。跟着指示走，您很容易就可以找到的。

A：明白了。还有什么是我需要知道或随身携带的吗?

B：没有了，这样就可以了。就等着您的行李送到传送带上，然后您就可以领取了。

A：太好了，谢谢你的帮助。

B：不客气。祝您度过愉快的一天! 旅途愉快!

重点词汇
及表达

☐ baggage *n.* 行李

☐ excess *adj.* 超额的

☐ weight limit 重量限制

☐ the baggage claim area 行李认领处

☐ conveyor belt 传送带

Scene 19　退票和改签

A: Can you help me with the refund and change of my flight ticket?

A：你能帮我退票和改签机票吗?

B: Yes, please provide me with your booking reference number.

B：可以，请提供您的订单编号。

A: Here it is. I need to change my flight to next week.

A：给你。我需要把航班改到下周。

B: Sure. Let me check the availability and the fare difference.

B：好的。我查一下是否有空位，再看看票价差额。

A: Can I also cancel one of my flights and get a refund?

A：我可以取消其中一趟航班并要求退款吗?

B: Yes, but there may be a cancellation fee. Let me check the terms and conditions of your ticket.

B：可以，但可能要收取消订单费。我查一下您所购机票的条款。

A: Thank you for your assistance.

A：谢谢你的帮助。

B: You're welcome. Let me process the changes and refund for you.

B：不客气。我来为您办理改签和退款。

129

Scene 20　帮忙放行李

A: Excuse me. Could you help me with my luggage?

A：打扰一下，你能帮我放一下行李吗?

B: Sure. What seems to be the problem?

B：当然可以。怎么了?

A: It's too heavy, and I can't put it in the overhead bin.

A：我的行李太重了，我无法把它放在头顶上方的行李架上。

B: Let me assist you with that. Here you go.

B：我来帮你。放好了。

A: Thank you so much.

A：非常感谢。

Scene 21　找地方放行李

A: Excuse me. Could you give me a hand with this?

A：打扰了，你能帮我一下吗?

B: Sure thing. What's the issue?

B：当然可以。有什么问题吗?

A: My bag is too big for the overhead bin.

A：我的包太大了，头顶上方的行李架上放不下。

☐ change *n.* 改签

☐ provide *v.* 提供

☐ term and condition 条款

☐ process *v.* 处理

☐ overhead *adj.* 上方的

☐ bin *n.* 行李架

☐ issue *n.* 问题

交通出行

B: Let's see if we can find a spot for it. Ah, there's one. Done.

A: Thank you so much. You're a lifesaver.

B：我们看看能不能找个地方放。啊，那边可以放。放好了。

A：非常感谢。你真是我的救星。

Scene 22　找座位（1）

A: Excuse me. Where's my seat?

B: What's your seat number?

A: It's 10A.

B: That's over here. Follow me.

A：打扰一下，请问我的座位在哪儿？

B：您的座位号是多少？

A：10A。

B：在这边。跟我来。

Scene 23　找座位（2）

A: Sorry, I can't find my seat.

B: What seat number are you looking for?

A: I have 33C.

B: That's on the other side. Let me guide you there.

A：抱歉，我找不到我的座位了。

B：您要找哪个座位？

A：我要找33C。

B：那个座位在另一边。我带您过去吧。

130

Scene 24　换座位（1）

A: Excuse me. Would you mind switching seats with me?

B: Sure. Which seat do you have?

A: I'm in the middle seat. I'd prefer the aisle.

B: No problem. I'll take the middle.

A: Thanks! You're a lifesaver!

B: You're welcome. Happy to help.

A：抱歉，你介意跟我换一下座位吗？

B：不介意。你的座位在哪儿？

A：我的座位在中间。我想换挨着过道的座位。

B：没问题。我坐中间的座位。

A：谢谢! 你真是我的救星!

B：不客气。我很乐意帮忙。

Scene 25　换座位（2）

A: Excuse me. Would you be willing to switch seats with me?

B: What's the issue with your current seat?

A：打扰了，你愿意和我换座位吗？

B：你现在的座位怎么了？

重点词汇
及表达

□ spot *n.* 地点

□ follow *v.* 跟随

□ guide *v.* 带领

□ switch *v.* 交换

□ aisle *n.* 过道

□ current *adj.* 目前的，现在的

A: I'm seated next to a crying baby, and it's been tough.

B: Oh, that's not fun. Which seat would you like?

A: Would you mind switching to the middle seat?

B: Sure, I don't mind. I hope you have a better flight now.

A: Thank you! You're very kind.

B: No problem. Happy to help out.

A: 我旁边有个哭闹的婴儿，这很难熬。

B: 哦，这可不好玩。你想要哪个座位？

A: 你介意换到中间的座位吗？

B: 没问题，我不介意。希望你现在能舒服些。

A: 谢谢！你真是太好了！

B: 不客气。我很乐意帮忙。

Scene 26 坐错座位

A: Excuse me. I'm afraid you are sitting in my seat.

B: I'm sorry. I made a mistake.

A: Never mind.

A: 抱歉，恐怕您坐的是我的座位。

B: 抱歉。我坐错了。

A: 没关系。

Scene 27 飞机上的餐饮

A: Excuse me. What are the meal options for this flight?

B: We have chicken and rice or vegetarian pasta.

A: I'll have the chicken and rice, please.

B: Would you like anything to drink with that?

A: Yes, I'll have a Coke, please.

B: Alright. I'll bring that to you shortly.

A: Thanks. By the way, do you have any snacks available for purchase?

B: Yes, we have chips, cookies, and sandwiches.

A: I'll have a bag of chips, please.

B: Alright! That will be $3.

A: Here you go.

B: Thank you.

A: 打扰一下，请问这趟航班有哪些餐点可供选择？

B: 我们有鸡肉饭或素食意大利面。

A: 我要鸡肉饭。

B: 您要喝点什么吗？

A: 要，请给我一杯可乐。

B: 好的。我很快就给您送过来。

A: 谢谢。顺便问一下，你们有零食出售吗？

B: 有，我们有薯片、饼干和三明治。

A: 我要一袋薯片。

B: 好的。3 美元。

A: 给你。

B: 谢谢。

131

交通出行

□ tough *adj.* 困难的

□ help out 帮忙

□ make a mistake 犯错

□ vegetarian pasta 素食意大利面

□ purchase *n.* 购买

Scene 28　索要毛毯

A: Excuse me. It's so cold in here. Do you have a blanket?

B: Sure. I'll fetch it for you.

A: Thanks. Can I have one for my friend too?

B: Of course. Here you go.

A: How can we return them?

B: Just leave them on your seat after the flight.

A: Got it. Thank you for your help.

B: You're welcome. Enjoy your flight.

A：打扰一下。这里太冷了。你们提供毛毯吗？

B：当然提供。我去给您拿过来。

A：谢谢。我能为我的朋友也要一条吗？

B：当然可以。给。

A：我们怎样归还毛毯呢？

B：飞行结束后把它们放在座位上就可以了。

A：明白了。谢谢你的帮助。

B：不客气。祝您旅途愉快。

Scene 29　转机

A: Excuse me. How much time does it take to transfer?

B: It depends on your connecting flight. Which airline are you flying with?

A: I'm flying with Delta. What's the procedure for transferring?

B: You need to go through security and then find your gate. Follow the signs for "Connecting Flights".

A: Thanks. Is there a shuttle bus to the connecting terminal?

B: No, but there is a train that runs between terminals.

A：打扰一下，请问转机需要多长时间？

B：这取决于您的转机航班。您乘坐的是哪家航空公司的航班？

A：我乘坐的是达美航空公司的航班。转机流程是怎么样的？

B：您需要通过安检，然后找到您的登机口。跟着"转机"标识走。

A：谢谢。请问有去中转航站楼的班车吗？

B：没有，但是有一列列车在航站楼之间运营。

Scene 30　去免税商店

A: Excuse me. Where is the duty-free shop in the airport?

A：打扰一下。请问机场免税商店在哪儿？

132

重点词汇
及表达

☐ blanket *n.* 毛毯
☐ fetch *v.* 去取
☐ connecting flight 转机航班

☐ procedure *n.* 流程
☐ duty-free shop 免税商店

B: It's on the third floor, near the departure gates.

A: How can I get there from here?

B: Just take the escalator over there and go up to the third floor.

A: Is it open 24 hours?

B: No, it closes at 9:00 pm.

B：在三楼，离登机口很近。

A：从这里怎么去那儿？

B：乘坐那边的自动扶梯上三楼就可以了。

A：店里是 24 小时营业吗？

B：不是，晚上 9 点停止营业。

Scene 31 抵达航站楼

A: Which terminal will the flight arrive in at the destination?

B: It'll arrive at Terminal 2, Sir.

A: OK, thank you. How do I get there?

B: You can take the shuttle bus or the train from the airport. They both go to Terminal 2.

A: Great. How long does it take to get there?

B: It takes about 10 minutes by shuttle bus and 15 minutes by train.

A：这趟航班会到达目的地的哪个航站楼？

B：先生，这趟航班将到达 2 号航站楼。

A：好的，谢谢。我怎么去那儿？

B：您可以从机场乘坐机场大巴或机场列车去。它们都开往 2 号航站楼。

A：太好了。去那里需要多长时间？

B：乘坐机场大巴大约 10 分钟，乘坐机场列车大约 15 分钟。

Scene 32 晕机寻求帮助

A: Excuse me. Can you help me, please?

B: Of course. What can I help you with?

A: I feel really sick and dizzy because of the flight. Do you have any airsickness pills?

B: Yes, we do. Here you are.

A: Thank you so much. Can I also have a plastic bag in case I need to vomit?

B: Sure. Here you go. Is there anything else I can do for you?

A: No, that's all. Thank you for your help.

A：打扰一下，你能帮我吗？

B：当然可以。我能帮您做些什么呢？

A：由于飞行的缘故，我感到很不舒服，头晕。你有晕机药吗？

B：有。给您。

A：非常感谢。我可以再要一个塑料袋吗？以防我想吐。

B：当然可以。给您。我还能为您做些什么吗？

A：没有了，就这些。谢谢你的帮助。

▢ departure gate 登机口

▢ at the destination 在目的地

▢ by train 乘坐列车

▢ airsickness pill 晕机药

▢ vomit *v.* 呕吐

Scene 33　晕机药

A: Excuse me. I'm not feeling well. Could you get me some medicine for airsickness?

B: Of course. Here's some airsickness medicine.

A: Could you get me an airsickness bag?

B: Yes, of course, Ma'am. Here is an airsickness bag for you.

A: Thank you. Can you get me some hot water?

B: Of course. Here is your hot water.

A: Thank you very much. I feel cold. Could you get me a blanket? Thank you.

B: Ma'am, here is your blanket.

A: Oh. Thank you so much.

B: You're welcome. What else do you need?

A: Could you get me a boyfriend?

B: All the single guys in the house, raise your hand.

A：打扰一下，我感觉不舒服。你能给我拿一些晕机药吗？

B：当然可以。给，这是晕机药。

A：能给我一个晕机袋吗？

B：当然可以，女士。这是给您的晕机袋。

A：谢谢。你能给我拿些热水吗？

B：没问题。这是给您的热水。

A：非常感谢。我觉得有点冷。你能给我拿条毯子吗？谢谢！

B：女士，这是您的毯子。

A：哦，非常感谢。

B：不客气。您还需要什么吗？

A：你能给我找个男朋友吗？

B：所有在场的单身男士，请举手。

Scene 34　飞机里程

A: Hi there. How many frequent flyer miles do I have?

B: You currently have 25,000 miles. You could use them to book a flight.

A: Can I book a flight to Chicago next month?

B: Absolutely. I can book a flight for you for 20,000 miles. There're a few options available. The earliest flight departs on May 5th at 10:00 am, and it arrives in Chicago at 1:30 pm. It has a layover of 1 hour in Dallas. Would you like me to book that one for you?

A: Yes, thank you.

B: Have a nice trip!

A：你好。请问我有多少飞行里程？

B：您目前的飞行里程是 25000 英里。你可以用它们来订机票。

A：我可以订一张下个月飞往芝加哥的机票吗？

B：当然可以。我帮你预订一张，用掉 20000 英里。有几个选项可供选择。最早的航班是 5 月 5 日上午 10 点起飞，下午 1 点 30 分抵达芝加哥。在达拉斯有一小时的中转时间。需要我帮您订这趟航班吗？

A：需要，谢谢。

B：祝您旅途愉快！

重点词汇
及表达

☐ airsickness medicine 晕机药

☐ airsickness bag 晕机袋

☐ currently *adv.* 目前

Scene 35　过海关

A: May I see your passport?

B: Here you are.

A: What's your final destination?

B: Thailand.

A: What's the purpose of your visit?

B: Tourism.

A: How long will you be staying?

B: One week.

A: Where will you be staying?

B: In the hotel.

A: How much currency are you carrying?

B: $200.

A: Do you have anything to declare?

B: Nothing.

A：我可以看一下您的护照吗?

B：给您。

A：您的最终目的地是哪里?

B：泰国。

A：您此行的目的是什么?

B：旅游。

A：您打算待多久?

B：一周。

A：您打算住在哪儿?

B：住在酒店。

A：您随身携带了多少现金?

B：200美元。

A：您有需要申报的物品吗?

B：没有。

Scene 36　健康检查

A: Health check. What do we need to do?

B: Fill out this form and have your temperature checked.

A: Are there any other requirements?

B: Remember: Wear a mask. Follow social distancing guidelines.

A: Got it! Thanks for letting us know.

B: No problem. Have a safe trip.

A：健康检查。我们需要做什么?

B：填写这张表，量一下体温。

A：还有其他要求吗?

B：记住戴上口罩。遵守社交距离准则。

A：明白了!谢谢告知。

B：不客气。祝您一路平安。

Scene 37　航班广播

A: Attention all passengers, welcome aboard Flight BA456 to Paris. We kindly remind you to fasten your seatbelts and ensure that your tray tables are stowed, and your seat backs are in the upright position for takeoff. We hope you have a comfortable flight, and thank you for choosing our airline.

A：各位乘客请注意，欢迎乘坐飞往巴黎的 BA456 航班。温馨提示，请您系好安全带，确保收好您的小桌板，让座椅靠背在起飞前处于直立状态。我们希望您拥有舒适的旅行。感谢您选择我们的航空公司。

135

交通出行

☐ purpose *n.* 目的

☐ currency *n.* 现金

☐ declare *v.* 申报

☐ temperature *n.* 体温

☐ social distancing 社交距离

☐ guideline *n.* 准则

☐ fasten one's seatbelt 系紧安全带

☐ upright *adj.* 直立的

☐ takeoff *n.* 起飞

Scene 38　催促登机

A: Attention all passengers, this is a final boarding call for Flight AA123 to New York. Please proceed to Gate 8 immediately, as the gate will be closing in 10 minutes. We kindly remind you to have your boarding pass and ID ready for boarding. Thank you for choosing our airline.

A：所有乘客请注意，这是飞往纽约的 AA123 航班的最后一次登机通知。请立即前往 8 号登机口，10 分钟后登机口将关闭。温馨提示，请您准备好登机牌和身份证件登机。感谢您选择我们的航空公司。

Scene 39　飞机晚点播报

A: Attention passengers, the flight from London to New York, scheduled to depart at 11:30 am, has been delayed by two hours due to bad weather conditions. We apologize for the inconvenience and will provide further updates as soon as possible.

A：乘客们请注意，原定于上午 11 点 30 分起飞的伦敦飞往纽约的航班，由于天气原因延误了两小时。对于给您带来的不便，我们深表歉意，并会尽快通知您此次航班的最新情况。

Scene 40　更改登机口

A: Dear passengers, please be informed that the gate for Flight BA321 to Paris has been changed from Gate 6 to Gate 12. We kindly ask all passengers to proceed to the new gate immediately for boarding.

A：尊敬的乘客们，请注意，飞往巴黎的 BA321 航班的登机口由 6 号登机口改为 12 号登机口。请所有乘客立即到新登机口登机。

Unit 6　Arriving at the Destination 到达目的地

Scene 1　接机

A: Hey, it's me. I'm arriving at the airport. Could you pick me up?

B: Sure. Which terminal are you at, and when will you land?

A：嘿，是我。我快到机场了。你能来接我吗？

B：当然可以。你在哪个航站楼？什么时候下飞机？

重点词汇
及表达

☐ remind v. 提醒
☐ schedule v. 安排，预定
☐ weather condition 天气条件
☐ inform v. 通知，告知

☐ immediately adv. 立刻，马上
☐ pick sb up 开车接某人
☐ land v. 降落，着陆

A: I'll be landing at Terminal 2 in about an hour.

B: OK, I'll be there in time. Safe flight!

A: 我大约一小时后在 2 号航站楼下飞机。

B: 好的，我会及时赶到的。一路平安!

Scene 2　酒店接机

A: Hello, do you offer airport pick-up service?

B: Yes, we do. Would you like to schedule one?

A: Yes, please. How can I make a reservation?

B: You can give us your flight details, and we'll arrange it for you.

A: Great, my flight arrives at 2:00 pm. Can you pick me up then?

B: Sure, we'll have a driver waiting for you at the airport.

A: 你好，请问你们有接机服务吗？

B: 有。您要预约吗？

A: 是的。我应该怎样预约呢？

B: 您可以告知我们您的航班信息。我们会为您安排的。

A: 太好了，我的航班下午 2 点抵达。到时候你们能来接我吗？

B: 当然可以。我们会派司机在机场等您。

Scene 3　出站信息

A: Hey, which terminal will you arrive at and when?

B: Terminal 3, arriving at 10:00 am.

A: Got it. I'll meet you at the baggage claim.

B: Sounds good. Do you need any flight details?

A: No, just text me when you land.

B: Will do. Looking forward to seeing you!

A: 嘿，你将抵达哪个航站楼？什么时候到？

B: 3 号航站楼，上午 10 点到。

A: 明白了。我在行李认领处等你。

B: 好的。你需要详细的航班信息吗？

A: 不需要，你落地后给我发短信就行了。

B: 好的。期待见到你!

Scene 4　去地铁站

A: Excuse me? Can you help me, please?

B: What can I do for you?

A: I'm trying to get to Shenzhen University metro station. And I don't know where to go.

A: 打扰了，请问你能帮我一下吗？

B: 我能为你做些什么？

A: 我想去深圳大学地铁站。但我不知道怎么去。

☐ offer v. 提供

☐ pick-up service 接机服务

☐ arrange v. 安排

☐ the baggage claim 行李认领处

☐ flight detail 详细的航班信息

☐ text v. 发信息

☐ metro station 地铁站

B: It's kind of far away. It is not within walking distance. You might want to take a bus first.

A: OK. How do I do that?

B: There's a bus stop right over there. Just go along this road for about 1,000 meters. Then turn left, and you won't miss the bus stop, and it's an orange bus. It's called B728. And it only costs 1 RMB.

A: I see. Thank you.

B: 有点远。它不在步行距离之内。你最好先坐公交车。

A: 好的。我该怎么乘坐公交车?

B: 那边有一个公交车站。沿着这条路走大约 1000 米,然后向左转,你就肯定能看到公交车站。你要乘坐的是一辆橙色公交车,编号是 B728。车费只要 1 元。

A: 我明白了。谢谢你!

Scene 5   找地铁站

A: Excuse me. Where is the nearest subway station?

B: The nearest subway station? Let me think... Oh, there's one just around the corner.

A: Great, thank you! How can I get there?

B: You can just walk straight ahead and take a left turn at the intersection. It's only a five-minute walk.

A: Thanks for your help! Is it easy to buy a ticket there?

B: Yes, you can buy a ticket at the ticket vending machines or from the ticket office.

A: OK, got it. Thanks again for your help!

B: You're welcome. Have a good trip!

A: 打扰一下,请问最近的地铁站在哪儿?

B: 最近的地铁站? 让我想想……哦,在拐角处就有一个。

A: 太好了,谢谢! 我怎么去那儿呢?

B: 你可以一直往前走,然后在十字路口左转。步行只要五分钟。

A: 谢谢你的帮助! 在那里购票容易吗?

B: 容易,你可以在自动售票机或售票处购票。

A: 好的,知道了。再次感谢你的帮助!

B: 不客气。祝你旅途愉快!

Scene 6   去火车站

A: Excuse me. How can I get to the train station?

B: Which train station are you going to?

A: The main train station.

A: 打扰一下,请问火车站怎么走?

B: 你要去哪个火车站?

A: 火车总站。

重点词汇
及表达

☐ within walking distance
   在步行距离之内

☐ subway station 地铁站

☐ straight adv. 径直

☐ ticket office 售票处

☐ train station 火车站

B: You can take the subway Line 2 and get off at the third stop. Then transfer to Line 1 and get off at the sixth stop. The train station is right there.

A: Thank you. Is it far from here?

B: No, it's not too far. It should take you around 20 minutes by subway.

Scene 7 去机场

A: Excuse me. Can you tell me how to get to the airport?

B: Sure. Which airport are you going to?

A: I'm going to the International Airport.

B: OK. You can take the subway to the airport. The subway station is just a few blocks from here.

A: That's great. How long does it take to get to the airport by subway?

B: It takes about 45 minutes, but it depends on the traffic.

A: Thanks for your help. Do I need to transfer to another line on the way?

B: No, it's a direct line to the airport. Just make sure you take the right direction.

A: Thank you so much for your help.

Scene 8 去市场

A: Excuse me. Do you know how to get to the market?

B: Sure. Which market are you looking for?

A: The local market, where they sell fruits and vegetables.

B: Ah, I know which one you're talking about. It's about two blocks that way.

B：你可以乘坐地铁 2 号线，在第三站下车。然后换乘 1 号线，在第六站下车。火车站就在那儿。

A：谢谢。离这儿远吗？

B：不太远。乘坐地铁大约 20 分钟。

A：打扰一下，你能告诉我怎么去机场吗？

B：当然可以。你要去哪个机场？

A：我要去国际机场。

B：好的。你可以乘坐地铁去机场。地铁站离这里只有几个街区。

A：太好了。乘坐地铁去机场需要多长时间？

B：大约 45 分钟，但要看交通状况。

A：谢谢你的帮助。我需要中途换乘其他线路吗？

B：不需要，这是直达机场的。只要确保走对方向就可以了。

A：非常感谢你的帮助。

A：打扰一下，你知道怎么去市场吗？

B：当然知道。你要去哪个市场？

A：当地市场，卖水果和蔬菜的地方。

B：啊，我知道你说的是哪个市场。往那边走大约两个街区。

☐ by subway 乘坐地铁

☐ block *n.* 街区

☐ traffic *n.* 交通

☐ direct *adj.* 直接的

☐ direction *n.* 方向

☐ market *n.* 市场

☐ vegetable *n.* 蔬菜

A: OK, and which direction should I turn at the end of the block?

B: You'll want to turn left, and then you'll see the market on your right-hand side.

A: Great. Thank you! Is it open every day?

B: Yes, it's open from 8:00 am to 6:00 pm every day except for Sundays.

A：好的。在这个街区的尽头我应该向哪个方向转弯？

B：你要向左拐，然后你会看到市场在你的右手边。

A：太好了，谢谢你！市场每天都营业吗？

B：是的，除了周日以外，每天从早晨8点营业到下午6点。

Scene 9 确认导航

A: Excuse me. Can you help me for a second?

B: Sure. What do you need help with?

A: I'm trying to find my way to the museum, but I'm not sure if my phone's navigation is accurate. Could you check it for me?

B: Sure, let me take a look. Hmm, it looks like the directions are correct. You just need to head down this street and turn left at the next intersection.

A: Thank you so much! I appreciate your help.

B: No problem. Glad I could assist you. Enjoy your visit to the museum!

A：打扰了，你能帮我一下吗？

B：当然可以。你需要什么帮助？

A：我正在找去博物馆的路，但我不确定我的手机导航是否准确。你能帮我查一下吗？

B：没问题，我看看。嗯，看起来方向是正确的。你只需要沿着这条街道往前走，在下一个十字路口向左拐。

A：太谢谢你了！谢谢你的帮助。

B：不客气。很高兴能帮到你。祝你有一次愉快的博物馆之旅！

140

Unit 7 Self-driving Travel 自驾游

Scene 1 规划路线

A: Let's plan our road trip. Where do you want to go?

B: I want to visit national parks.

A: OK, we can start with Yosemite and then go to Yellowstone.

A：我们计划一下自驾游吧。你想去哪里？

B：我想参观国家公园。

A：好的，我们可以从优胜美地公园开始，然后去黄石公园。

重点词汇
及表达

☐ navigation *n.* 导航

☐ accurate *adj.* 准确的

☐ intersection *n.* 十字路口

☐ road trip 公路旅行

B: Sounds great. How long will the trip take?

A: About two weeks. We can also stop at Grand Canyon and Zion.

B: Perfect, let's book accommodations and rent a car.

Scene 2　轮流开车

A: Who's going to drive on our road trip?

B: I don't mind driving, but we should switch off.

A: That's a good idea. How many hours do you think you can drive at a time?

B: Probably around 3 hours before I need a break.

A: OK, we can switch it off every 3 hours then. Do you want to start the first leg of the trip?

B: Sure, I'll take the first shift. Do we need to get additional insurance for extra drivers?

A: Yes, let's check with the rental car company about that.

Scene 3　极端天气

A: Look at the weather forecast. It's going to snow heavily tomorrow.

B: Yeah, we need to be prepared. Do we have snow chains?

A: I don't think so. Should we buy some?

B: It's better to have them, just in case. What about changing to winter tires?

A: Good idea. Let me check if there's a nearby garage that can do it for us.

B: And don't forget to drive slower and keep a safe distance from other cars.

B：听起来不错。这次旅行要花多长时间？

A：大约两周。我们也可以在大峡谷和锡安停留。

B：太好了，我们预订住宿和租车吧。

A：我们的自驾游谁来开车？

B：我不介意开车，但我们应该轮流开。

A：好主意。你觉得你一次能开几个小时的车？

B：可能大约三个小时后我就需要休息了。

A：好的，那我们可以每三个小时轮换一次。你想第一个开车吗？

B：当然，我排在第一个。我们需要为额外的司机购买额外的保险吗？

A：需要，我们跟租车公司核实一下。

A：看天气预报。明天将会下大雪。

B：是的，我们需要做好准备。我们有雪天的防滑链吗？

A：我想我们没有。我们要买一些吗？

B：最好买一些，以防万一。换上冬季轮胎怎么样？

A：好主意。我看看附近有没有修车厂可以帮我们换。

B：别忘了开慢点，和其他车保持安全距离。

□ accommodation *n.* 住宿

□ switch off 轮流，交换

□ break *n.* 休息

□ insurance *n.* 保险

□ weather forecast 天气预报

□ chain *n.* 链子，链条，锁链

□ garage *n.* 修车厂

Scene 4 　找加油站

A: We're running out of gas. How far is the nearest gas station?

B: Only a few kilometers. Don't worry.

A：我们快没油了。最近的加油站有多远？

B：只有几公里。别担心。

Scene 5 　汽车加油

A: Fill it up, please.

B: What kind of gas would you like to have? Regular or premium?

A: Regular, please.

B: OK.

A: How much?

B: $70.

A: Thank you.

A：请加满油。

B：您要加哪种汽油？普通的还是高级的？

A：普通的。

B：好的。

A：多少钱？

B：70美元。

A：谢谢。

Scene 6 　油价优惠

A: Let's stop at this gas station to fill up.

B: Sure. Do you know how much the gas is per gallon?

A: I'm not sure. Let's ask the attendant.

B: Excuse me. How much is the gas per gallon?

C: It's $3.50 per gallon.

A: Do you have any discounts or promotions available?

C: Yes, if you use our loyalty card, you can get 10 cents off per gallon.

A：我们在这个加油站停下加油吧。

B：好的。你知道每加仑汽油多少钱吗？

A：我不确定。我们问问工作人员吧。

B：打扰了，请问每加仑汽油多少钱？

C：每加仑3.5美元。

A：你们有折扣或促销活动吗？

C：有，如果您使用我们的会员卡，每加仑汽油可以优惠10美分。

Scene 7 　洗车服务

A: Wash my car, please.

B: Sure. What kind of wash would you like?

A: Just a basic wash. How much does it cost?

B: It's $15. Do you have a membership card?

A: No, I don't. Can I pay by credit card?

B: Yes, we accept all major credit cards.

A：请帮我洗车。

B：好的。您想要哪种洗车服务？

A：简单清洗一下就可以了。多少钱？

B：15美元。您有会员卡吗？

A：没有。我可以用信用卡支付吗？

B：可以，我们接受所有主流信用卡。

重点词汇
及表达

☐ run out of 用光，耗尽
☐ gas station 加油站
☐ regular adj. 常规的
☐ premium adj. 高级的

☐ fill up 加油
☐ gallon n. 加仑
☐ discount n. 折扣
☐ promotion n. 促销

☐ loyalty card 会员卡
☐ basic wash 基本的清洗
☐ membership card 会员卡

Scene 8　汽车保养

A: My car needs maintenance.

B: Should we take it to the 4S store?

A: Yes, what do they offer?

B: They provide regular checkups, oil changes, tire rotations, and more.

A: How much does it cost?

B: It depends on which services you choose. For example, a regular checkup can cost around $50–$100, an oil change can cost $30–$70, and a tire rotation can cost $20–$50. It's best to check with the local 4S store for specific pricing.

A：我的车需要保养了。

B：我们要把它送到 4S 店吗？

A：是的，他们提供什么服务？

B：他们提供定期检查、换油、更换轮胎等服务。

A：需要多少钱？

B：这取决于你选择哪种服务。例如，定期检查的费用约为 50~100 美元，换油的费用为 30~70 美元，更换轮胎的费用为 20~50 美元。你最好向当地 4S 店询问具体价格。

Scene 9　汽车事故

A: Oh no, we just got into a minor car accident!

B: Is everyone OK?

A: Yes, we're all fine, but the car is damaged.

B: Let's exchange insurance information and take pictures.

A: Great idea! I'll also call the police.

B: I hope it won't take too long to sort everything out.

A：哦，天哪，我们刚刚出了一场小车祸!

B：所有人都没事吧？

A：没事，我们都很好，只是车损坏了。

B：我们交换一下保险信息，然后拍照。

A：好主意! 我也会报警的。

B：希望解决这一切不用花太长时间。

Scene 10　安全驾驶

A: Are you sure we are on the right route?

B: Yes, just keep on driving. We'll get to the hotel in an hour.

A: An hour? That's a long time. I'm totally exhausted. Let's speed up. Wait, what's the speed limit in the city?

A：你确定我们走的路线是正确的吗？

B：确定，继续开。我们一小时后到达酒店。

A：一个小时？ 时间太长了。我累坏了。我们加速吧。等一下，这个城市的限速是多少？

□ maintenance *n.* 保养

□ regular checkup 定期检查

□ tire rotation 更换轮胎

□ minor *adj.* 微小的

□ sort out 处理

□ exhausted *adj.* 筋疲力尽的

□ speed limit 速度限制

B: 30 miles per hour. Don'drive too fast. It's not safe. There're too many cars and buses on the way.

A: The car is making some strange noise. I think there's something wrong. Let's check it out.

Scene 11 拖车服务

A: Let's park it under the tree.

B: Gosh, it's so hot.

A: Damn! There is something wrong with the brakes.

B: We've also got a flat tire. Do you know how to change tires?

A: I do. But we don't have extra tires.

B: What bad luck!

A: Let's push the car to a repair shop.

B: Keep on pushing. I think we need to call somebody to help us.

A: Hey, can you send someone to tow my car away?

(Ten minutes later)

C: Hey, could you please tell me where you are?

A: We are at Xuefu Road. No.14.

C: Yes, Ma'am. We'll send someone there immediately. Please wait for 10 minutes.

Scene 12 出行堵车

A: Ugh, there's so much traffic. We should consider taking a different route.

B: Would that be faster?

B：每小时 30 英里。不要开得太快。不安全。路上有太多的小汽车和公交车。

A：车子在发出一些奇怪的声音。我觉得有点不对劲。我们检查一下吧。

A：我们把车停在树下吧。

B：天哪，太热了。

A：该死! 刹车出故障了。

B：我们的轮胎也爆了。你知道怎么更换轮胎吗?

A：知道。但是我们没有备用轮胎。

B：真倒霉。

A：我们把车推到修理店吧。

B：继续推。我想我们需要找人来帮忙。

A：嘿，你能派人把我的小汽车拖走吗?

（10 分钟后）

C：嘿，你能告诉我你在哪儿吗?

A：我们在学府路 14 号。

C：好的，女士。我们马上派人过去。请等 10 分钟。

A：啊，交通太拥挤了。我们应该考虑走另一条路。

B：那样会更快吗?

144

重点词汇
及表达

□ brake *n.* 刹车

□ extra tire 备用轮胎

□ consider *v.* 考虑

A: Yes, according to Google Maps, it's a quicker option.

B: Alright, let's give it a shot.

A: 是的，根据谷歌地图，那是更快的选择。

B: 好吧，我们试试。

Scene 13   收费标识

A: What does the sign with the construction symbol mean?

B: It means there's road work ahead.

A: OK. And what about the sign with the toll booth?

B: It means we have to pay a fee to use the road ahead.

A: I see. Thanks for explaining.

B: No problem. Make sure to drive carefully in construction areas, and you should have change ready for tolls.

A: 这个带有建筑物图标的标识是什么意思？

B: 意思是前面在修路。

A: 好的。那带有收费站图标的标识是什么意思？

B: 那意味着我们付费后才能通过前面的路。

A: 明白了。谢谢你的解释。

B: 不客气。在施工区域开车一定要小心，并且要准备好交过路费的零钱。

145

Scene 14   限速标识

A: Did you see that sign with the speed limit number?

B: Yeah, we should make sure not to go over that speed.

A: Exactly. What about the sign with the rest area symbol?

B: It means there's a spot ahead where we can take a break and stretch our legs.

A: Got it. Thanks for letting me know.

B: No problem. Remember to take frequent breaks to stay alert while driving.

A: 你看到那个写着限速数字的标识了吗？

B: 看到了，我们应该确保不要超过那个速度。

A: 没错。那带有休息区图标的标识呢？

B: 意思是前面有个地方，我们可以在那里休息一下，伸伸腿。

A: 明白了。谢谢你告诉我。

B: 不客气。记得开车时要经常休息以保持警觉性。

□ shot n. 尝试

□ construction symbol 建筑物图标

□ pay a fee 付费

□ stay alert 保持警觉

□ road sign 路牌标识

□ turn left 向左转

□ turn left ahead 前面左转

□ no entry 禁止通行

□ speed limit 限速

□ no turn left 禁止左转

□ no cycling 禁止非机动车通行

□ no stopping 禁止停车

□ go straight 直行

□ turn around 掉头

□ maximum speed 最高速度

□ one-way traffic 单向交通

□ traffic light 交通指示灯

□ pull over 靠边停车

□ caution *n.* 警示标识

□ safety first 安全第一

□ ahead only 限直行

□ stop sign 停车标志

□ minimum speed 最低速度

□ no U-turn 禁止掉头

□ no overtaking 禁止超车

□ no motor vehicles 禁止机动车通行

□ no waiting 禁止停留

□ stop and yield 停车和让行

□ turn right 右转

□ speed bump 减速带

□ parking lot 停车场

□ dead-end street 死胡同

□ no parking 禁止停车

□ pedestrian crossing 人行横道

□ honk *v.* 鸣喇叭

Unit 8 Renting a Car 租车

Scene 1 预订租车

A: Hi, I'd like to rent a car for next weekend.

B: Sure. What type of car are you looking for?

A: Something compact and good on gas.

B: We have a few options available. When do you need it, and for how long?

A: I need it from Saturday morning until Sunday evening.

B: Got it. I'll make the reservation for you.

A：你好，我想租一辆车下周末用。

B：好的。您想要什么类型的车？

A：小巧又省油的车。

B：我们有几种选择。您什么时候需要？需要多长时间？

A：我周六早晨到周日晚上需要。

B：明白了。我来为您预订。

□ rent a car 租车

□ compact *adj.* 体积小的

146

Scene 2 租车类型

A: I'd like to rent a car.

B: May I see your driver's license?

A: Here is my international driver's license. What kind of cars do you have?

B: We have Honda, Ford, and Toyota. Which make and model do you prefer?

A: Ford, Please. I'd like to have an automatic car.

B: Sure, Ford Fiesta hatchback, then.

A: 我想租一辆车。

B: 我可以看一下您的驾驶执照吗?

A: 这是我的国际驾照。你们有什么样的车?

B: 我们有本田、福特和丰田。您喜欢哪个品牌和型号的车?

A: 请给我福特。我想要一辆自动挡的车。

B: 没问题，那就福特嘉年华掀背车吧。

Scene 3 车型选择

A: What type of car should we rent for our trip?

B: Well, how many people will be traveling with us? And how much luggage do we have?

A: It's just the two of us, and we have two small suitcases.

B: In that case, maybe we can go for a smaller car, like a sedan.

A: Sounds good. But do you think we should rent a car with GPS navigation?

B: It could be useful. Let me check if it's an additional cost.

A: 我们这次旅行应该租什么样的车呢?

B: 嗯，有多少人和我们一起旅行? 有多少行李?

A: 只有我们两人，还有两个小行李箱。

B: 那样的话，也许我们可以租一辆小一点的车，比如小轿车。

A: 听起来不错。但是你认为我们应该租一辆装载 GPS 导航系统的车吗?

B: 可能会有用。让我查一下是不是额外收费。

Scene 4 租车费用

A: What's the rate for the car per day?

B: $60 per day. Do you want insurance?

A: Yes, full coverage, please.

B: That is 10 extra dollars per day.

A: That's fine. Is there any mileage limit?

B: Yes, 50 miles. After that, we charge $1 per mile.

A: 这辆车每天的租金是多少?

B: 60 美元一天。您要保险吗?

A: 要，全额承保。

B: 那样每天多收 10 美元。

A: 好的。有里程限制吗?

B: 有，50 英里。超出限制，我们每英里收费 1 美元。

147

交通出行

☐ driver's license 驾驶执照

☐ make *n.* 品牌

☐ model *n.* 型号

☐ sedan *n.* 小轿车

☐ GPS（Global Positioning System）全球定位系统

☐ useful *adj.* 有用的

☐ rate *n.* 费用

☐ full coverage 全险

☐ mileage limit 里程限制

Scene 5 协议与付款

A: How do we finalize the car rental agreement?

B: We'll need to sign the rental contract and provide a deposit.

A: How much is the deposit?

B: It depends on the type of car you choose. For a standard sedan, the deposit is $500.

A: How can I pay the deposit and the rental fee?

B: You can pay by credit card or cash. Do you have a preference?

A: I'll pay with my credit card. When do I need to pay the rental fee?

B: The rental fee is due at the end of the rental period when you return the car.

A：我们如何确定租车协议呢？

B：我们需要签订租赁合同并支付押金。

A：押金是多少？

B：这要看您选什么车了。一辆标准轿车的押金是 500 美元。

A：我怎样支付押金和租金？

B：您可以用信用卡或现金支付。您想以哪种形式付款？

A：我用信用卡支付。我什么时候需要支付租金？

B：租期结束时，您还车的时候交租金。

Scene 6 取车与还车

A: When can I pick up the car, and where can I return it?

B: You can pick up the car at our office at 9:00 am and return it thereby 6:00 pm on the due date.

A: Can I return it after 6:00 pm?

B: Yes, but there'll be a late fee if you return it after our office is closed.

A: OK, got it. And how do I return the car? Do I need to fill up the gas?

B: Yes, please fill up the gas tank before returning the car, and park it in our designated area.

A: Alright, thanks for the information.

A：我什么时候可以取车，在哪儿还车？

B：您可以在上午 9 点到我们的车行取车，在归还日下午 6 点前还车。

A：我可以在下午 6 点以后还吗？

B：可以，但是如果您在我们车行下班后还车的话，需要付滞纳金。

A：好的，知道了。我怎么还车呢？我需要把油加满吗？

B：需要，还车前请加满油，并把车停在我们指定的位置。

A：好的，谢谢你提供的信息。

重点词汇
及表达

☐ rental agreement 租赁协议

☐ rental contract 租赁合同

☐ rental fee 租金

☐ due *adj.* 到期的

☐ gas tank 油箱

☐ designated area 指定区域

Scene 7　还车

A: Do I have to fill it up when I check in?

B: Yes.

A: Where should I return the car?

B: You can return it at any of our branches.

A: Is there anyone near the airport?

B: Yes.

A: OK, I'll rent one.

A：我需要在办理还车手续时加满油吗？

B：需要。

A：我应该在哪儿还车？

B：您可以到我们的任何一家分店还。

A：机场附近有分店吗？

B：有。

A：好的，我租一辆。

Scene 8　保险与事故

A: Can you tell me about car insurance options?

B: We have basic and comprehensive coverage. Basic covers damage to the car and liability. Comprehensive covers theft and personal injury.

A: How much more is comprehensive?

B: It costs more, but it helps you more in case of problems.

A: What should I do if there's an accident?

B: Call 911 for emergencies; then call us for help.

A: Thanks for your help!

A：你能告诉我汽车保险有哪些选择吗？

B：我们提供基本险和综合险。基本险包括汽车损坏险和责任险。综合险包括盗窃和人身伤害。

A：综合险会多出多少钱？

B：费用会高一些，但遇到问题时它能为你提供更多的帮助。

A：如果遇上事故我该怎么办？

B：遇上紧急情况请拨打 911，然后向我们求助。

A：谢谢你的帮助!

☐ branch *n.* 分店

☐ comprehensive coverage 综合险

☐ liability *n.* 责任险

☐ emergency *n.* 紧急情况

Part 8　Consumer Life
消费生活

Unit 1 At a Supermarket 在超市

Scene 1 寻找商品

A: Hi, do you know where I can find sunglasses, sunscreen, hats, and umbrellas?

B: Sure, sunglasses are in Aisle 6; sunscreen is in Aisle 10; hats are in Aisle 12; and umbrellas are in Aisle 14.

A: Thank you. Do you know if there are any sales going on?

B: Let me check. Yes, hats and umbrellas are on sale this week.

A: Great, I'll take a look.

B: Alright. Let me know if you need any assistance.

A: Will do. Thanks for your help.

B: No problem. Happy shopping!

A：嗨，你知道我在哪儿可以找到太阳镜、防晒霜、帽子和雨伞吗？

B：知道，太阳镜在 6 号货道，防晒霜在 10 号货道，帽子在 12 号货道，雨伞在 14 号货道。

A：谢谢。你知道有什么促销活动吗？

B：我查一下。嗯，帽子和雨伞这周大减价。

A：太好了，我看看。

B：好的。如果您需要帮助，请告诉我。

A：好的。谢谢你的帮助。

B：不客气。购物愉快!

Scene 2 询问新鲜度

A: Excuse me. Are the fruits and vegetables fresh here?

B: Yes, they're very fresh. We receive daily shipments.

A: How about the berries? Are they sweet?

B: Definitely, we only sell ripe ones.

A: Thank you. How long do they usually last?

B: Most of our products have a shelf life of 3–5 days.

A: Alright. Thanks for your help.

A：打扰一下，这里的水果和蔬菜新鲜吗？

B：是的，很新鲜。我们是每天进新货。

A：浆果怎么样？它们甜吗？

B：当然，我们只卖成熟的浆果。

A：谢谢。它们通常能放多久？

B：我们大多数产品的保质期是 3~5 天。

A：好的。谢谢你的帮助。

重点词汇
及表达

☐ sunglasses *n.* 太阳镜

☐ sunscreen *n.* 防晒霜

☐ sale *n.* 促销

☐ shipment *n.* 运输，运输的货物

☐ ripe *adj.* 成熟的

☐ shelf life 保质期

Scene 3　特价活动

A: Hi, what are the current promotions in the store?

B: We have a sale on snacks and beverages. And a buy-one-get-one-free deal on select beauty products.

A: Sounds good. Is there anything else on sale?

B: Yes, we have a clearance on winter clothing and accessories.

A: That's great. I'll check those out.

B: Let me know if you need any help.

A: Thank you.

B: Have a nice day!

A：嗨，现在店里有什么促销活动吗？

B：我们的零食和饮料在打折。还有精选美容产品"买一送一"的优惠。

A：听起来不错。还有别的东西在打折吗？

B：有，冬装和配饰在清仓甩卖。

A：太好了。我会去看看的。

B：如果需要帮助，请告诉我。

A：谢谢。

B：祝您过得愉快!

Scene 4　超市结账

A: How much is it in total?

B: That'll be $45.50, please.

A: Can I pay by credit card?

B: Yes, we accept all major credit cards.

A: Great, here you go.

B: Thank you! Your receipt is in the bag.

A：总共多少钱？

B：一共是 45.5 美元。

A：我可以用信用卡支付吗？

B：可以，我们接受所有主流信用卡。

A：好的，给你。

B：谢谢! 您的收据在袋子里。

153

Unit 2　Lost and Found 失物招领

Scene 1　失物招领处

A: Excuse me. Where is the lost and found?

B: It's on the first floor near the entrance.

A: Thank you. Is it open now?

B: Yes, it's open from 9:00 am to 5:00 pm.

A: Great! Thanks for your help.

B: No problem. Have a nice day.

A：打扰了，请问失物招领处在哪儿？

B：在一楼，靠近入口。

A：谢谢。现在开门了吗？

B：开了，从早晨 9 点开到下午 5 点。

A：太棒了! 谢谢你的帮助。

B：不客气。祝您过得愉快。

☐ beverage *n.* 饮料

☐ select *adj.* 精选的

☐ beauty product 美容产品

☐ accessory *n.* 配饰

☐ in total 总共

☐ major *adj.* 主要的，主流的

☐ entrance *n.* 入口

消费生活

Scene 2 捡到手机

A: Excuse me. I found a phone. Can I give it to the lost and found?

B: Sure. Where did you find it?

A: I found it on the bench near the fountain.

B: Thank you. We'll take care of it.

A：打扰了，我捡到了一部手机。我可以把它交到失物招领处吗？

B：当然可以。你是在哪儿捡到的？

A：我是在喷泉旁边的长凳上捡到的。

B：谢谢。我们会处理的。

Scene 3 领取失物

A: Hi, I lost my bag, and I heard it was found. Can I retrieve it at the lost and found?

B: Sure! Can you describe your bag and where you lost it?

A: It's a black backpack with a red zipper. I lost it at the library.

B: Great! We have a black backpack with a red zipper. Can you identify the contents?

A: Yes, there's a laptop and a notebook inside.

B: That's it! You can retrieve your bag at the front desk.

A：你好，我的包丢了，而且我听说它被找到了。我可以去失物招领处认领吗？

B：当然可以！您能描述一下您的包的样子，以及您是在哪儿丢失的吗？

A：那是一个带有红色拉链的黑色背包。我把它落在图书馆了。

B：好的。我们找到了一个带有红色拉链的黑色背包。您能跟我确认一下包里有什么东西吗？

A：好的，包里有一台笔记本电脑和一个笔记本。

B：就是这个！您可以去前台取包。

Unit 3 Deposit Service 寄存服务

Scene 1 行李寄存

A: Excuse me. Where can I store my bag?

B: We have a baggage storage area right over there. It costs $5 per bag.

A: OK. Thanks. How long can I store it?

A：打扰了，请问我可以把包存在哪儿？

B：那边有行李寄存区。每个包收费 5 美元。

A：好的。谢谢，我可以存多久？

重点词汇
及表达

☐ bench *n.* 长凳

☐ fountain *n.* 喷泉

☐ retrieve *v.* 取回

☐ describe *v.* 描述

☐ identify *v.* 确定，识别

☐ store *v.* 存放

☐ storage area 寄存区

B: You can store it for up to 8 hours. After that, there's an additional charge.

A: Got it. Can I pay with cash?

B: Yes, we accept both cash and card.

A: Great! Thank you.

B：您可以存8个小时。超时要另外收费。

A：知道了。我可以付现金吗？

B：可以，我们接受现金和银行卡。

A：太好了！谢谢。

Scene 2 寻找存放物品

A: Excuse me. I can't find my bag. Can you help me?

B: Sure. Can you tell me which locker it was in?

A: I forgot. Can you check the security camera footage?

B: Of course, let me take a look. Oh, here it is! Locker 23.

A: Thank you so much!

A：打扰了，我找不到我的包了。你能帮我吗？

B：当然。您能告诉我它在哪个储物柜吗？

A：我忘了。你能查看一下监控录像吗？

B：当然可以，让我看看。哦，在这儿！23号储物柜。

A：太谢谢你了！

Unit 4 Purchasing Cosmetics 购买化妆品

Scene 1 购买化妆品

A: Hi, I'm looking for some new cosmetics.

B: Of course! What kind of products are you interested in?

A: I need a new foundation and maybe a new lipstick.

B: Great! What's your skin type? Do you have any particular concerns?

A: I have combination skin, and I'm looking for something with good coverage.

A：嗨，我想买一些新化妆品。

B：没问题！您对什么样的产品感兴趣？

A：我需要一盒新粉底，也许还需要一支新口红。

B：好的。您的皮肤是什么类型？您有什么特别的需求吗？

A：我是混合性皮肤。我想买遮瑕效果好的粉底。

□ locker *n.* 储物柜
□ security camera footage 监控录像
□ cosmetics *n.* 化妆品
□ foundation *n.* 粉底
□ lipstick *n.* 口红
□ skin type 皮肤类型
□ combination skin 混合性皮肤

B: I recommend this foundation. It's great for combination skin and has great coverage.

A: Sounds good. What about lipstick?

B: What kind of color are you interested in?

A: I'm looking for something that's bold but not too bright.

B: How about this one? It's a deep red. That's very popular right now.

A: Hmm, that might be a bit too dark for me.

B: No problem. What about this one? It's a little lighter.

A: That's perfect!

B：我推荐这款粉底。它非常适合混合性皮肤，而且遮瑕效果很好。

A：听起来不错。口红呢？

B：您喜欢什么颜色的？

A：我想要一支颜色醒目但不过于鲜艳的口红。

B：这支口红怎么样？是深红色的。现在很流行。

A：嗯，这对我来说可能有点太暗了。

B：没关系。这支怎么样？颜色稍微亮一点。

A：太好了！

Scene 2 购买香水

A: Do you have this perfume scent?

B: Which perfume scent are you looking for?

A: I want something floral and light.

B: Yes, we have a few floral scents available. Let me show you.

A：你们有这种气味的香水吗？

B：您想要哪种香味的香水？

A：我想要淡雅的花香。

B：哦，我们有一些花香型的。我拿给您看看。

Scene 3 索要样品

A: Can I get some samples with my purchase?

B: Sure, we have a few options available.

A: Thank you! What samples do you have?

B: We have skincare and fragrance samples. Which would you prefer?

A: Skincare, please.

B: No problem. I'll include some with your purchase.

A：我买产品时能送我一些样品吗？

B：当然可以，我们提供几种选择。

A：谢谢！你们有哪些样品？

B：我们有护肤品和香水样品。您更喜欢哪种？

A：请给我护肤品。

B：没问题。我会把一些样品加在您购买的产品中。

重点词汇
及表达

☐ perfume *n.* 香水

☐ scent *n.* 气味

☐ floral *adj.* 花的

☐ sample *n.* 样品

☐ skincare *n.* 护肤

☐ fragrance sample 香水样品

Scene 4　购买护肤品

A: Hi there, I'm looking for some skincare products.

A：你好，我想买一些护肤品。

B: Absolutely! What kind of products are you interested in?

B：当然可以! 您对哪类产品感兴趣?

A: I need a good moisturizer and maybe a cleanser too.

A：我需要一款好用的保湿霜，也许还需要一支洗面奶。

B: We have some great options. Are you looking for something specifically for dry or oily skin?

B：我们有一些不错的选择。您想要干性或油性皮肤专用的吗?

A: My skin tends to be on the dry side.

A：我的皮肤偏干性。

B: In that case, I'd recommend this moisturizer. It's very hydrating and will help lock in moisture.

B：那样的话，我推荐这款保湿霜。它保湿效果好，有助于锁住水分。

A: That sounds perfect. What about a cleanser?

A：听起来很不错。洗面奶有什么样的?

B: This one is great for dry skin as well. It's very gentle.

B：这款对干性皮肤也很好。非常温和。

A: Great, I'll take both of them.

A：太好了，这两款我都买了。

B: Fantastic! Do you need anything else today?

B：太棒了! 您今天还要点什么?

A: No, that's all. Thank you so much for your help.

A：不要了，就这些。非常感谢你的帮助。

B: You're welcome! Don't hesitate to come back if you need anything else. Have a great day!

B：不客气! 如果您还需要什么，尽管来找我。祝您过得愉快!

Scene 5　皮肤类型

A: Is this lotion OK for oily skin?

A：这款乳液适合油性皮肤吗?

B: Actually, that one is good for dry skin. This one is better for oily skin.

B：事实上，那款乳液对干性皮肤很有效。这款更适合油性皮肤。

157

消费生活

☐ skincare product 护肤品

☐ lotion *n.* 乳液

☐ moisturizer *n.* 保湿霜

☐ oily skin 油性皮肤

☐ cleanser *n.* 洗面奶

☐ gentle *adj.* 温和的

Scene 6　过敏退货

A: Excuse me. Can I return this skincare if I have an allergic reaction?

B: Yes, you can return or exchange within 30 days with the receipt.

A: Great, thank you.

B: No problem. Is there anything else I can help you with?

A: No, that's all. Thank you again.

B: You're welcome. Have a nice day!

A：打扰了。如果出现过敏反应，我可以退货吗？

B：可以。您可以凭收据在30天内退换货。

A：太好了，谢谢。

B：不客气。还有什么需要我帮忙的吗？

A：没有了，就这些。再次感谢你。

B：不客气。祝您过得愉快!

Unit 5　Membership Cards 会员卡

Scene 1　会员卡优惠

A: Hi, what are the benefits of your membership card?

B: You can get discounts, rewards, and special offers.

A: How much does it cost to become a member?

B: It's free to join. Would you like to sign up?

A: Yes, please. How do I sign up?

A：你好，会员卡有什么福利吗？

B：您可以享受折扣、奖励和特别优惠。

A：成为会员要花多少钱？

B：加入是免费的。您想加入吗？

A：想。我如何加入呢？

Scene 2　开通会员卡

A: Hi, how do I sign up for a membership card?

B: You can fill out an application at the customer service desk.

A: What information do I need to provide?

B: Just your name, address, and email.

A: Is there anything else I need to know?

A：嗨，我如何办会员卡呢？

B：您可以在客户服务台填写申请表。

A：我需要提供什么信息？

B：只需要您的姓名、地址和电子邮件。

A：还有什么我需要知道的吗？

要点词汇
口表达

☐ allergic reaction 过敏反应

☐ return or exchange 退换

☐ benefit *n.* 福利

☐ special offer 特别优惠

☐ application *n.* 申请表

☐ customer service 客户服务

B: Yes, you'll receive a card, and you can start using it right away.

A: Great! Thanks for your help.

B: You're welcome. Have a nice day!

B：哦，您会收到一张卡，您可以马上开始使用。

A：太棒了！谢谢你的帮助。

B：不客气。祝您过得愉快！

Scene 3　会员卡积分

A: Hi, can I earn points with my purchase?

B: Yes, our membership program allows you to earn points.

A: How many points can I earn per purchase?

B: It depends on the amount of your purchase.

A: Can I redeem the points for rewards or discounts?

B: Yes, you can redeem your points for rewards and discounts.

A: Sounds great. Thank you for the information.

B: You're welcome. Happy shopping!

A：嗨，我可以通过购物来赚取积分吗？

B：是的，我们的会员计划可以让您赚取积分。

A：每次购买可以获得多少积分？

B：这要看您的购买量。

A：我可以用积分兑换奖励或折扣吗？

B：可以，您可以用积分兑换奖励和折扣。

A：听起来不错。谢谢你提供的信息。

B：不客气。祝您购物愉快！

Scene 4　积分兑换

A: Excuse me. Can I use my membership points to redeem items here?

B: Yes, you can use your points to redeem items in-store.

A: How many points do I need to redeem something?

B: It depends on the item's value and the points you have.

A: Can I combine my points with other payment methods?

B: Yes, you can pay with a combination of points and cash or a card.

A: OK! Thank you for letting me know.

B: No problem. Happy shopping!

A：打扰一下，我可以用我的会员积分在这里兑换商品吗？

B：可以，您可以用积分兑换店内商品。

A：兑换商品需要多少积分？

B：这取决于商品的价格和您的积分。

A：我可以把积分和其他支付方式结合使用吗？

B：可以，您可以用积分加现金或银行卡支付。

A：好的！谢谢你告诉我这些。

B：不客气。祝您购物愉快！

消费生活

- □ earn points 赚取积分
- □ redeem v. 兑换
- □ membership point 会员积分
- □ value n. （商品）价值

- □ combine...with...
  把……与……结合

Unit 6 Having the Check 结账

Scene 1 何处结账

A: Excuse me. Where can I pay?

B: Over there, by the cashier.

A: Thanks. Do I need to wait in line?

B: No, you can go straight there.

A: Great! Thanks for your help!

B: You're welcome! Have a nice day!

A: 打扰一下，我可以在哪儿付款？

B: 在那边，收银台旁边。

A: 谢谢。我需要排队等候吗？

B: 不用，您可以直接去那儿。

A: 太棒了！谢谢你的帮助！

B: 不客气！祝您过得愉快！

Scene 2 支付方式

A: Where do I check out?

B: The cashier is right there.

A: Can I pay with a credit card?

B: Yes. We accept payment by credit card, cash, and WeChat Pay.

A: 我应该在哪儿结账？

B: 收银台就在那边。

A: 我可以用信用卡支付吗？

B: 可以。我们接受信用卡、现金和微信支付。

Scene 3 分期付款

A: What are the payment options?

B: Cash or credit card.

A: Can I pay in installments with my card?

B: Yes, you can. Is it a credit card?

A: Yes, it is.

B: Then you can choose the installment option.

A: Thank you for your help.

B: You're welcome. Have a nice day!

A: 付款方式有哪些？

B: 现金或信用卡。

A: 我能用信用卡分期付款吗？

B: 可以。这张是信用卡吗？

A: 是的。

B: 那么您可以选择分期付款。

A: 谢谢你的帮助。

B: 不客气。祝您过得愉快！

Scene 4 线上预订

A: Hi, I'd like to place an order for pickup.

B: Sure. What would you like to order?

A: 你好，我想下一个线下提货的订单。

B: 好的。您想订购什么？

重点词汇
及表达

☐ cashier n. 收银台

☐ wait in line 排队等候

☐ payment n. 支付

☐ installment n. 分期付款

☐ pickup n. 提货

全场景英语口语

A: I'd like to order a laptop and a printer.

B: OK, and how would you like to pay?

A: I'll pay online. Is that OK?

B: Sure. We'll send you a payment link. When would you like to pick it up?

A: Tomorrow at 2:00 pm.

B: Alright, we'll have it ready. Thank you!

A: Thank you, bye!

A：我想订购一部笔记本电脑和一台打印机。

B：好的。您想怎样付款呢？

A：我在网上付款。这样可以吗？

B：当然可以。我们会给您发送一个付款链接。您想什么时候来提货呢？

A：明天下午2点。

B：好的，我们会准备好的。谢谢您！

A：谢谢，再见！

Unit 7 Asking for Help 寻求帮助

Scene 1 寻找商店

A: Excuse me. Where's the Huawei store?

B: It's on the second floor, next to the escalator.

A: Other electronics stores nearby?

B: Best Buy on the third floor, Microsoft on the first.

A: Thanks.

B: Enjoy shopping!

A：打扰一下，华为商店在哪儿？

B：在二楼，在自动扶梯旁边。

A：附近还有其他电子产品商店吗？

B：百思买商店在三楼，微软商店在一楼。

A：谢谢。

B：祝您购物愉快！

161

Scene 2 广播寻人

A: Excuse me. Can you help me? My son is lost somewhere in the store.

B: Of course. We'll do everything we can. Can you tell me his name and what he looks like?

A: His name is Tommy, and he's a little boy with blond hair and blue eyes. He was wearing a red shirt and blue shorts.

A：打扰了，你能帮帮我吗？我儿子在商场走失了，不知道在哪儿。

B：当然会帮忙，我们会尽力帮助您的。您能告诉我他的名字和长相吗？

A：他叫汤米，他是一个金发蓝眼睛的小男孩。他穿着红色衬衫和蓝色短裤。

☐ payment link 付款链接

☐ electronics store 电子产品商店

B: Alright, we'll make an announcement over the store intercom, and we'll have our staff keep an eye out for him. In the meantime, can you stay here at the service desk in case he comes back?

A: Yes, of course. Thank you so much for your help.

B: No problem, we'll do everything we can to make sure he's found safe and sound. Please don't hesitate to let us know if you need anything else.

B：好的，我们会通过商场广播系统进行公告，并让我们的员工留意他。在此期间，您能不能待在服务台，以防他回来找不到人？

A：好的，没问题。非常感谢你的帮助。

B：不客气，我们会尽一切努力确保他能安全找到。如果您还需要什么帮助，请随时告诉我们。

Scene 3　找洗手间

A: Excuse me. Where is the restroom?

B: It's just over there to the left.

A: Thank you. Is it easy to find?

B: Yes, it's clearly marked, and there are signs.

A: Great! Thanks for your help.

B: You're welcome.

A：打扰一下，请问洗手间在哪儿？

B：就在那儿，在左边。

A：谢谢。容易找到吗？

B：容易，洗手间标记得很清楚，而且有标识。

A：太棒了！谢谢你的帮助。

B：不客气。

162

Unit 8　Business Hours 营业时间

Scene 1　营业时间

A: Excuse me. What are the business hours of the store?

B: We open from 10:00 am to 9:00 pm on weekdays.

A: What about weekends?

B: On Saturdays and Sundays, we open at 9:00 am and close at 10:00 pm.

A：打扰了，请问商店的营业时间是什么时候？

B：工作日的营业时间是上午10点到晚上9点。

A：周末呢？

B：周六和周日，我们早晨9点开门，晚上10点关门。

重点词汇
及表达

☐ make an announcement 通知
☐ keep an eye out 留意
☐ safe and sound 安然无恙

☐ hesitate v. 犹豫
☐ mark v. 标记
☐ business hour 营业时间

A: Do the hours change during holidays?

B: Yes, they do. We'll post notices in advance.

A：节假日工作时间有变化吗？

B：有。我们会提前发布通知。

Scene 2 冬季与夏季营业时间

A: Excuse me. What are the operating hours for the mall during winter and summer?

B: During winter, we open at 10:00 am and close at 9:00 pm. During summer, we open at 9:00 am and close at 10:00 pm.

A: Thank you. Are there any changes in the operating hours on weekends?

B: No, our operating hours on weekends are the same as on weekdays.

A: Alright. Thanks for your help.

B: You're welcome.

A：打扰了。请问商场冬季和夏季的营业时间是怎样的？

B：在冬季，我们上午10点开门，晚上9点关门。在夏季，我们上午9点开门，晚上10点关门。

A：谢谢。周末的营业时间有什么变化吗？

B：没有，我们周末的营业时间和平时一样。

A：好的。谢谢你的帮助。

B：不客气。

Scene 3 开业时间

A: Hi, could you tell me if the new store is open yet?

B: Sure. Which store are you referring to?

A: The one on Main Street.

B: Let me check. Yes, it opened last week. Would you like the hours?

A: Yes, please.

B: It's open from 10:00 am to 9:00 pm Monday through Saturday and 11:00 am to 7:00 pm on Sunday.

A：嗨，你能告诉我这家新店是否开业了吗？

B：当然可以。您指的是哪家店？

A：位于主街的那家。

B：我查一下。开业了，这家店上周开业了。您想知道营业时间吗？

A：想。

B：周一至周六上午10点至晚上9点，周日上午11点至晚上7点。

Scene 4 夜间入口

A: Is the cinema open 24x7?

B: No, it closes at midnight.

A：这家电影院是一周7天每天24小时营业吗？

B：不是，它在午夜不营业。

☐ post notices 发布通知

☐ in advance 提前

☐ operating hour 营业时间

☐ the same as 与······相同

☐ refer to 指，提及

☐ at midnight 在午夜

消费生活

A: Where is the entrance that is open late at night?

B: The entrance at the back is open 24x7.

A: Oh, I see. Thanks for letting me know.

B: You're welcome. Enjoy your movie!

A：深夜开放时入口在哪儿?

B：后面的入口是一周7天每天24小时开放的。

A：哦,知道了。谢谢你告诉我。

B：不客气。享受观影吧!

Unit 9 Purchasing New Products 购买新品

Scene 1　预订商品

A: Do you know if we can make a reservation for the new bag?

B: Yes, you can. Let me check availability and schedule a visit for you.

A: That would be great. Thank you so much.

B: You're welcome. Can I have your name and phone number, please?

A: Sure, my name is Alice, and my number is 1234567890.

B: Thank you, Alice. I will confirm your appointment shortly.

A：你知道我们是否可以预订这个新款包包吗?

B：可以预订。我查一下是否有货,然后为您安排到店时间。

A：那太好了。非常感谢。

B：不客气。能告诉我您的名字和电话号码吗?

A：当然,我叫爱丽丝,电话号码是1234567890。

B：谢谢您,爱丽丝。我很快就会确认您的预约。

Scene 2　请求调货

A: Excuse me. Do you have any more stock of this black leather bag?

B: I'm sorry. We're currently out of stock.

A: Is there any way to order it or get it from another store?

B: Yes, we can check if it's available at another location or order it for you.

A: That would be great! Could you please help me with that?

A：打扰一下,这种黑色皮包还有现货吗?

B：抱歉。我们现在缺货了。

A：有什么办法可以订购或从其他店铺调货吗?

B：嗯,我们可以查一下其他店是否有货,或者为您订购。

A：那太好了!你能帮我安排一下吗?

□ confirm one's appointment 确认预约

□ stock *n.* 库存

□ out of stock 缺货

B: Of course. What's your contact information?

A: My number is 5551234. Thank you!

B：当然可以。您的联系方式是什么？

A：我的电话号码是5551234。谢谢你！

Scene 3　礼盒包装

A: Do you have gift bags? I wanna give this as a present.

B: Yes. Just down the jewelry shelf.

A: I'll buy this gift bag.

A：你们有礼品袋吗？我想把这个作为礼物送人。

B：有。就在珠宝货架下面。

A：我要买这个礼品袋。

Unit 10　Buying Clothes 购买服饰

Scene 1　寻找衣服

A: Hey. What're you looking for today?

B: I need a coat. I want the coat to be very warm.

A: OK. Do you have any other requirements?

B: Yes. Also, I want the coat to be very formal, so that I can wear it for the interview.

A: OK. Great. Well, we have this coat here, which is very beautiful and formal. Enough to wear for an interview.

A：嘿。您今天想买点什么？

B：我需要一件外套。我希望这件外套非常暖和。

A：好的。您还有别的要求吗？

B：有。我也希望这件外套非常正式，这样我就可以穿它去面试了。

A：哦，好的。嗯，这里有这件外套，非常漂亮，也很正式。穿上它面试很合适。

165

Scene 2　衣服尺码

A: This size is too small. Can you find a larger one?

B: Sure. What size are you looking for?

A: Maybe one size up.

B: I'll see what we have in stock.

A: Thanks! I appreciate it.

B: No problem. Happy to help.

A：这个尺码太小了。你能找到大一点的吗？

B：当然可以。您要多大尺码的？

A：可能大一号吧。

B：我看看我们的库存还有些什么。

A：谢谢! 非常感谢。

B：不客气。我很乐意帮忙。

☐ contact information 联系信息

☐ jewelry *n.* 珠宝

☐ shelf *n.* 架子

☐ requirement *n.* 要求

☐ formal *adj.* 正式的

☐ interview *n.* 面试

☐ in stock 库存

Scene 3　找试衣间

A: Excuse me. Where are the fitting rooms?

B: They're in the back of the store, to your left.

A: Thank you.

B: You're welcome. Let me know if you need a different size or color.

A: Will do.

B: Happy shopping!

A：打扰一下，请问试衣间在哪儿？

B：在商店靠里面，在您的左边。

A：谢谢。

B：不客气。如果您需要不同的尺码或颜色，请告诉我。

A：好的。

B：祝您购物愉快!

Scene 4　试穿衣服

A: Oh. I like it. Let me try it. Oh, what size do you have?

B: We have sizes S, M, L, and XL.

A: This one is Medium. I don't know if it's suitable for me. But I'll try it first. Can you hold this for me?

B: Of course.

A: Thank you.

A：哦。我喜欢这件。让我试试。哦，你们有什么尺码的？

B：我们有小码、中码、大码和加大码的。

A：这是中码的。我不知道它是否适合我。不过我还是先试试吧。你能帮我拿一下这个吗？

B：当然可以。

A：谢谢。

Scene 5　鞋子挤脚

A: I like these. But they're too tight on me. They're pinching my toes. Do you have them in size seven?

B: Yes. We have them in the warehouse. I'll fetch them for you right away. Please wait for a second.

A：我喜欢这双鞋。但是我穿太紧了。这双鞋挤脚。你们有七号的吗？

B：有。我们的仓库里有。我马上给您取过来。请稍等。

Scene 6　圆点上衣

A: That polka dot top there. Can you take it down for me, so I can try it on?

B: Of course. The fitting room is right over there.

A：那边那件带有圆点花纹的上衣。你能帮我取下来，让我试穿一下吗？

B：当然可以。试衣间就在那边。

重点词汇
及表达

☐ fitting room 试衣间

☐ try v. 试穿

☐ tight adj. 紧的

☐ warehouse n. 仓库

☐ try on 试穿

Scene 7 裙子太大

A: This dress is too big for me. I think I'm gonna pass on it.

B: No problem. We have a lot of good choices. Let me show you the other dresses.

A：这条裙子我穿太大了。我想我还是不要了。

B：没问题。我们有很多不错的选择。我给您看看其他的裙子。

Scene 8 当季新品

A: Excuse me. What are the newest products this season?

B: We just got in some new arrivals. Would you like me to show you?

A: Yes, please. Thank you.

B: Follow me. I'll show you the latest styles.

A: Great! I'm excited to see them.

B: I think you'll really like them.

A：打扰一下，这一季的最新服装是什么？

B：我们刚进了一些新货。要我展示给您看看吗？

A：好的。谢谢你！

B：跟我来。我给您看看最新的款式。

A：太棒了！我很激动能见到这些新款。

B：我想您一定会喜欢的。

167

Scene 9 讨论衣服

A: How do you like it?

B: Wow. I actually like it a lot. What do you think?

A: It looks great.

B: Is it formal enough for the interview?

A: Yes. You can definitely wear it to an interview.

B: Oh! That's great! How much is it?

A: It's 500 dollars.

A：您觉得怎么样？

B：哇。我真的很喜欢。你觉得怎么样？

A：看起来很棒。

B：穿这件衣服去面试够正式吗？

A：够正式。您绝对可以穿它去面试。

B：哦！太好了！多少钱？

A：500 美元。

Scene 10 颜色搭配

A: Hey, what do you think of this hat with this shirt?

B: I think they go well together. The colors complement each other.

A：嘿，你觉得这顶帽子配这件衬衫怎么样？

B：我觉得它们很配。这些颜色相辅相成。

☐ pass on 传递，将……交给

☐ arrival *n.* 抵达物

☐ latest style 最新款式

☐ actually *adv.* 事实上，确实

☐ complement *v.* 补充

A: That's what I was thinking too. Thanks for your opinion.

B: No problem. Happy to help with your outfit.

A：我也是这么想的。谢谢你的意见。

B：不客气。很高兴帮您选衣服。

Scene 11　买帽子

A: Oh, this hat looks great on me. I'll take it. Do you have one in pink too?

B: Sorry. We only have it in creamy white.

A：哦，这顶帽子我戴起来真好看。我要买。你们也有粉红色的吗？

B：抱歉。我们只有乳白色的。

Scene 12　颜色选择

A: Do you have this in another color?

B: Yes, we also have light green and black. But I think you look great in pink.

A：这件还有别的颜色吗？

B：有，还有浅绿色和黑色的。但我觉得您穿粉红色很好看。

Scene 13　肤色搭配

A: This color doesn't really match my skin tone. Do you have other options?

B: What color are you looking for?

A: Maybe something warmer, like a deep red?

B: Let me check if we have that in stock.

A: Thanks. I appreciate it.

B: No problem. Happy to help.

A：这种颜色和我的肤色不太相配。还有其他可选的吗？

B：您想要什么颜色的？

A：也许颜色更暖的吧，比如深红色？

B：我看看有没有现货。

A：谢谢。我很感激。

B：不客气。我很乐意帮忙。

Scene 14　询问材质

A: Are these real gold?

B: Not really. That's why they are so cheap. But they are very pretty, and they are very light.

A: Is this one hundred percent cotton?

B: Yes, it's very comfortable to wear.

A: Is this bag real leather?

B: Yes, I can guarantee that.

A：这些是真金的吗？

B：算不上是，所以它们才这么便宜。但是它们很漂亮，也很轻。

A：这是百分之百纯棉的吗？

B：是的，穿起来很舒服。

A：这个包是真皮的吗？

B：是的，我可以保证。

重点词汇
及表达

- □ outfit *n.* 衣服
- □ creamy white 乳白色
- □ light green 浅绿色
- □ match *v.* 搭配
- □ skin tone 肤色
- □ real gold 真金
- □ cotton *n.* 棉花
- □ real leather 真皮
- □ guarantee *v.* 保证

Scene 15 活动优惠

A: Wow! That's a lot. That's definitely over my budget.

B: OK. Well. We actually have a promotion now. If you buy this coat, you can also get our best-selling design for 50% off. And this is also formal enough to wear for an interview as well.

A: Wow. You're such a good salesgirl. I really wanna buy it.

B: OK. Great! Do you want this in size L or M?

A: I think Medium is better for me.

B: OK. Great. Two Ms.

A: Yes. Definitely.

A: 哇! 太贵了，明显超出了我的预算。

B: 哦。好的。事实上我们现在有促销活动。如果您买这件外套，您还可以五折买到我们最畅销的款式。而且这款也够正式，适合参加面试。

A: 哇。你真是一位非常棒的售货员。我真的很想买。

B: 好的。太棒了! 你要大号还是中号的?

A: 我想中号比较适合我。

B: 好的。太好了。两件中号的。

A: 是的。没错。

Scene 16 讨价还价

A: And do you have any other gift for me? Actually, I need a hat.

B: OK. Great. We actually have a discount on hats now as well.

A: Great, I'll take both. Can you pack them for me?

B: Yes, of course.

A: 你还会送我别的赠品吗? 事实上，我需要一顶帽子。

B: 嗯。好的。事实上目前我们的帽子也在打折。

A: 太好了，两样我都要。你能帮我包起来吗?

B: 当然可以。

Scene 17 退换政策

A: Excuse me. If I try this on at home and it doesn't fit, can I return or exchange it?

B: Yes, as long as you have the receipt and it's within our return policy timeframe.

A: What if I don't have the receipt?

B: We can still try to process the return or exchange, but it may be more difficult without the receipt.

A: 打扰了，如果我在家里试穿不合身，可以退换吗?

B: 可以，只要您有收据，而且在我们的退货政策期限内。

A: 如果我没有收据该怎么办?

B: 我们仍然会尽力办理退货或换货，但没有收据可能会麻烦一些。

☐ promotion *n.* 促销

☐ best-selling design 最畅销的款式

☐ pack *v.* 包装

☐ receipt *n.* 收据

☐ return policy 退货政策

☐ timeframe *n.* 时间表

A: OK. I'll make sure to keep it safe. Thank you.

A：好的。我会确保它完好无损的。谢谢你!

B: You're welcome. Let us know if you need any further assistance.

B：不客气。如果您需要更多的帮助,请告诉我们。

Scene 18   退换货时间

A: Can I return this if it doesn't fit?

A：如果不合身我可以退货吗?

B: Yeah. As long as you keep the receipt and do not damage it, you can return it within seven days.

B：可以。只要您保存好收据并且商品没有破损,您可以在七天内退货。

A: Can I exchange this for a larger size if it's too small?

A：如果太小,我可以换一件大一点的吗?

B: Yes, as long as it's not damaged, you can exchange it within a month.

B：可以,只要没有破损,一个月内可以换。

Scene 19   衣物保养

170

A: I really like this T-shirt. Can I put it in the washing machine?

A：我很喜欢这件 T 恤。我可以把它放进洗衣机里洗吗?

B: Yes, you can put it in the washing machine. The color doesn't fade, and the material doesn't shrink.

B：可以,您可以把它放进洗衣机里洗。它不会褪色,而且这种面料不会缩水。

Unit 11   After-sales Service 售后服务

Scene 1   退货

A: Excuse me. I need to exchange these shoes for my child.

A：打扰了,我要把这双给孩子买的鞋换掉。

B: What's the issue with the shoes?

B：这双鞋有什么问题吗?

A: They don't fit well.

A：不太合脚。

B: Alright. Do you have the receipt and tags?

B：好的。您有收据和吊牌吗?

重点词汇
及表达

☐ keep the receipt 保存收据

☐ damage v. 损坏

☐ shrink v. 缩水

☐ fit v. 合身

☐ tag n. 标签,标牌

A: Yes, I have them with me.

B: Great! You can pick out a replacement pair.

A: Thank you for your help.

B: No problem. Happy to assist.

A：有，我随身带着呢。

B：太好了！您可以挑一双想换的。

A：谢谢你的帮助。

B：不客气。我很乐意帮忙。

Scene 2 换货

A: Hi, I bought a phone from your store, but it has a quality issue.

B: Sure. Do you have the receipt?

A: I'm sorry. I can't seem to find it.

B: We need the receipt for the return process.

A: Can you still help me with the return, even without the receipt?

B: I'm afraid not. The receipt is necessary for returns.

A: Alright. Thank you anyway.

A：你好，我在你们店里买了一部手机，但是有质量问题。

B：嗯。您有收据吗？

A：抱歉。我好像找不到了。

B：办理退货手续时需要收据。

A：即使没有收据，你也能帮我处理退货吗？

B：恐怕不行。退货时必须有收据。

A：好吧。不管怎样都谢谢你。

Scene 3 上门安装

A: Hi, I just bought a washing machine from your store. But I don't know how to install it. Can I request for a technician to come and install it for me?

B: Of course. Please provide your order number and address.

A: My order number is 123456, and my address is 123 Main Street.

B: Alright, we will schedule a technician to come to your house as soon as possible.

A: Thank you so much! I appreciate your help.

B: You're welcome. Please let us know if you need any further assistance.

A：你好，我刚从你们店里买了一台洗衣机。但我不知道怎样安装。我可以要求技术人员来帮我安装吗？

B：当然可以。请提供您的订单号和地址。

A：我的订单号是123456，我的地址是主街123号。

B：好的，我们会尽快安排技术人员上门。

A：太谢谢你了！谢谢你的帮助。

B：不客气。如果您需要更多帮助，请告诉我们。

☐ replacement *n.* 替换

☐ quality issue 质量问题

☐ return *n.* 退货

☐ install *v.* 安装

☐ technician *n.* 技术人员

☐ assistance *n.* 帮助

Scene 4　开箱验货

A: Can you open the box for me to inspect the vase?

B: Sure! Let me get my box cutter.

A: I want to make sure it's not broken.

B: No problem. We want you to be satisfied.

A: Thank you. Everything looks good.

B: You're welcome. Enjoy your new vase!

A：你能打开盒子让我检查一下花瓶吗？

B：没问题！我去拿美工刀。

A：我想确保它没有破损。

B：没问题。我们希望您能满意。

A：谢谢。一切看起来都很好。

B：不客气。好好欣赏您的新花瓶吧！

Scene 5　要求赔偿

A: Hi, I received my order, but it's not what I expected.

B: I'm sorry to hear that. What seems to be the problem?

A: The item I received is not the one I ordered.

B: I apologize for the inconvenience. We'll make it right. Can you provide me with your order number?

A: Sure. It's 123456.

B: Thank you. We'll send you the correct item right away and offer you compensation for the inconvenience.

A：你好，我收到了我预订的东西，但它不是我想要的。

B：听到这个消息我很抱歉。出了什么问题？

A：我收到的货物不是我订购的。

B：给您带来不便，我深表歉意。我们会处理好的。您能提供一下您的订单号吗？

A：当然可以。我的订单号是123456。

B：谢谢。我们马上会把正确的货物寄给您，并补偿给您带来的不便。

Scene 6　免费送货

A: Can you deliver the cabinet for free?

B: Sorry, we don't offer free delivery.

A: How much is the delivery fee?

B: It depends on your location. Where are you located?

A: I'm located in the city center.

B: The delivery fee for that area is $50.

A：这个储物柜你们能免费送货吗？

B：抱歉，我们不提供免费送货服务。

A：配送费是多少？

B：这要看您所处的位置。您住在哪儿？

A：我住在市中心。

B：那个地区的配送费是50美元。

重点词汇
及表达

☐ inspect v. 检查

☐ box cutter 美工刀

☐ expect v. 期待

☐ compensation n. 补偿

☐ free delivery 免费送货

☐ delivery fee 配送费

Unit 12   Coupons 优惠券

Scene 1   使用优惠券

A: Can I use a coupon for this purchase?

B: Yes, you can. Do you have it with you?

A: Yes, here it is.

B: Great, we can apply it to your total.

A: Thank you! I appreciate it.

B: You're welcome! Happy shopping!

A：我这次可以用优惠券购买吗？

B：可以。您随身携带优惠券了吗？

A：带了，给你。

B：好的，我们可以在您结账的时候用上。

A：谢谢! 我很感激。

B：不客气! 祝您购物愉快!

Scene 2   获取优惠券

A: Hi, how can I get a coupon?

B: You can sign up for our email newsletter.

A: Is there any other way?

B: You can also follow us on social media.

A: OK! Thanks for letting me know.

B: No problem! Happy to help.

A: Thank you. Have a good day!

A：嗨，我怎样才能得到优惠券呢？

B：您可以订阅我们的电子邮件简报。

A：还有别的获取方式吗？

B：您也可以在社交媒体上关注我们。

A：好的! 谢谢你告诉我。

B：不客气。我很乐意帮忙。

A：谢谢。祝你过得愉快!

Scene 3   优惠券信息

A: Excuse me. What's the expiration date for this coupon?

B: It expires on the 30th of this month.

A: Thanks. Is there a minimum purchase amount to use it?

B: Yes, the minimum is $20.

A: Got it. Thank you for the information.

B: You're welcome. Happy shopping!

A: Thanks. Have a good day!

A：打扰一下，这张优惠券的有效期是什么时候？

B：本月 30 号到期。

A：谢谢。请问有最低消费金额限制吗？

B：有，最低 20 美元。

A：明白了。谢谢你提供的信息。

B：不客气。祝您购物愉快!

A：谢谢。祝你过得愉快!

- ☐ coupon *n.* 优惠券
- ☐ apply *v.* 应用
- ☐ newsletter *n.* 简报
- ☐ social media 社交媒体
- ☐ expiration date 有效期
- ☐ minimum purchase amount 最低消费金额

Unit 13　Hairdressing 理发美发

Scene 1　染发

A: I'm thinking about dyeing my hair.

B: What color are you considering?

A: I'm not sure. Maybe blonde?

B: Do you want to go to a salon or do it yourself?

A: I'll go to a salon. I don't want to mess it up.

B: Good idea. Let me know how it turns out!

A：我在考虑染头发。

B：你考虑染成什么颜色?

A：我不确定。也许金黄色?

B：你想去美发店染还是自己染?

A：我要去美发店染。我不想弄得一团糟。

B：好主意。染完了告诉我效果怎么样。

Scene 2　美发会员

A: Have you tried the new hair salon down the street?

B: No. Is it any good?

A: Yeah, they have great deals for members.

B: How much does it cost to be a member?

A: Just $50 a year, and you get discounted prices.

B: That sounds like a good deal. Thanks!

A：你去过街道那头新开的那家美发店吗?

B：没去过。那家店好吗?

A：挺好的,他们对会员很优惠。

B：会员费是多少?

A：一年只要50美元,还可以打折。

B：听起来很划算。谢谢!

Scene 3　换发型

A: Hi, can I help you with your hair?

B: Yes, I want to change my hairstyle.

A: Sure. What do you have in mind?

B: I was thinking about getting a short bob.

A: Great! Let's start with a consultation.

B: Sounds good. Thank you!

A：您好,您的发型有什么需要我帮忙的吗?

B：哦,我想换个发型。

A：当然可以,您有什么想法?

B：我想剪个短波波头。

A：好的! 我们先沟通一下。

B：听起来不错。谢谢你!

174

重点词汇
及表达

□ dye v. 染色

□ salon n. 美容院

□ mess up 弄糟

□ discounted price 折扣价

□ hairstyle n. 发型

□ have...in mind 在考虑,想要

□ consultation n. 商讨,咨询

Scene 4　剪发和洗发

A: Hi, I'd like a haircut and shampoo.

B: Sure. What style do you want?

A: Just a trim and a basic wash, please.

B: OK. Take a seat, and let me get started.

A: Great! Thanks. How long will it take?

B: About 30 minutes. Are you in a hurry?

A: No, I have some time.

A：你好，我想理发和洗发。

B：好的。您想要什么样的发型？

A：只用修剪一下，再洗一下就可以了。

B：好的。请坐。那我开始了。

A：好的! 谢谢。要花多长时间？

B：大约 30 分钟。您赶时间吗？

A：不赶，我有时间。

Scene 5　洗发和吹发

A: Hi, can I get a wash and blowout?

B: Sure. Do you want any treatment with that?

A: No, just a regular wash, please.

B: OK! Please follow me to the shampoo station.

A: Wow! This blowout looks amazing. Thank you!

B: You're welcome. Have a great day!

A：嗨，我能洗一下头发，吹个造型吗？

B：当然可以。您需要护理吗？

A：不需要，就是普通的洗发。

B：好的! 请跟我来洗发台。

A：哇! 吹出的造型看起来很棒。谢谢你!

B：不客气。祝您过得愉快!

175

☐ haircut *n.* 理发

☐ shampoo *n.* 洗头发

☐ style *n.* 式样

☐ trim *v.* 修整，剪下

☐ blowout *n.* 吹头发

☐ treatment *n.* 护理

Part 9　Banking Business
银行业务

Unit 1 Deposits and Withdrawals 存钱和取款

Scene 1 开户

A: Hi, I want to open a savings account.

B: Sure, we have several options available. What kind of account are you interested in?

A: I'm not sure. Could you give me some information about the interest rates?

B: Of course, our current rates range from 0.5% to 1.5%, depending on the account type and balance.

A: That sounds good. What documents do I need to bring to open an account?

B: You'll need to bring your ID, proof of address, and your initial deposit.

A: OK. Thank you for your help.

A：你好，我想开一个储蓄账户。

B：好的，我们有几种选择。您想开哪种账户？

A：我不确定。你能提供与利率相关的信息吗？

B：当然可以，我们目前的利率根据账户类型和余额的不同，从 0.5% 到 1.5% 不等。

A：听起来不错。开户需要带什么文件？

B：您需要带上您的身份证、地址证明和您的初始存款。

A：好的。谢谢你的帮助。

Scene 2 存钱

A: Can I help you?

B: Yes, I want to deposit some money.

A: How much would you like to deposit?

B: $500.

A: Alright, do you have an account with us?

B: Yes, here's my account number.

A: Great. Let me process that for you.

A：有什么我能帮忙的吗？

B：有的，我想存一些钱。

A：您想存多少钱？

B：500 美元。

A：好的，您在我们这里有账户吗？

B：有，这是我的账号。

A：好的。我来帮您处理一下。

178

□ open a savings account 开账户

□ interest rate 利率

□ balance *n.* 余额

□ initial deposit 初始存款

□ deposit some money 存钱

□ account number 账号

Scene 3　自动取款机

A: Excuse me. Do you know where the ATM is?

B: Yes, it's just around the corner, next to the supermarket.

A: Great! Thanks! Is it a 24-hour machine?

B: Yes, it is.

A: Perfect! That's exactly what I need. Thanks again.

B: You're welcome. Have a nice day!

A：打扰一下，你知道自动取款机在哪儿吗？

B：知道，就在拐角处，在超市旁边。

A：太棒了！谢谢！这台机器是24小时工作吗？

B：是的。

A：完美！这正是我需要的。再次感谢。

B：不客气。祝您过得愉快！

Scene 4　取款

A: I need to withdraw some cash.

B: Sure, how much do you need?

A: Just $100.

B: OK, your card and ID, please.

A: Here you are.

B: Here's your cash. Anything else I can help you with?

A: No, that's all. Thanks!

B: You're welcome. Have a good day!

A：我需要取一些现金。

B：没问题，您需要多少钱？

A：只要100美元。

B：好的，请出示您的银行卡和身份证。

A：给你。

B：这是您的现金。还有什么需要我帮忙的吗？

A：没有了，就这个。谢谢！

B：不客气。祝您过得愉快！

银行业务

□ ATM (automated teller machine)
自动取款机

□ withdraw v. 取出

Unit 2 **Transferring Money** 转账

Scene 1　跨国转账

A: Excuse me. Can I transfer money to another country from here?

A：打扰一下，我可以从这里汇款到另一个国家吗？

B: Yes, you can. Do you have all the necessary information?

B：可以。您有所有必要的信息吗？

A: What information do I need?

A：我需要什么信息呢？

B: You'll need the recipient's name, address, and bank account number.

B：您需要收款人姓名、地址和银行账号。

A: OK. Thank you. Is there a fee for international transfers?

A：好的。谢谢。跨国转账要收费吗？

B: Yes, there is. The fee depends on the amount and the destination country.

B：要收费。费用取决于汇款金额和目的地国家。

Scene 2　转账手续费

A: Does the bank charge a fee for transfers?

A：银行转账要收费吗？

B: It depends on the type of transfer.

B：这要看转账的类型。

A: What are the options?

A：有哪些选择？

B: There are domestic and international transfers.

B：有国内转账和国际转账。

A: And what about fees for each type?

A：每种类型的收费是多少？

B: Let me check on that for you.

B：我帮您查一下。

重点词汇
与表达

- ☐ transfer money 转账，汇款
- ☐ recipient 收款人
- ☐ international transfer 跨国转账
- ☐ charge a fee 收费
- ☐ domestic *adj.* 国内的

Unit 3 *Current Exchange* 兑换货币

Scene 1   兑换外币

A: What's the current exchange rate for US dollars?

B: It's 6.5 *yuan* per dollar today.

A: Thanks. What's the maximum amount of dollars I can exchange in one day?

B: The daily limit is 50,000 *yuan* equivalent.

A: 美元目前的兑换率是多少？

B: 今天 1 美元兑换 6.5 元人民币。

A: 谢谢。我一天最多能兑换多少美元？

B: 每日限额是与 5 万元人民币等值的美元。

Scene 2   汇率

A: Good morning. May I help you?

B: I would like Chinese RMB. Can you exchange this for me?

A: Oh, OK. What kind of currency have you got?

B: I have US dollars. What's today's exchange rate for US dollars?

A: It's 6.80 RMB for 1 US dollar.

B: OK. I'd like to exchange 20 US dollars.

A: Oh. That's good. That's 136 RMB. So would you please fill in this form?

B: Thank you.

A: What denominations would you like to have?

B: I would like 2 50-RMB bills. And for the rest, I would like coins because I want to take the bus.

A: OK, no problem. So here are 2 50-RMB bills, and here are the coins.

A: 早上好。有什么能为您效劳吗？

B: 我要兑换人民币。你能帮我兑换吗？

A: 哦，好的。您持有哪种货币？

B: 美元。今天美元的兑换率是多少？

A: 1 美元兑换 6.8 元人民币。

B: 好的。我想兑换 20 美元。

A: 哦。好的。也就是 136 元人民币。请您填一下这张表好吗？

B: 谢谢。

A: 您想要什么面值的？

B: 我想要 2 张 50 元的纸币。余下的我想要硬币，因为我想乘坐公交车。

A: 好的，没问题。这是 2 张 50 元的纸币。这些是硬币。

181

银行业务

- □ current *adj.* 目前的，当前的
- □ exchange rate 兑换率
- □ maximum *adj.* 最大的
- □ equivalent *n.* 等同物，对应物

- □ currency *n.* 货币
- □ denomination *n.* 面值
- □ coin *n.* 硬币

B: Thank you.

A: So, is there anything else I can do for you?

B: No, that's all. Thank you.

A: OK. Thank you very much. Have a nice day.

B: You too. Bye.

B: 谢谢。

A: 嗯，我还能为您做些什么吗？

B: 没有了，就这些。谢谢你！

A: 好的。非常感谢。祝您过得愉快！

B: 你也是。再见。

Unit 4　Credit Cards 信用卡

Scene 1　办理信用卡

A: Excuse me. What documents do I need to apply for a credit card?

B: You'll need to bring your ID card, proof of income, and address.

A: Do I need to bring anything else?

B: No, that's all. Would you like to apply now?

A: Yes, please.

A: 打扰一下，申请信用卡需要什么文件？

B: 您需要携带身份证、收入证明和地址证明。

A: 我还需要携带别的东西吗？

B: 不需要了，就这些。您想现在申请吗？

A: 是的。

182

Scene 2　信用额度

A: Hi, how much is my credit limit?

B: Your credit limit is $5,000.

A: Can I increase it?

B: Yes, you can request a credit limit increase. We'll review your request and notify you of the result.

A: 嗨，我的信用额度是多少？

B: 您的信用额度是 5000 美元。

A: 我可以增加额度吗？

B: 可以增加，您可以申请提高信用额度。我们将审核您的请求并通知您结果。

重点词汇
及表达

☐ document *n.* 文件

☐ proof of income 收入证明

☐ credit limit 信用额度

☐ request *v.* 申请

☐ review *v.* 审核

☐ notify *v.* 通知

A: OK. I'll do that.

B: Great. Let me know if you need any assistance.

A: Thank you.

B: You're welcome. Have a nice day!

A：好的。我会申请的。

B：好的。如果您需要帮助，请告诉我。

A：谢谢。

B：不客气。祝您过得愉快！

Scene 3 信用卡分期

A: Hi, do you accept credit cards here?

B: Yes, we do. Visa and Mastercard.

A: Can I pay in installments with my credit card?

B: Yes, you can. We have 3- and 6-month installment plans.

A: That sounds great. Thank you!

B: You're welcome. Just let me know when you're ready to pay.

A：嗨，你们接受信用卡吗？

B：接受。我们接受维萨信用卡和万事达卡。

A：我能用信用卡分期付款吗？

B：可以。我们有3个月和6个月的分期付款计划。

A：听起来不错。谢谢你！

B：不客气。您打算付钱的时候告诉我一声。

183

□ Visa 维萨（信用卡品牌）

□ Mastercard 万事达（信用卡品牌）

Part 10　Home Life
居家生活

Unit 1 Watching TV 看电视

Scene 1 　找遥控器

A: Have you seen the remote control?

B: No, I haven't.

A: Mom wants to know where it is.

B: Maybe Dad knows.

A: Dad, do you know where the remote is?

A：你看到遥控器了吗？

B：没有，我没看到。

A：妈妈想知道它在哪儿。

B：也许爸爸知道。

A：爸爸，您知道遥控器在哪儿吗？

Scene 2 　请求看电视

A: Can I watch TV now?

B: Did you finish your homework?

A: Not yet.

B: Then no TV until it's done.

A: Okay, I'll finish it.

A：我现在可以看电视吗？

B：你做完作业了吗？

A：还没有。

B：那在做完作业之前不许看电视。

A：好的，我会做完作业的。

Scene 3 　电视投屏

A: How can I cast my phone screen to the TV?

B: Do you have a smart TV or a casting device?

A: I have a smart TV.

B: You can connect your phone and TV to the same Wi-Fi network and use the screen mirroring function.

A: Thanks. I'll try that.

B: No problem. Let me know if you need help.

A：我怎样才能把手机屏幕投屏到电视上呢？

B：你有智能电视或投屏设备吗？

A：我有一台智能电视。

B：你可以把手机和电视连接到同一个无线网络，然后使用屏幕镜像功能。

A：谢谢，我试试。

B：不客气，如果你需要帮助就告诉我。

重点词汇
及表达

☐ remote control 遥控

☐ done *adj.* 做完的

☐ cast *v.* 投射

☐ casting device 投屏设备

☐ network *n.* 网络

☐ screen mirroring function 屏幕镜像功能

Scene 4　付费节目

A: Can you cancel my paid TV program?

B: Sure, may I know your account number?

A: It's 123456.

B: Alright, which program do you want to cancel?

A: The movie channel, please.

B: Alright, it's canceled.

A：你能取消我的付费电视节目吗？

B：当然可以。请问您的账号是什么？

A：123456。

B：好的，您想取消哪个节目？

A：电影频道。

B：好的，取消了。

 ## Unit 2　Using an Air Conditioner 使用空调

Scene 1　开空调

A: It's getting hot. Can you turn on the air conditioner?

B: Sure. Where's the remote?

A: I think it's on the coffee table.

B: Found it! Click. The air conditioner is on.

A: Great. Thanks! It's much cooler now.

B: You're welcome! Enjoy the cool air.

A：天越来越热了。你能把空调打开吗？

B：当然可以。遥控器在哪儿？

A：我想它在咖啡桌上。

B：找到了！咔哒。空调开了。

A：太好了。谢谢！现在凉爽多了。

B：不客气！享受凉爽的空气吧。

187

Scene 2　调节温度

A: It's getting too cold. Can you turn up the air conditioner?

B: Sure. What temperature would you like?

A: Maybe around 23 degrees Celsius?

B: Got it. Adjusting to 23 degrees now.

A: Thanks. That's perfect! Much better now.

B: You're welcome! Let me know if you need anything else.

A：太冷了。你能把空调温度调高一点吗？

B：当然可以。你想要调到多少度？

A：大约 23 摄氏度？

B：好的。现在就调到 23 摄氏度。

A：谢谢。完美！现在好多了。

B：不客气！如果你有什么别的需求，请告诉我。

□ paid TV program 付费电视节目

□ turn on the air conditioner 打开空调

□ remote *n.* 遥控器

□ turn up 调高（温度）

Scene 3　调换模式

A: It's getting too cold in here. Can you adjust the air conditioner mode?

B: Sure, let me switch to energy-saving mode.

A: That's better. Thanks!

B: No problem. I can also set it to sleep mode.

A: Perfect! Let's keep it on that setting.

B: Agreed. Enjoy the comfortable temperature!

A：这儿越来越冷了。你能调一下空调模式吗？

B：当然可以。我来调到节能模式。

A：好多了。谢谢！

B：不客气。我也可以设置为睡眠模式。

A：完美！我们保持这种设置就可以了。

B：好的。享受舒适的温度吧！

 Unit 3 **Using a Microwave Oven** 使用微波炉

Scene 1　加热与解冻

A: Hey, can you heat up the leftovers in the microwave?

B: Sure. What setting should I use? High?

A: No, use medium to avoid overcooking. Thanks!

B: Got it. And for defrosting frozen meat?

A: Use the defrost mode. It's more efficient.

B: Great, thanks for the tips! Love the energy-saving features.

A: No problem. Happy to help. Enjoy your meal!

A：嘿，你能把剩菜用微波炉热一下吗？

B：好的。我应该怎么设置？高火吗？

A：不是，用中火，以免加热过头。谢谢！

B：明白了。那解冻冻肉呢？

A：使用解冻模式。这样更有效率。

B：好的。谢谢你的建议！我喜欢它的节能性能。

A：不客气。我很乐意帮忙。用餐愉快！

Scene 2　温度与模式

A: What temperature and time should I set for the microwave?

B: For reheating, try 60 seconds on high.

A: And for defrosting?

B: Maybe 5 minutes on low, depending on the size.

A：我应该把微波炉的温度和时间设置成多少？

B：重新加热的话，试试开高火60秒。

A：那解冻呢？

B：大概低火5分钟，要看食物量的大小。

重点词汇
及表达

☐ energy-saving mode 节能模式

☐ sleep mode 睡眠模式

☐ setting *n.* 设置

☐ leftover *n.* 剩菜

☐ microwave *n.* 微波炉

☐ defrost *v.* 解冻

☐ reheat *v.* 重新加热

全场景英语口语

A: Is there an energy-saving mode?

B: Yes, it's called "Eco Mode".

A: Great, I'll try that. Thanks!

B: You're welcome! Enjoy your meal!

A：有节能模式吗?

B：有，它叫"生态模式"。

A：太好了，我试试。谢谢!

B：不客气! 用餐愉快!

Scene 3 安全问题

A: Set microwave to medium-high and 5 minutes for popcorn.

B: No, it's too hot! Set to low and 3 minutes.

A: But it won't pop well. How about 4 minutes?

B: OK. But check for sparks or smoke.

A: Got it! Safety first! 4 minutes on low. Thanks!

B: You're welcome. Enjoy your popcorn!

A：制作爆米花的话，要把微波炉调到中高火，5分钟。

B：不行，温度太高了! 设置为低火，3分钟。

A：但是爆米花会爆不好。4分钟怎么样?

B：可以 。但要注意是否有火花或烟雾。

A：明白了! 安全第一! 低火4分钟。谢谢!

B：不客气。享受你的爆米花吧!

189

Unit 4 Laundry 洗衣服

Scene 1 洗衣粉与洗衣液

A: Do you prefer laundry powder or liquid detergent?

B: I usually use laundry powder for my clothes.

A: I find liquid detergent more convenient and less messy.

B: But I heard laundry powder is more effective in removing stains.

A: Yes, it depends on personal preference and the type of clothes.

B: True. I'll try liquid detergent next time. Thanks!

A：你喜欢用洗衣粉还是洗衣液?

B：我通常用洗衣粉洗衣服。

A：我觉得洗衣液更方便，也不会弄得很凌乱。

B：但我听说洗衣粉去渍更有效。

A：是的，用什么取决于个人喜好和衣服的类型。

B：没错。下次我试试洗衣液。谢谢!

- medium-high *n.* 中高火
- pop *v.* 爆破
- spark *n.* 火花
- laundry powder 洗衣粉
- liquid detergent 洗衣液
- stain *n.* 污渍
- personal preference 个人喜好

Scene 2　消毒剂与柔顺剂

A: Do we have any disinfectant for laundry?

B: Yes, we do. It's in the cupboard.

A: Great! And do we have fabric softener?

B: Yes, it's on the shelf beside the detergent.

A: Perfect! I'll add some to the washing machine.

B: Sounds good! Let's make sure our clothes are clean and soft.

A：我们有衣物消毒液吗?

B：有。在橱柜里。

A：太棒了!我们有织物柔顺剂吗?

B：有,在架子上的洗衣液旁边。

A：完美!我要加一些到洗衣机里。

B：听起来不错!我们要确保我们的衣服干净柔软。

Scene 3　甩干与烘干

A: I love using the dryer for my clothes!

B: Me too! It saves so much time.

A: I usually do a spin dry before using the dryer.

B: That's a good idea! It helps clothes dry faster.

A: Yeah, and then I set it to medium heat.

B: I prefer low heat to be safe.

A: Good point! Safety first!

A：我喜欢用烘干机烘干衣服!

B：我也是!这样能节省很多时间。

A：我通常在使用烘干机之前先甩干衣服。

B：好主意!这样可以让衣服干得更快。

A：是的,然后我把烘干机调到中温。

B：为了安全,我倾向于调到低温。

A：很好!安全第一!

Scene 4　找洗衣店

A: Hey, do you know where the nearest laundry is?

B: Yeah, there's one on Main Street. Just a few blocks away.

A: Is it self-serve, or do they offer drop-off service?

B: It's self-serve, but they do have an attendant on duty during certain hours.

A: OK! Thanks for the info. Do you know if they have a change machine?

B: Yes, they do. You can also use a credit or debit card to pay.

A: Great! Thanks for your help!

A：嘿,你知道最近的洗衣店在哪儿吗?

B：知道,主街上有一家。离这儿就几个街区。

A：那儿提供自助服务还是送洗服务?

B：自助服务,但在特定时段有服务员值班。

A：好的!谢谢你提供的信息。你知道他们是否有找零机吗?

B：有。你也可以用信用卡或借记卡支付。

A：太棒了!谢谢你的帮助!

重点词汇
及表达

☐ disinfectant *n.* 消毒液

☐ cupboard *n.* 橱柜

☐ softener *n.* 柔顺剂

☐ dryer *n.* 烘干机

☐ spin dry 甩干

☐ self-serve *n.* 自助服务

☐ drop-off service 送洗服务

☐ on duty 值班

☐ debit card 借记卡

Scene 5 上门取衣

A: Hi, I was wondering if you offer pick-up and delivery for laundry?

B: Yes, we do offer that service for an additional fee.

A: Great.

B: We wash, dry, and fold the clothes before delivering them.

A: That sounds perfect. Can I schedule a pick-up for tomorrow?

B: Sure. What's your address and preferred time?

A: My address is 123 Main Street. Can we do 11:00 am?

B: Sounds good. We'll see you tomorrow at 11:00 am.

A：嗨，我想知道你们是否提供上门取衣送衣服务？

B：嗯，我们确实提供这项服务，但要额外收费。

A：太好了。

B：我们在送衣服之前会清洗、晾干、叠好。

A：听起来很不错。我能约明天的取衣服务吗？

B：当然可以。您的地址和想约的时间是？

A：我的地址是主街123号。我们可以约在上午11点吗？

B：可以。我们明天上午11点见。

191

Scene 6 干洗衣物

A: Hi, I need to drop off a wool coat for dry cleaning.

B: Sure, we can take care of that. It will be ready in three days.

A: Great! Do I need to fill out any forms?

B: Just a quick form with your name and phone number.

A: OK. Here it is. Is there a deposit required?

B: No, payment is due when you pick up your coat.

A: Perfect! Thank you for your help.

B: You're welcome. Have a great day!

A：你好，我需要送一件羊毛大衣去干洗。

B：没问题，我们会处理好的。三天内就可以洗好。

A：太棒了！我需要填写什么表格吗？

B：只需要快速填写一张包含您的姓名和电话号码的表格就可以了。

A：好的。给你。需要预付费吗？

B：不需要，您取大衣的时候再付款。

A：太棒了！谢谢你的帮助。

B：不客气。祝您过得愉快！

居家生活

□ pick-up and delivery 取件送件

□ additional fee 额外的费用

□ dry cleaning 干洗

□ fill out 填写

□ deposit *n.* 订金

□ due *adj.* 应支付

Scene 7 取衣服

A: I forgot my claim ticket. Can I still pick up my clothes?

B: Sure. What's your name and phone number?

A: My name is Lily, and my number is 5551234.

B: Let me check... Yes, we have your clothes. Here you go.

A: Thank you so much!

B: No problem. Have a nice day!

A：我忘了拿取衣票。我还能取我的衣服吗？

B：当然可以。请问您的姓名和电话号码是什么？

A：我叫莉莉，电话号码是 5551234。

B：我查一下……嗯，我们有您的衣服。给您。

A：太感谢了！

B：不客气。祝您过得愉快！

Unit 5 Cooking 做饭

Scene 1 关燃气灶

A: Is the stove on? I smell gas.

B: Oh no! I forgot to turn it off!

A: Quick! Turn it off and open the windows!

B: Done. Sorry about that.

A: It's OK. Safety first! Double-check next time.

B: Definitely. Thank you for reminding me!

A：燃气灶是开着的吗？我闻到燃气的气味了。

B：哦，天哪！我忘了关了！

A：快！把它关掉，打开窗户！

B：关上了。抱歉。

A：没关系。安全第一！下次检查两次。

B：我一定会的。谢谢你的提醒！

Scene 2 选择温度与时间

A: What temperature should we set for the oven?

B: 350°F for 30 minutes should be good.

A: What about the stovetop?

B: Medium heat for 10 minutes.

A: Should we use high heat for boiling water?

B: Yes, that's usually the best option.

A: Alright, let's get cooking then!

A：烤箱的温度应该设定为多少？

B：350 华氏度烤 30 分钟就可以了。

A：那灶台呢？

B：中火 10 分钟就可以了。

A：烧开水需要调到高火吗？

B：需要，这通常是最好的选择。

A：好的。我们开始做饭吧！

重点词汇
及表达

☐ claim ticket 取衣票

☐ Safety first! 安全第一！

☐ double-check v. 再次检查

☐ oven n. 烤箱

☐ stovetop n. 灶台

Scene 3　洗菜切菜

A: Wash the vegetables thoroughly. Then chop them finely.

B: OK, got it. Should I use cold water?

A: Yes, cold water is fine. Make sure to remove any dirt.

B: Alright. I'll be careful. Should I peel the carrots?

A: No need to peel them. Just wash and chop them.

B: Understood. I'll start right away. Thanks!

A：把蔬菜彻底洗干净，然后把它们切碎。

B：好的，我知道了。我应该用冷水洗吗？

A：是的，冷水就可以了。一定要把所有污垢都洗掉。

B：好的。我会认真洗的。胡萝卜要削皮吗？

A：不用削皮。把它们洗干净切碎就可以了。

B：明白了。我马上就开始。谢谢!

Scene 4　蔬菜去皮

A: Can you help me peel these potatoes?

B: Sure. Should I use a knife or a peeler?

A: Use a peeler for the potatoes and a knife for the carrots.

B: Got it! I'll get to work on peeling them.

A: Great! Thanks for your help!

B: No problem. Happy to help!

A：你能帮我削土豆皮吗？

B：当然可以。我应该用刀还是削皮器？

A：用削皮器削土豆，用刀削胡萝卜。

B：明白了! 我要开始削皮了。

A：太棒了! 谢谢你的帮助!

B：不客气。我很乐意帮忙!

Scene 5　奶酪在哪儿

A: Dad, where's the cheese?

B: Check the top shelf of the fridge.

A: I already checked. It's not there.

B: Did you check the cheese drawer?

A: Oh, I found it! Thanks, Dad.

B: No problem. Enjoy your snack.

A：爸爸，奶酪在哪儿？

B：看看冰箱最上面的架子。

A：我已经看过了。那上面没有。

B：你检查过放奶酪的抽屉了吗？

A：哦，我找到了! 谢谢爸爸。

B：不客气。好好享用你的点心。

Scene 6　做烤鸡

A: How do you make roasted chicken?

B: Well, first, you need to preheat the oven.

A：你是怎么做烤鸡的？

B：嗯，首先，需要预热烤箱。

☐ chop v. 切碎

☐ remove v. 去除

☐ peel v. 去皮

☐ peeler n. 削皮器

☐ fridge n. 冰箱

☐ roasted chicken 烤鸡

☐ preheat v. 预热

A: What temperature should it be?

B: Around 400 degrees Fahrenheit.

A: And how long should it cook for?

B: Usually about an hour and a half.

A: OK. Thanks. I'll give it a try!

A：温度应该设定成多少?

B：大约 400 华氏度。

A：要烤多久?

B：通常是一个半小时左右。

A：好的。谢谢。我要试试!

Scene 7　微波加热

A: Mom's not home tonight. You can microwave leftovers for dinner.

B: OK. Do we have anything to eat?

A: Yeah. There's some leftover pizza in the fridge.

B: Great! I'll heat that up then.

A: Just be careful not to overheat it.

B: I know. Thanks for letting me know.

A：妈妈今晚不在家。晚饭你可以用微波炉加热剩饭剩菜。

B：好的。我们有什么可吃的吗?

A：有。冰箱里还有一些吃剩的比萨饼。

B：太好了!我到时候把它加热一下。

A：只是要小心,不要加热过头了。

B：我知道的。谢谢你提醒我。

Scene 8　年夜饭

A: What dishes should we prepare for the Chinese New Year's Eve dinner?

B: How about dumplings, fish, and hotpot?

A: I think we should also make some vegetable dishes.

B: Agreed. What about stir-fried broccoli and eggplant with garlic?

A: Sounds good. Let's add those to the menu.

B: Great！We'll have a delicious feast!

A：年夜饭应该准备什么菜呢?

B：饺子、鱼和火锅怎么样?

A：我想我们还应该做些蔬菜。

B：好的。炒西兰花和蒜蓉茄子怎么样?

A：听起来不错。我们把这些加到菜单上吧。

B：太好了,我们将会有一顿美味的大餐!

重点词汇
及表达

□ give it a try 尝试

□ microwave v. 微波加热

□ overheat v. 加热过头

□ dumpling n. 饺子

□ hotpot n. 火锅

□ stir-fried broccoli 炒西蓝花

□ eggplant with garlic 蒜蓉茄子

烹饪用具

- knives *n.* 刀具
- cookware *n.* 炊具
- spoons *n.* 勺子
- mixer *n.* 搅拌器
- pastry tools 糕点工具
- can opener 开罐器
- peeler *n.* 削皮器
- bowl *n.* 碗
- kettle *n.* 水壶
- pot *n.* 锅
- microwave stove 微波炉

- cutting board 切菜板
- oven *n.* 烤箱
- utensils *n.* 餐具
- blender *n.* 搅拌机
- grinder *n.* 研磨器
- bottle opener 开瓶器
- chopsticks *n.* 筷子
- plate *n.* 碟子
- coffee machine 咖啡机
- frying pan 煎锅
- fork *n.* 叉子

烹饪动词

- chop *v.* 切碎
- slice *v.* 切片
- sauté *v.* 煸炒
- grill *v.* 烤
- bake *v.* 烘烤
- boil *v.* 煮沸
- stir-fry *v.* 炒

- dice *v.* 切丁
- mince *v.* 切细
- fry *v.* 煎
- roast *v.* 烤炙
- simmer *v.* 炖
- steam *v.* 蒸
- blend *v.* 搅拌

195

居家生活

Unit 6 Using a Fridge 使用冰箱

Scene 1　保鲜与冷冻

A: Where should I put the milk?

B: In the fridge, on the middle shelf.

A: What about the chicken in the freezer?

B: Bottom drawer. Label it with today's date.

A: And the veggies?

B: In the crisper. Keep them in the bag.

A: Got it!

A：我应该把牛奶放在哪儿?

B：放进冰箱里，放在中间的架子上。

A：冷冻柜里的鸡肉怎么办?

B：放进最下面的抽屉里。标上今天的日期。

A：蔬菜呢?

B：放进保鲜盒里。把它们装在袋子里。

A：明白了!

Scene 2　冻品解冻

A: What's for dinner tomorrow?

B: I'm thinking about making some frozen fish.

A: OK. How do we thaw it?

B: Just leave it in the fridge overnight.

A: Got it. Should we cover it?

B: Yes, with plastic wrap.

A: Sounds good. Thanks!

A：明天吃什么?

B：我想做一些冻鱼。

A：好的。我们怎么解冻它?

B：在冰箱里放一个晚上就可以了。

A：明白了。要把鱼包起来吗?

B：是的，用保鲜膜包起来。

A：听起来不错。谢谢!

Scene 3　翻找冰箱

A: Can you grab the milk from the fridge?

B: Sure. Let me open it.

A: While you're there, can you find the butter?

B: Got it! It was in the back.

A: Thanks! Could you also close the door?

B: No problem! All done.

A：你能从冰箱里拿点牛奶吗?

B：当然可以。我来打开冰箱。

A：你打开冰箱时能找找黄油吗?

B：找到了。它在靠里的地方。

A：谢谢! 你能把冰箱门关上吗?

B：没问题! 关好了。

重点词汇
及表达

□ freezer *n.* 冷冻柜

□ thaw *v.* 解冻

Unit 7 Doing Housework 做家务

Scene 1   铺床

A: Mom, can you teach me how to make the bed?

B: Sure! First, we need to straighten the sheets.

A: OK. I got it. What's next?

B: Next, we tuck in the sides and foot of the bed.

A: Oh, I see. Then we fold the top sheet and comforter.

B: Yes, and finally, we place the pillows at the head of the bed.

A: Thanks, Mom. That was easy!

A：妈妈，您能教我怎么铺床吗？

B：当然！首先，我们需要把床单拉直。

A：好的。我明白了。接下来呢？

B：接下来，我们把侧边和床脚掖起来。

A：哦，我明白了。然后我们叠好上面的床单和被子。

B：没错，最后，我们把枕头放在床头。

A：谢谢妈妈。这很简单！

Scene 2   收拾桌子

A: Your desk is very messy. Please clean it up.

B: OK. I'll clean it now.

A: Make sure you put everything in its proper place.

B: I will, Dad. Sorry for the mess.

A: It's OK. Just try to keep it organized in the future.

B: I will. Thanks for reminding me.

A：你的桌子太乱了。请把它清理干净。

B：好的。我现在就清理。

A：一定要把物品摆放在合适的位置。

B：我会的，爸爸。很抱歉弄得这么乱。

A：没关系。以后尽量保持井然有序。

B：我会的。谢谢您提醒我。

Scene 3   擦玻璃

A: Windows need cleaning. Pass me the cloth.

B: Sure. Here you go. Be careful!

A: Thanks. I'll open the window for better reach.

B: Great, I'll close it when you're done.

A：窗户需要擦一擦。把抹布递给我。

B：好的，给你。小心！

A：谢谢。为了够得着，我得把窗户打开。

B：好的，你擦完窗户我就关上。

居家生活

197

□ make the bed 铺床

□ fold *v.* 折叠

□ sheet *n.* 床单

□ comforter *n.* 被子

□ messy *adj.* 凌乱的

□ organized *adj.* 有条理的

A: All done. You can close it now. Thanks!

B: You're welcome. Windows look sparkling now!

A：都擦完了。你现在可以关上了。谢谢!

B：不客气。窗户现在看起来闪闪发光!

Scene 4 扫地拖地

A: Can you sweep the floor? It's messy.

B: Sure, I'll sweep and mop the floor.

A: Thanks! Don't forget the corners and under the sofa.

B: Got it! I'll make sure it's clean and tidy.

A: Great! Let me know if you need any help.

B: Will do! Thanks for the offer. I got this.

A：你能扫一下地吗? 地上脏兮兮的。

B：当然可以,我会扫地拖地的。

A：谢谢! 别忘了角落和沙发下面。

B：知道了! 我会确保地面干净整洁。

A：太棒了! 如果需要帮助,请告诉我。

B：好的。谢谢你的好意。我能搞定。

Scene 5 垃圾分类

A: Time to take out the trash!

B: Sure thing! Let's sort this garbage out.

A: Recyclables go in the blue bin, and food waste goes in the green bin.

B: Got it! I'll take care of it.

A: Awesome job! Let's do our part to keep the environment clean and green.

B: You got it, sweetie! We gotta take care of our planet.

A：该扔垃圾了!

B：没问题! 我们把这些垃圾分类吧。

A：可回收垃圾放进蓝色垃圾箱里,食物残渣放进绿色垃圾箱里。

B：明白了! 我会处理的。

A：干得好! 让我们尽自己的一份力量来保持环境整洁和绿色。

B：没错,亲爱的! 我们要保护好我们的地球。

Scene 6 除尘

A: The house is so dusty. We need to clean it.

B: Yeah, it's been a while. Let's start dusting.

A: I'll get the duster and sweep the floors.

B: I'll use the vacuum cleaner to clean the carpets.

A: Great. Let's make our home dust-free again!

A：房子里满是灰尘。我们需要清扫干净。

B：是啊,有段时间没打扫了。我们开始擦灰尘吧。

A：我去拿抹布,然后扫地。

B：我要用吸尘器清洁地毯。

A：好的。我们把家里打扫得一尘不染吧!

□ sparkling *adj.* 闪亮的

□ sweep the floor 扫地

□ mop the floor 拖地

□ tidy *adj.* 整洁的

□ sort *v.* 分类

□ recyclable *n.* 可回收物

□ do one's part 尽力

□ dusty *adj.* 布满灰尘的

□ dust *v.* 擦去灰尘

□ vacuum cleaner 吸尘器

Unit 8　At the Bathroom 在浴室

Scene 1　递送物品

A: Could you pass me a towel?

B: Sure, here you go.

A: Thanks. Do you mind if I take a shower now?

B: Not at all. Go ahead.

A: Can you hand me my clothes after I'm done?

B: Of course. No problem.

A：你能递给我一条毛巾吗?

B：当然可以，给你。

A：谢谢。你介意我现在洗澡吗?

B：不介意。去吧。

A：我洗好后你能把衣服递给我吗?

B：当然可以。没问题。

Scene 2　调节水温

A: Is the water too hot?

B: No, it's too cold, actually.

A: Turn the knob to the left.

B: OK, now it's perfect. Thanks!

A: Glad to help. Enjoy your shower!

B: Will do. Thanks again!

A：水是不是太热了?

B：不，事实上是太凉了。

A：把旋钮转到左边。

B：好的，现在完美了。谢谢!

A：很高兴能帮上忙。好好享受你的淋浴吧!

B：好的。再次感谢!

Scene 3　浴室暖气

A: Can you turn on the bathroom heater?

B: Sure, where's the switch?

A: It's on the wall near the door.

B: Got it. How long should I keep it on?

A: Just until the mirror defogs, about 5 minutes.

B: OK. I'll turn it off when it's done.

A：你能把浴室里的浴霸打开吗?

B：当然可以。开关在哪儿?

A：在门附近的墙上。

B：看到了。应该开多久?

A：直到镜子上的雾气消散，大约5分钟。

B：好的。雾气消散后我会关掉浴霸。

Scene 4　在洗手间

A: Where's the toilet paper?

A：卫生纸在哪儿?

居家生活

199

☐ take a shower 洗澡，淋浴

☐ knob *n.* 旋钮

☐ heater *n.* 取暖器

☐ defog *v.* 除雾

B: On the shelf next to you.

A: Do you have any air fresheners?

B: Yeah, they're in the cabinet under the sink.

A: I'm done. Can you bring me a towel?

B: Sure, I'll grab one for you.

B：在你旁边的架子上。

A：有空气清新剂吗？

B：有，在水槽下面的柜子里。

A：我上完了。你能给我拿条毛巾吗？

B：当然可以，我给你拿一条。

Scene 5　冲马桶

A: The toilet won't flush again.

B: Did you try plunging it?

A: Yes, but it's still not working.

B: I'll get the plunger and try again.

(After a few minutes of plunging)

B: It's working now.

A: Thank you so much!

A：马桶又不能冲水了。

B：你试过疏通吗？

A：试过，但还是不能冲水。

B：我去拿马桶疏通器，然后再试一次。

（疏通几分钟后）

B：现在能冲水了。

A：太谢谢你了！

Scene 6　等待使用洗手间

A: Hey, are you almost done in there?

B: Just a minute. I'm almost finished.

A: I really need to go. Can you hurry up?

B: Sorry, I'm almost done. Just give me a second.

A: Come on. I can't hold it much longer!

B: OK, OK. I'm coming out now!

A：嘿，你快结束了吗？

B：请稍等。我马上就好了。

A：我真的憋不住了。你能快点吗？

B：抱歉，我马上就好了。稍等一会儿。

A：拜托。我真的憋不住了！

B：好的，好的。我现在就出来！

Scene 7　占用洗手间

A: Is the bathroom still occupied?

B: I'm not sure. Let me check.

(After a moment)

B: Yes, someone's in there.

A: OK. Thanks for checking.

B: No problem.

A：洗手间里还有人吗？

B：我不确定。我看看。

（过了一会儿）

B：是的，有人在里面。

A：好的。谢谢你去查看。

B：不客气。

重点词汇
及表达

☐ air freshener 空气清新剂

☐ sink n. 水槽

☐ flush v. 冲洗

☐ plunger n. 马桶疏通器

☐ hurry up 赶快

☐ occupied adj. 占用的

Unit 9 Making a Move 搬家

Scene 1   搬家需求

A: Hi, I need to move to a new apartment soon. Can you help me?

A：嗨，我很快就要搬去新公寓了。你们能提供帮助吗？

B: Sure. When do you need to move?

B：当然可以。您什么时候需要搬家？

A: Next month. I have a lot of stuff. Can you provide boxes?

A：下个月。我有很多东西。你们能提供一些箱子吗？

B: Yes, we can provide boxes and help you pack. Do you have any fragile items?

B：可以，我们可以提供箱子，帮您打包。请问您有易碎物品吗？

A: Yes, a few. And I need help with disassembling furniture.

A：有一些。我需要你们帮我拆卸家具。

B: Not a problem. We can provide disassembly and assembly services. Anything else I should know?

B：没问题。我们可以提供拆卸与组装服务。还有什么我需要了解的吗？

Scene 2   乔迁派对

A: Hey! I want to invite you to my housewarming party!

A：嘿! 我想邀请你参加我的乔迁派对!

B: Wow, that's exciting! When's the big day?

B：哇，太令人兴奋了! 搬家的好日子是哪天？

A: Next Saturday, starting at 6:00 pm. Are you free to swing by?

A：下周六，下午6点开始。你有空过来吗？

B: Absolutely! I'd love to come. Should I bring anything?

B：当然! 我很乐意来。我要带什么东西吗？

A: Just yourself! I'll have all the food and drinks taken care of.

A：什么都不用带! 我会准备好所有的食物和饮料。

B: Sounds like a plan. Looking forward to checking out your new digs!

B：听起来不错。期待参观你的新居!

A: Thanks, me too! Appreciate you coming out.

A：谢谢，我也很期待! 谢谢你能过来。

□ apartment *n.* 公寓

□ fragile item 易碎物品

□ disassemble furniture 拆卸家具

□ housewarming party 乔迁派对

□ swing by 经过，绕过去

居家生活

Unit 10　Using the Elevator 使用电梯

Scene 1　帮按电梯

A: Excuse me. Could you please help me press the elevator button?

B: Sure. Which floor do you need to go to?

A: I'm going to the 6th floor. Thank you!

B: No problem. Happy to help.

A: Sorry, I have a lot of things in my hands.

B: Don't worry about it. Let me know if you need any more help.

A: Thanks. You're very kind.

A: 打扰一下，你能帮我按一下电梯按钮吗？

B: 当然可以。你要去几楼？

A: 我要去6楼。谢谢!

B: 不客气。我很乐意帮忙。

A: 抱歉，我手上的东西太多了。

B: 别担心。如果你还需要什么帮助，请告诉我。

A: 谢谢。你真好。

Scene 2　电梯暂停

A: Hold the elevator, please!

B: Sure. Come on in.

A: Thanks. What floor are you going to?

B: 10th floor. How about you?

A: 14th floor. Thanks.

B: Here we are, the 10th floor. Have a good day!

A: You too, bye!

A: 请让电梯停一下!

B: 好的。进来吧。

A: 谢谢。你要去几楼？

B: 10楼，你呢？

A: 14楼，谢谢。

B: 到了，10楼。祝你过得愉快!

A: 你也是，再见!

Scene 3　如何乘坐电梯

A: Press the button to call the elevator.

B: Now, we wait for it to arrive?

A: Yes! Once it's here, we step inside.

B: Now, I should press the button for the floor we need, right?

A: Yes, here we are! See, it's easy.

B: Wow, we made it! Can I press the button next time?

A: 按这个按钮呼叫电梯。

B: 现在我们就等它来吗？

A: 是的! 电梯一到，我们就进去。

B: 现在我应该按下我们要去的楼层按钮，对吗？

A: 是的，我们到了! 你看，很简单。

B: 哇，我们成功了! 下次还可以让我按按钮吗？

□ press the button 按下按钮

□ hold v. 使保持（在某位置）

□ call the elevator 呼叫电梯

202

Scene 4　乘坐电梯（1）

A: Let's get on the elevator.

B: I'm scared. Can you hold my hand?

A: Sure, I'll be right here with you the whole time.

B: How do I press the button for our floor?

A: Just reach up and push the number 5.

B: Is it going to move now?

A: Yes, we're going up! Look at the numbers changing.

B: Wow, this is fun!

A: See, there's nothing to be afraid of. Now we're here!

A：我们乘坐电梯吧。

B：我很害怕。你能握住我的手吗?

A：当然可以，我会一直陪在你身边。

B：我们楼层的按钮怎么按?

A：把手伸上去，按下 5 号键。

B：电梯要移动了吗?

A：是的，我们正在往上升! 看看数字的变化。

B：哇，真有趣!

A：瞧，没什么可怕的。现在我们到了!

Scene 5　乘坐电梯（2）

A: Let's take the elevator. Press the "up" button.

B: The elevator is here.

A: The door is open. Let's get on the elevator, then.

A: Can you hit "25" for me?

B: Sure, Mom.

A: The elevator is going up. Don't jump in the elevator, baby. It's not safe.

B: Here we are.

A: Let's get off.

A：我们乘坐电梯吧。按向上键。

B：电梯到了。

A：门开了。那我们上电梯吧。

A：你能帮我按一下 25 吗?

B：当然可以，妈妈。

A：电梯正在上升。别在电梯里跳，宝贝。不安全。

B：我们到了。

A：我们出电梯吧。

203

居家生活

Unit 11　**Express Delivery** 快递

Scene 1　国际包裹

A: Hello, can you help me? I have a package to send internationally.

A：你好，你能帮帮我吗? 我有一个国际包裹要寄。

☐ scared *adj.* 恐惧的

☐ reach up 向上伸手

☐ take the elevator 乘坐电梯

☐ safe *adj.* 安全的

☐ package *n.* 包裹

B: Of course, we offer international shipping. What's the destination country?

A: It's going to Japan. Can you tell me the shipping cost?

B: Yes, we can calculate that for you. Can I have the weight and dimensions of the package, please?

A: Sure, it's 2 kilograms and 30cm x 20cm x 15cm.

B: Alright, based on that, the shipping cost is $50. Is that OK?

A: Yes, that sounds good. Can you tell me how long it'll take to arrive?

B: It should take around 7–14 business days for delivery.

B：当然可以，我们提供国际运输。请问目的地是哪个国家？

A：是去日本的。你能告诉我运费吗？

B：可以，我们可以为您计算一下。请问能告诉我包裹的重量和尺寸吗？

A：当然可以，重 2 千克，长宽高分别是 30 厘米、20 厘米、15 厘米。

B：好的，这样算下来，运费是 50 美元。这个价格能接受吗？

A：能接受，听起来不错。你能告诉我多久才能到吗？

B：寄送大约需要 7~14 个工作日。

Scene 2 物流信息

A: How can I receive updates on my package after it's been shipped?

B: We'll send you a tracking number via email.

A: How long will it take to receive the email?

B: It should be sent within 24 hours of shipment.

A: Can I also receive updates via text message?

B: Yes, just provide us with your mobile number.

A: Thank you. That's all I need to know.

B: You're welcome. Have a great day!

A：在我的包裹发货后，我怎样才能收到物流更新信息？

B：我们会通过电子邮件给您发一个运单号。

A：我多长时间能收到邮件？

B：应该是在包裹装运后 24 小时内发出。

A：我也可以通过短信收到最新消息吗？

B：可以，只需要提供您的手机号码就行了。

A：谢谢。我了解这些就够了。

B：不客气。祝您过得愉快！

Scene 3 包裹信息

A: Hi, I need to send this package to Thailand.

B: Sure. What's in the package?

A：你好，我要把这个包裹寄到泰国。

B：好的，包裹里有什么？

□ shipping cost 运费

□ update *n.* 最新信息

□ track *v.* 追踪

□ via *prep.* 通过

A: It's some souvenirs and snacks.

B: Alright, we'll need the weight and dimensions.

A: Let me check. It's 2 kg and 30 x 25 x 20 cm.

A：是一些纪念品和小吃。

B：好的，我们需要知道重量和尺寸。

A：我查一下。重 2 千克，长宽高分别是 30 厘米、25 厘米、20 厘米。

Scene 4　投递方式

A: Do you want it shipped express or regular?

B: Express, please.

A: OK, any fragile items inside?

B: Yes, a vase. Can you pack it securely?

A: Sure thing! We'll take good care of it.

A：您要速运还是普通快递？

B：速运。

A：好的。里面有易碎物品吗？

B：有一个花瓶。你能把它包好吗？

A：当然可以! 我们会包好的。

Unit 12　Keeping Early Hours 早睡早起

Scene 1　早点休息

205

A: I have something to do tomorrow morning. I need to rest early tonight.

B: OK. What time do you want to sleep?

A: Can we finish everything by 9:00 pm?

B: Sure, no problem. We'll wrap things up early.

A: Thanks! I appreciate it. I really need a good night's sleep.

A：明天上午我有事要做。今晚我需要早点休息。

B：好的。你想什么时候睡觉？

A：我们能在晚上 9 点前完成所有事情吗？

B：当然可以，没问题。我们会早点做完的。

A：谢谢! 我很感激。我真的需要好好睡一觉。

Scene 2　催促睡觉

A: It's getting late. You should go to bed soon.

B: I want to stay up a little longer.

A: You need to get enough rest for school tomorrow.

B: But I'm not sleepy.

A: Come on. Let's get ready for bed now.

A：时间不早了。你应该尽快上床睡觉。

B：我想晚点儿睡。

A：明天上学，你需要好好休息。

B：但我一点也不困。

A：来吧。现在准备去睡觉吧。

☐ souvenir *n.* 纪念品

☐ dimension *n.* 尺寸

☐ express *adj.* 特快的，快速的

☐ regular *adj.* 普通的

☐ securely *adv.* 安全地

☐ wrap things up 把事情整理一番

☐ stay up 熬夜，深夜不睡

☐ sleepy *adj.* 困倦的

Scene 3　作息时间

A: What time do you usually go to bed?

B: Around midnight. How about you?

A: I usually go to bed around 11:00 pm.

B: How many hours of sleep do you get?

A: I try to get at least 7 hours.

B: Yeah. I need to work on getting more sleep.

A：你通常几点睡觉?

B：差不多午夜。你呢?

A：我通常晚上 11 点左右上床睡觉。

B：你每天睡几个小时?

A：我尽量至少睡 7 个小时。

B：哦。我得尽力多睡一会儿了。

Scene 4　睡前习惯

A: Do you prefer reading or having a nightcap before bed?

B: I usually read. What about you?

A: I like to unwind with a drink sometimes.

B: That can be relaxing, but I try to avoid it.

A: Yeah. I understand. Reading is a good way to wind down too.

A：你就喜欢睡前阅读还是小酌一杯呢?

B：我通常会阅读。你呢?

A：我有时喜欢喝一杯放松一下。

B：那确实可以放松，但我尽量避免喝酒。

A：嗯。我理解。阅读也是一种很好的放松方式。

Scene 5　睡眠问题

A: I'm having trouble falling asleep lately.

B: What's been keeping you up?

A: I think it's stress from work.

B: Have you tried meditating or reading before bed?

A: I haven't, but that sounds like a good idea.

B: You should also turn off your phone earlier.

A：我最近很难入睡。

B：什么事让你睡不着?

A：我想是工作压力。

B：你试过睡前冥想或阅读吗?

A：没试过，不过听起来是个好主意。

B：你也应该早点关掉手机。

Scene 6　叫人起床

A: Hey, it's getting late. You should wake up.

B: Just a few more minutes, please?

A: No, you need to start your day.

B: Alright. I'm getting up.

A: Good! I'll make breakfast for you.

A：嘿，时间不早了。你该醒醒了。

B：让我再睡几分钟好吗?

A：不行，你需要开始新的一天。

B：好吧。我这就起床。

A：很好。我给你做早餐。

重点词汇
及表达

☐ work on 努力

☐ have a nightcap 喝点睡前酒

☐ wind down 放松

☐ have trouble (doing sth)（做某事）有困难

☐ meditate v. 冥想

☐ make breakfast 做早餐

Scene 7 叫孩子起床

A: Wakey, wakey. Rise and shine.

B: (Sleepily) Five more minutes, Mommy, please?

A: You know, we have a lot to do today, and we can't be late for school. It's important to start the day on time.

B: (Yawns) OK, Mommy. I'll get up now.

A: Great! I'll help you get ready for the day.

A：醒醒，醒醒。起床了。

B：（困倦地）妈妈，我再睡五分钟，好吗？

A：你知道的，我们今天有很多事要做，上学不能迟到。准时开始新的一天是很重要的。

B：（打呵欠）好的，妈妈。我现在起床。

A：太棒了! 我来帮你准备好迎接新的一天。

Scene 8 叫妻子起床

A: Good morning, honey. Are you awake? It's time to get up.

B: (Mumbling) Not really. Why?

A: Honey, it's already 8:00 o'clock, and we need to leave in an hour. Would you mind waking up?

B: (Groans) OK, give me a few more minutes.

A: I'm sorry to rush you, but we have a lot to do today. Can you please try to get up now?

B: (Sighs) Alright, I'll get up.

A: Thank you, love. I'll make some coffee for you.

B: (Smiling) That sounds good.

A：早上好，亲爱的。你醒了吗? 该起床了。

B：（喃喃自语）没完全醒。为什么现在就要起床？

A：亲爱的，已经8点了，我们需要在一个小时内出发。你介意现在就起床吗？

B：（呻吟）好吧，我再睡几分钟。

A：很抱歉催你起床，但我们今天有很多事情要做。你能尽力起床吗？

B：（叹气）好吧，我起床。

A：谢谢你，亲爱的。我给你煮点咖啡。

B：（微笑）听起来不错。

Scene 9 叫孩子吃早餐

A: Hey, sweetie, breakfast is all set.

B: Awesome, thanks, Mom! Pancakes, you know me too well.

A：嘿，亲爱的，早餐准备好了。

B：太棒了，谢谢妈妈! 是煎饼啊，你太了解我了。

207

居家生活

☐ yawn *v.* 打呵欠

☐ get ready for 为……做准备

☐ awake *adj.* 醒着的

☐ rush *v.* 催促

☐ pancake *n.* 煎饼

A: Hold on. Did you remember to wash your hands?

B: Yes, Mom. Of course.

A: And brush your teeth?

B: Yup, already done.

A: Great. Dig in and enjoy your meal!

A：等等，你记得去洗手了吗？

B：洗了，妈妈。当然记得。

A：你刷牙了吗？

B：哦，已经刷过了。

A：很好。尽情享用吧。

Unit 13 Property Management 物业管理

Scene 1 维修水电

A: Hi, do you know how to contact the property maintenance?

B: Yes, what's the problem?

A: I need some help with the water and electricity.

B: I can give you the number. Do you have a pen?

A: Yes, I'm ready.

B: It's 1234567890. Good luck!

A: Thanks a lot!

A：你好，你知道怎样联系物业维修吗？

B：知道。怎么了？

A：我需要有人帮我维修水电。

B：我可以给您电话号码。您有笔吗？

A：有，我准备好了。

B：1234567890。祝您好运！

A：非常感谢！

Scene 2 噪声投诉

A: Hi, I want to file a noise complaint about my neighbor.

B: OK! What seems to be the issue?

A: They play loud music late at night, and it's affecting my sleep.

B: I see. We will notify them about the complaint.

A: Thank you. I appreciate it.

B: No problem. Have a good day.

A：你好，我想投诉我邻居家的噪声问题。

B：好的。怎么回事？

A：他们在深夜播放很大声的音乐，影响了我的睡眠。

A：知道了。您的投诉我们会告知他们。

A：谢谢。我很感激。

B：不客气。祝您过得愉快。

重点词汇
及表达

□ hold on 等一下

□ property maintenance 物业维修

□ electricity n. 电

□ file a complaint 投诉

□ affect v. 影响

Scene 3　缴纳物业费

A: How do I pay my property fee?

B: You can pay online or at the property management office.

A: Can I get a receipt or invoice?

B: Yes, you can ask for it at the office.

A: When is the deadline?

B: The deadline is the 10th of each month.

A: Thank you for your help.

B: You're welcome.

A：我要怎样缴交物业费？

B：您可以在网上或者去物业管理处缴费。

A：我可以索要收据或发票吗？

B：可以，您可以去物业管理处取发票。

A：缴费截止日期是什么时候？

B：截止日期是每月 10 日。

A：谢谢你的帮助。

B：不客气。

Scene 4　垃圾点

A: Hey, can you tell me where the trash goes in our neighborhood?

B: Yeah. There's a bin around the corner.

A: Oh, I see it now. Thanks!

B: No problem. Just make sure to separate the recycling.

A: Got it. Will do. Ugh, the bin smells terrible.

B: Yeah. It's due for a cleaning.

A：嘿，你能告诉我我们小区的垃圾倒在哪儿吗？

B：可以。拐角处有个垃圾桶。

A：哦，我这会看到了。谢谢！

B：不客气。只用确保将可回收物分开就行了。

A：明白。我会这么做的。啊，垃圾桶的气味很难闻。

B：是的。该清理一下了。

Scene 5　小区停车

A: Excuse me. Where can I park in the community?

B: You can park in the underground garage or roadside parking.

A: Is there any extra cost?

B: Yes, you need to pay for the parking space.

A: Can I buy a monthly parking card?

A：打扰一下，请问小区里哪儿可以停车？

B：您可以把车停在地下车库或路边停车场。

A：要额外收费吗？

B：是的，您需要支付使用停车场的费用。

A：我可以购买一张停车月卡吗？

209

居家生活

- ☐ property fee 物业费
- ☐ invoice *n.* 发票
- ☐ separate *v.* 分开
- ☐ the recycling 可回收物
- ☐ park *v.* 停车
- ☐ community *n.* 小区
- ☐ parking space 停车场

B: Yes, you can get a membership card at the property office.

A: OK. Thank you for your help.

B: You're welcome.

B：可以，您可以在物业管理处办一张会员卡。

A：好的。谢谢你的帮助。

B：不客气。

Scene 6 小区门禁卡

A: How can I apply for a community access card?

B: Please fill out this form and provide your ID card.

A: Can I get it today?

B: Sorry, it takes 2–3 business days.

A: OK. Thanks.

B: You're welcome.

A：我该怎样申请小区门禁卡？

B：请填写这张表，并提供您的身份证。

A：我今天能拿到吗？

B：抱歉，需要2~3个工作日。

A：好的。谢谢。

B：不客气。

Unit 14 House Decoration 房屋装修

210

Scene 1 选购物品

A: Let's buy a new sofa for the living room.

B: Sounds good. What style do you prefer?

A: How about a modern one? And we also need new curtains.

B: I agree. What color and material do you suggest?

A: How about a light gray sofa and linen curtains?

B: Perfect. Let's go shopping for them this weekend.

A：我们买一张新沙发放在客厅里吧。

B：听起来不错。你喜欢什么风格的？

A：现代风格的怎么样？我们还需要购买新窗帘。

B：我同意。你建议选择什么颜色和布料的？

A：浅灰色的沙发和亚麻窗帘怎么样？

B：棒极了！我们这周末去买吧。

Scene 2 购买电器

A: What size fridge do we need?

B: I think a medium one would be fine.

A: And what about the air conditioner?

A：我们需要多大的冰箱？

B：我想中等大小的就可以了。

A：那空调呢？

□ access card 门禁卡

□ business day 工作日

□ linen curtain 亚麻窗帘

□ medium *adj.* 中等的

B: We should get one for the bedroom too.

A: Should we look for sales?

B: Yes, let's compare prices online.

B：我们应该也买一个放在卧室里。

A：我们要看看特价活动吗？

B：要，我们在网上比较一下价格吧。

Scene 3 买床及床上用品

A: Let's buy a new bed for the bedroom.

B: What kind of bed do you want?

A: Something comfortable and not too expensive.

B: How about this one? It comes with a mattress.

A: Looks good. Let's also get new sheets and pillows.

B: Sure, and we need a new comforter too.

A：我们买一张新床放在卧室里吧。

B：你想要什么样的床？

A：舒服又不太贵的。

B：这张床怎么样？它带有一个床垫。

A：看起来不错。床单和枕头也买新的吧。

B：好的，我们还需要一条新被子。

Scene 4 买桌椅

A: How about this wooden desk?

B: Looks nice, but maybe too big.

A: What about this glass one?

B: Too modern for my taste.

A: OK, let's move on to chairs.

B: I like this armchair. It's comfortable.

A: How about a matching desk for the armchair?

B: Good idea. Let's go for it.

A：这张木桌怎么样？

B：看起来不错，但是可能太大了。

A：这张玻璃的呢？

B：对我的口味来说太现代了。

A：好的，我们继续看看椅子。

B：我喜欢这把扶手椅。很舒适。

A：为这把椅子选择一张相配的书桌怎么样？

B：好主意，就这么办。

Scene 5 买厨房用具

A: Let's look at some kitchenware.

B: How about this set of pots and pans?

A: Looks good. And we need a rice cooker.

B: What about a dishwasher?

A: Good idea. Do you prefer a built-in or portable one?

A：我们来看看厨房用具吧。

B：这套锅碗瓢盆怎么样？

A：看起来不错。我们还需要一个电饭煲。

B：洗碗机怎么样？

A：好主意。你喜欢内嵌的还是可移动的？

居家生活

211

□ compare prices 比较价格

□ mattress *n.* 床垫

□ pillow *n.* 枕头

□ wooden *adj.* 木制的

□ armchair *n.* 扶手椅

□ kitchenware *n.* 厨房用具

□ pots and pans 锅碗瓢盆

□ rice cooker 电饭煲

□ dishwasher *n.* 洗碗机

B: A built-in one. Let's take this one.

A: Sure, let's check out now.

B：内嵌的。就买这个吧。

A：好的。我们现在结账吧。

Scene 6 买柜子

A: What style of wardrobe do you like?

B: I prefer a modern style with sliding doors.

A: Good choice. How about a bedside table?

B: I want something functional with drawers.

A: What about this one? It matches the wardrobe.

B: Yes, that's perfect. Let's take them.

A：你喜欢什么风格的衣柜?

B：我更喜欢带滑动门的现代风格。

A：不错的选择。这个床头柜怎么样?

B：我想要带抽屉的实用款。

A：这个怎么样? 它和衣柜很相配。

B：是的，太好了。我们买下这些吧。

Scene 7 装修需求

A: What do you want to do with this space?

B: I want to make it a cozy area for reading.

A: Do you have a color scheme in mind?

B: Yes, warm earthy tones would be nice.

A: What about lighting?

B: I'd like a lamp and maybe some fairy lights.

A: Sounds lovely. Let's make it happen!

A：你想利用这个空间做什么?

B：我想把它改造成一个舒适的读书角。

A：你想好配色方案了吗?

B：想好了，温暖的大地色系会很好。

A：那照明呢?

B：我想要一盏灯，也许还要装一些彩色小灯。

A：听起来不错。我们来动手实现这些吧!

Scene 8 装修风格

A: What kind of decoration style do you like?

B: I prefer a modern and minimalist style.

A: Any specific colors or materials you want to use?

B: I like light colors and natural materials like wood and stone.

A: How about the furniture and lighting?

A：你喜欢什么样的装修风格?

B：我更喜欢现代、简约的风格。

A：你想用什么特别的颜色或材料吗?

B：我喜欢浅色，喜欢天然材料，比如木材和石头。

A：家具和照明要选什么样的呢?

重点词汇
及表达

□ wardrobe *n.* 衣柜

□ bedside table 床头柜

□ color scheme 配色方案

□ earthy tone 大地色系

□ decoration style 装修风格

□ minimalist *adj.* 简约的

□ lighting *n.* 照明

B: I want something simple and functional, with good lighting.

B：我想要简单实用、照明效果好的。

A: Great. We can work on a detailed plan together.

A：好的。我们一起制订详细的计划吧。

Scene 9 安装家电

A: How's the installation going?

A：安装得怎么样了？

B: Still working on the TV. What's next?

B：还在安装电视。接下来要安装什么？

A: The fridge and oven are being delivered tomorrow.

A：冰箱和烤箱明天会送到。

B: OK, I'll be here. Anything else?

B：好的，我会在这儿。还有别的事吗？

A: The dishwasher comes in a few days. That's it.

A：洗碗机过几天就送来了。就这些了。

B: Got it. It should be done by the weekend.

B：知道了。周末前应该能完成。

Scene 10 安装洗衣机

A: Have you finished installing the washing machine?

A：洗衣机安装好了吗？

B: Not yet. I can't find the water inlet.

B：还没有。我找不到进水口。

A: It's behind the machine. You need to move it.

A：在洗衣机后面。你需要移动它。

B: OK, got it. How about the power cord?

B：好的，我知道了。电源线呢？

A: Just plug it into the socket on the wall.

A：把它插进墙上的插座就行了。

B: Great, thanks for your help.

B：太好了，谢谢你的帮助。

Scene 11 安装灯具

A: Have you installed the light yet?

A：灯装好了吗？

B: Not yet. Do we have all the parts?

B：还没有。所有的零件都在吗？

A: Yes, but I'm not sure how to wire it.

A：都在，但我不知道怎样接线。

B: Let me check the instructions.

B：我看一下说明书。

A: Great, I'll get the ladder.

A：好的，我去拿梯子。

B: Perfect. Let's get started.

B：太好了，我们开始安装吧。

□ installation *n.* 安装

□ deliver *v.* 递送

□ water inlet 进水口

□ power cord 电源线

□ part *n.* 零件

□ wire *v.* 接线

□ ladder *n.* 梯子

Unit 15　Renting an Apartment 租房

Scene 1　租房需求

A: Hi, I'm looking for a place to rent.

B: Great! What're you looking for?

A: I need a one-bedroom apartment in a safe area.

B: Sure. What's your budget?

A: Around $1200 per month.

B: Got it. Would you like to live in a specific neighborhood?

A: Not really, but I prefer something close to public transportation.

B: OK, I'll check our listings and get back to you.

A：你好，我想租房。

B：好的。您想租什么样的房子？

A：我想租位于安全地带的一居室公寓。

B：好的。您的预算是多少？

A：每月大约 1200 美元。

B：明白了。您想住在哪个特定的小区吗？

A：没有特定的，但我更喜欢附近有公共交通的房子。

B：好的，我查一下我们的房源清单，然后回复您。

214

Scene 2　约看房

A: Hi, I'm interested in the apartment listing.

B: Great! When would you like to schedule a viewing?

A: How about this weekend?

B: Sure, let me check the available times.

B: How about 11:00 am on Saturday?

A: Sounds good. I'll see you then.

A：你好，我对这份公寓清单很感兴趣。

B：好的。您想安排什么时间看房？

A：这周末怎么样？

B：当然可以，我查一下可约的时段。

B：周六上午 11 点怎么样？

A：听起来不错。到时候见。

Scene 3　检查房子

A: Let's check the house.

B: OK, what should we check?

A: The walls, floors, and appliances.

B: Alright! I'll start with the walls.

A：我们去看看房子吧。

B：好的，我们应该检查什么？

A：墙壁、地板和电器。

B：好的。我先从墙开始。

重点词汇
及表达

□ public transportation 公共交通

□ schedule v. 安排

□ viewing n. 观看

□ appliance n. 电器

A: I'll check the appliances.
B: Everything looks good to me.
A: Great. Let's move on to the next room.

A：我来检查一下电器。
B：我看一切都很好。
A：太好了。我们去下一个房间吧。

Scene 4   租房条件

A: What are the conditions for renting this place?
B: We require a security deposit and proof of income.
A: Is there a lease agreement?
B: Yes, it's a one-year lease.
A: Can I have a copy to review?
B: Sure, let me print one for you.

A：租这间房需要什么条件？
B：我们要求提供押金和收入证明。

A：有租赁协议吗？
B：有，租约是一年。
A：能给我一份看一下吗？
B：当然可以，我帮你打印一份。

Scene 5   签订租约

A: Hi, can we chat about rent and the lease?
B: Sure. What are you thinking?
A: I want to renew my lease for another year.
B: Sounds good. When can you pay rent?

A: On the first of every month. Is that OK?
B: Perfect, let's sign the lease agreement.

A：嗨，我们能谈谈租金和租约吗？
B：当然可以。您有些什么考虑？
A：我想再续一年的租约。
B：听起来不错。您什么时候能付房租？

A：每个月的第一天，可以吗？
B：很好。我们签订租约吧。

Scene 6   续约

A: Hey, can we chat about rent and the lease?
B: Yeah, what's up?
A: I want to extend my lease for another year.
B: Cool. When's the rent due?
A: First of each month, works for you?
B: Great, let's sign the lease agreement.

A：嘿，我们能谈谈租金和租约吗？
B：可以。怎么了？
A：我想把我的租约再延长一年。
B：很好。房租什么时候交？
A：每个月的第一天，行吗？
B：很好。我们签订租约吧。

215

□ condition *n.* 条件
□ security deposit 押金
□ lease agreement 租约

□ renew one's lease 续约
□ sign *v.* 签订

Unit 16   Visiting a Doctor 看病

Scene 1   感染流感

A: Hi, Doctor.

B: What seems to be the problem today?

A: I've had a very bad headache for a number of days.

B: Have you taken any medication, like aspirin?

A: Yes, but the pain doesn't go away.

B: Do you have any other symptoms?

A: Yes. I have a fever and nausea once in a while.

B: Colds are going around these days. Show me your tongue and say, "Ah."

A: "Ah."

B: I'll schedule you a blood test and urine test first. Then let's see what we can do.

A: When can I get the result of my test?

B: In about 4 hours.

(Four hours later)

A: These are the results of my blood test and urine test.

B: Ah, you have a terrible flu. I'll give you a fever shot first; then prescribe you some antibiotics. You'll be fine in three days.

A: Thanks.

A：您好，医生。

B：今天你哪里不舒服？

A：这几天我头痛得很厉害。

B：你吃过什么药吗？比如阿司匹林？

A：吃过，但是疼痛并没有消失。

B：你还有其他症状吗？

A：有。我偶尔发烧和恶心。

B：最近感冒在流行。伸出你的舌头说："啊。"

A："啊。"

B：我先给你安排验血和尿检。然后我们看看能做些什么。

A：我什么时候能知道检测结果？

B：大约 4 小时后。

（4 小时后）

A：这些是我的验血和尿检结果。

B：嗯，你得了严重的流感。我先给你打一针退烧针，然后给你开一些抗生素。三天后你就会好的。

A：谢谢。

216

重点词汇
及表达

- medication *n.* 药物
- symptom *n.* 症状
- nausea *n.* 恶心
- blood test 验血
- urine test 尿检
- prescribe *v.* 开处方
- antibiotics *n.* 抗生素

Scene 2　头痛

A: Hi, Doctor. I have a terrible headache. I was hoping you could help me.

B: Hi there. Tell me more about your headache. Does it feel like a dull ache or a sharp pain?

A: It's a dull ache, and it's mostly around my forehead.

B: I see. Let me check your medical history. Have you had headaches before?

A: Yeah, I've had headaches before, but this one is really bothering me.

B: I see. How has your sleep been lately? Are you getting enough rest?

A: Not really. I've been working on a big project, and it's been causing a lot of stress.

B: Alright. Based on what you're telling me, it could be a tension headache. I'll check you over to be sure.

(Doctor performs the exam)

B: It looks like you have tension headaches. Stress and tight muscles can cause them. Try deep breathing, relax, and take pain medicine.

A: OK, I'll try those things. Thanks, Doctor.

A：您好，医生。我头痛得厉害。我希望您能帮帮我。

B：你好。你再告诉我一些关于你头痛的细节。是隐隐作痛还是刺痛？

A：隐隐作痛，而且主要在额头周围。

B：我知道了。我查一下你的病史。你以前出现过头痛症状吗？

A：出现过，我以前也出现过头痛症状，但是这次真的很困扰我。

B：我明白了。你最近睡眠怎么样？有充分的休息吗？

A：休息不太够。我一直在做一个大项目，这给我带来了很大压力。

B：好的。根据你告诉我的情况来看，可能是紧张性头痛。我给你检查一下，以防万一。

（医生进行检查）

B：看起来你是紧张性头痛。压力和肌肉紧绷会导致这些症状。试着深呼吸，放松，然后服用止痛药。

A：好的，我试试这些办法。谢谢您，医生。

Scene 3　膝盖疼

A: Doctor, I feel pain behind my knee after running.

B: How long has it been bothering you?

A：医生，我跑步后觉得膝盖后面疼。

B：你感觉不适有多久了？

217

居家生活

□ headache *n.* 头痛

□ dull ache 隐隐作痛

□ sharp pain 剧痛

□ medical history 病史

□ tension headache 紧张性头痛

□ pain medicine 止痛药

□ bother *v.* 困扰

A: It started right after I finished running.

B: Is it swollen or bruised?

A: No, it's not swollen or bruised.

B: OK, let's do an exam to see what's going on.

A：我刚跑完步就开始了。

B：肿了吗？有瘀伤吗？

A：没有肿，也没有瘀伤。

B：好的，做个检查看看是怎么回事吧。

Scene 4 牙疼

A: My left tooth is hurting a lot.

B: How long has it been hurting?

A: It started hurting yesterday.

B: Is the pain constant, or does it come and go?

A: It's constant.

B: I recommend you schedule a dental appointment.

A：我左边的一颗牙疼得厉害。

B：疼多久了？

A：昨天开始疼的。

B：疼痛是持续性的还是时断时续的？

A：是持续性的。

B：我建议你预约看牙医。

Scene 5 呼吸困难

A: Sometimes I have trouble catching my breath.

B: How often does that happen?

A: It's happened a few times in the past week.

B: Have you experienced any other symptoms?

A: No, just the shortness of breath.

A：有时候我感觉呼吸困难。

B：多久发生一次？

A：过去这一周里发生过几次。

B：你还有其他症状吗？

A：没有，只是呼吸急促。

Scene 6 季节性流感

A: Hi there, what brings you in today?

B: I've been running a fever and experiencing headaches.

A：你好，你今天怎么过来了？

B：我一直在发烧，还头疼。

重点词汇
及表达

☐ swollen *adj.* 肿痛的

☐ bruised *adj.* 擦伤的

☐ constant *adj.* 持续的

☐ come and go 时断时续

☐ dental appointment 牙医预约

☐ shortness of breath 呼吸急促

A: Oh, I'm sorry to hear that. Have you noticed any other symptoms, like a runny or stuffy nose?

B: Yeah, my nose won't stop running.

A: I understand. It could be seasonal flu. Have you taken any medication for it?

B: No, not yet.

A: Alright, let's take a look and see what we can do to help you feel better.

A：哦，听到这个消息我很难过。你注意到其他症状了吗？比如流鼻涕或鼻塞？

B：注意到了，我的鼻涕流个不停。

A：知道了。可能是季节性流感。你服用过什么药物吗？

B：没有，还没有服药。

A：好的，我们来看看能做些什么让你感觉好点。

Scene 7 嗓子疼与咳嗽

A: Hello, what seems to be the problem today?

B: My throat hurts, and I have a cough.

A: How long have you had these symptoms?

B: About a week.

A: Alright, let's examine your throat.

A：你好，今天身体有什么不舒服吗？

B：我嗓子疼，还咳嗽。

A：这些症状持续多久了？

B：大约一周。

A：好的，我们检查一下你的咽喉。

Scene 8 睡眠困难

A: Hi there, what's been bothering you?

B: I've been feeling really tired lately.

A: Have you been sleeping well?

B: Not really. I wake up several times during the night.

A: OK, let's check your blood pressure and run some tests.

A：你好，有什么病痛困扰你吗？

B：我最近一直觉得很疲惫。

A：你睡得好吗？

B：不太好。我夜里醒了好几次。

A：好的，我们来测一下你的血压，然后做一些检查。

219

居家生活

□ runny or stuffy nose 流鼻涕或鼻塞

□ seasonal flu 季节性流感

□ throat *n.* 咽喉

□ cough *n.* 咳嗽

□ blood pressure 血压

□ test *n.* 检查

Unit 17 Buying Medicine 买药

Scene 1 处方配药

A: Hi, I'd like to have this prescription filled.

B: Can I see your medical care card, please?

A: Here you are.

B: Are you allergic to any medications?

A: No.

B: Please wait about 30 minutes.

A：您好，我想按照这张处方配药。

B：我能看一下您的医疗卡吗？

A：给您。

B：您对什么药物过敏吗？

A：没有。

B：请等待大约 30 分钟。

Scene 2 处方取药

A: Hi, I'd like to pick up my prescription, please.

B: OK. Here you are. Take 2 times per day, before, during, or after meals.

A: OK.

B: Oh, remember, do not eat any spicy or greasy food. And drink a lot of hot water.

A: OK. Thank you.

B: Bye.

A: Bye.

A：您好，我想取我的处方药。

B：好的。给您。每天两次，餐前、餐中或餐后服用。

A：好的。

B：哦，记住，不要吃辛辣和油腻的食物。多喝热水。

A：好的。谢谢您！

B：再见。

A：再见。

220

Scene 3 胃痛

A: Excuse me. Can you recommend a medicine for stomach pain?

B: Is it acute or chronic pain?

A: Just acute pain.

B: I suggest taking an antacid. Do you have any allergies?

A：打扰一下，您能推荐一种治胃痛的药吗？

B：是急性疼痛还是慢性疼痛？

A：急性疼痛。

B：我建议您吃点抗酸药。您对什么过敏吗？

重点词汇
及表达

☐ prescription n. 处方

☐ medical care card 医疗卡

☐ greasy adj. 油腻的

☐ acute adj. 急性的

☐ chronic adj. 慢性的

☐ antacid n. 抗酸药

A: No, I don't.

B: Then you can try this one.

Scene 4　止痛药

A: Excuse me. What can I take for a headache?

B: Ibuprofen, Tylenol, or aspirin work well.

A: Which one is better?

B: Ibuprofen is best for me.

A: OK, can I find them here?

B: Yes, they are on the shelf to your right.

A: Thank you. I'll take the ibuprofen.

Scene 5　服药方式

A: How should I take this medicine?

B: It's written on the label. What did the doctor say?

A: I forgot to ask. Should I take it with food?

B: Yes, it's better to take it with food. And don't skip doses.

A: Thanks, I'll be careful.

Scene 6　药物副作用

A: Does this medication have any side effects?

B: It's possible. Common ones include nausea and dizziness.

A: When should I avoid taking it?

B: If you have liver or kidney problems or are allergic to it.

A：不，我不过敏。

B：那您可以试试这个。

A：打扰一下，请问我吃什么药可以治头痛？

B：布洛芬、泰诺或阿司匹林都很有效。

A：哪种更好？

B：布洛芬最适合我。

A：好的，我能在这里找到这些药吗？

B：可以，在您右边的架子上。

A：谢谢。我要布洛芬。

A：我该怎样服用这种药？

B：标签上写着呢。医生怎么说？

A：我忘了问。我应该和食物一起服用吗？

B：是的，最好随餐服用。不要忘了服药。

A：谢谢。我会注意的。

A：这种药有副作用吗？

B：可能会有。常见症状包括恶心和头晕。

A：什么情况下应该避免服用？

B：如果您有肝脏或肾脏问题或对这种药物过敏。

居家生活

221

☐ aspirin *n.* 阿司匹林

☐ on the shelf 在架子上

☐ label *n.* 标签

☐ dose *n.* 剂量

☐ side effect 副作用

☐ dizziness *n.* 头晕

☐ liver *n.* 肝脏

☐ kidney *n.* 肾脏

A: Thanks for letting me know.

B: Always read the label and follow the instructions.

A：谢谢您告诉我这些。

B：一定要阅读标签并按照说明服用。

Scene 7　药物副作用症状

A: I feel dizzy after taking this medicine.

B: What medicine did you take?

A: I bought some painkillers for my headache.

B: Did you check the side effects before taking them?

A: No, I didn't think of it.

B: You should always read the label before taking any medication.

A：服用这种药物后我觉得头晕。

B：您服用了什么药？

A：我买了些止痛药治头痛。

B：您服用前查看过副作用吗？

A：没有，我没想到。

B：您在服用任何药物之前应该阅读它的标签。

Unit 18　Caring for Patients 照顾病人

Scene 1　探视病人

A: Can I visit my friend in the hospital?

B: Yes, visiting hours are from 10:00 am to 8:00 pm.

A: Are there any restrictions on the number of visitors?

B: Only two visitors are allowed at a time.

A: Are there any rules or regulations I should be aware of?

B: Yes, visitors need to follow hospital guidelines, such as wearing a mask and washing hands.

A: Thank you for letting me know.

A：我可以去医院看望我的朋友吗？

B：可以，探视时间是上午10点到晚上8点。

A：探视人数有限制吗？

B：一次只允许两人探视。

A：有什么规章制度是我应该知道的吗？

B：有，访客需要遵守医院指南，比如戴口罩和洗手。

A：谢谢您告诉我这些。

重点词汇
及表达

□ painkiller *n.* 止痛药

□ visiting hour 探视时间

□ restriction *n.* 限制

□ regulation *n.* 规定

Scene 2　物品清单

A: Do you have a list of items needed?

A：您有所需物品的清单吗?

B: Yes, we have a list prepared.

B：有，我们准备了一份清单。

A: Can you please provide it to me?

A：您能提供给我吗?

B: Sure, I'll give it to you right away.

B：当然可以，我马上给你。

A: Thank you so much. I'll take care of it.

A：非常感谢。我会处理好的。

B: You're welcome. Let us know if you need anything else.

B：不客气。如果你还需要什么，请告诉我们。

Scene 3　忌口食物

A: Are there any dietary restrictions I should follow?

A：有什么饮食限制需要我遵守的吗?

B: Yes, please avoid spicy and greasy foods for now.

B：有，现在请不要吃辛辣和油腻的食物。

A: Anything else?

A：还有别的吗?

B: It's best to avoid alcohol and smoking too.

B：最好也不要喝酒和吸烟。

A: Alright. I'll keep that in mind. Thanks.

A：好的，我会记住的。谢谢。

B: You're welcome.

B：不客气。

Scene 4　祝愿早日康复

A: I heard your friend is in the hospital.

A：我听说你的朋友住院了。

B: Yes, unfortunately, he is not doing well.

B：是的，很不幸，他的情况不太好。

A: I'm so sorry to hear that. I hope him recover soon.

A：听到这个消息我很难过。希望他早日康复。

B: Thank you. I appreciate it. I hope so too.

B：谢谢。我很感激。我也希望如此。

A: If there's anything I can do to help, please let me know.

A：如果有什么我能帮忙的，请告诉我。

B: Thank you, I will. That means a lot to me.

B：谢谢，我会的。我深感宽慰。

223

居家生活

- □ a list of items 物品清单
- □ right away 立刻，马上
- □ dietary restriction 饮食限制
- □ keep...in mind 记住
- □ recover v. 康复

Unit 19 Hospital Registration 医院挂号

Scene 1 医院挂号

A: Excuse me, Doctor. I have a headache. What kind of **specialist** should I see?

A：打扰一下，医生。我头痛。请问我应该看什么专科医生？

B: You can see a **neurologist**. Which hospital do you prefer?

B：你可以去看神经科医生。你想去哪家医院？

A: Can you recommend one nearby?

A：您能推荐一家附近的吗？

B: You can go to the General Hospital. Do you want me to **make an appointment** for you?

B：你可以去综合医院。需要我帮你预约吗？

A: Yes, please. Thank you.

A：需要。谢谢您。

Scene 2 挂号就诊

A: Excuse me, Doctor. I have chest pain.

A：打扰一下，医生。我胸口痛。

B: Have you seen a **cardiologist** before?

B：你以前看过心脏病医生吗？

A: No, I haven't.

A：我没看过。

B: You can go to the Cardiology Department for registration.

B：你可以去心内科挂号。

A: Where is it located?

A：心内科在哪里？

B: On the third floor. Turn right after the elevator.

B：在三楼，出了电梯右转。

A: Thank you. I'll go there now.

A：谢谢，我现在就去。

Scene 3 支付挂号费

A: Excuse me. Where can I pay my **registration fee**?

A：打扰一下，请问我在哪儿缴纳挂号费？

B: You can pay at the cashier over there.

B：您可以去那边的收银台付款。

A: Can I pay with my credit card?

A：我可以用信用卡支付吗？

重点词汇
及表达

☐ specialist *n.* 专科医生
☐ neurologist *n.* 神经科医生
☐ make an appointment 预约
☐ cardiologist *n.* 心脏病医生

☐ registration *n.* 挂号
☐ registration fee 挂号费

B: Yes, we accept all major credit cards.

A: How much is the registration fee?

B: It's $50 for adults and $30 for children.

A: Alright, I'll pay for myself and my child.

B：可以，我们接受所有的主流信用卡。

A：挂号费是多少？

B：成人 50 美元，儿童 30 美元。

A：好的，我会支付孩子和我自己的挂号费。

Scene 4　更改预约时间

A: Hello, may I ask how to change my appointment time?

B: Sure, you can either call the registration hotline or go to the registration office in person.

A: What if I can't change it? Can I get a refund?

B: I'm sorry, refunds are not allowed. You can try to reschedule your appointment.

A: OK, thanks for your help.

B: You're welcome. Have a nice day!

A：你好，请问如何更改我的预约时间？

B：哦，您可以拨打挂号热线，也可以亲自去挂号处。

A：如果改不了怎么办？我可以要求退款吗？

B：抱歉，不能退款。您可以试着重新安排预约时间。

A：好的，谢谢你的帮助。

B：不客气。祝您过得愉快！

225

Scene 5　更改挂号时间

A: Hi, I need to change my appointment time. Can you help me?

B: Sure, you can call our registration desk.

A: I tried but couldn't get through. Is there any other way?

B: You can come to the hospital and change it in person.

A: What if I can't make it at all? Can I get a refund?

A：你好，我需要更改我的挂号时间。你能帮我吗？

B：当然可以，您可以打电话给我们的挂号台。

A：我试过了，但是打不通。还有别的办法吗？

B：您可以亲自来医院更改。

A：如果我根本不能来怎么办？可以申请退款吗？

☐ adult *n.* 成年人

☐ hotline *n.* 热线

☐ in person 亲自

☐ registration desk 挂号台

☐ get through（电话）接通

☐ refund *n.* 退款

B: Yes, if you cancel 24 hours before your appointment.

B：如果您在约定时间 24 小时之前取消预约的话，可以申请退款。

A: Thank you for your help.

A：谢谢你的帮助。

B: You're welcome.

B：不客气。

Scene 6 过号

A: Excuse me. I think I missed my turn.

A：打扰一下，我觉得我应该过号了。

B: What number are you?

B：您是多少号？

A: 234.

A：234。

B: Sorry, we're already at 250.

B：抱歉，我们已经到 250 号了。

A: Oh no, can I still see the doctor?

A：哦，天哪，我还能看病吗？

B: You'll have to go back to the front desk and re-register.

B：您得回到前台重新登记。

A: OK, thank you.

A：好的，谢谢。

Unit 20 Disease Prevention 预防疾病

Scene 1 天冷加衣

A: Don't forget to wear a coat. It's cold outside.

A：别忘了穿件外套。外面很冷。

B: OK, Mom. I'll put on a jacket.

B：好的，妈妈。我会穿上夹克衫的。

A: Make sure to wear a hat and gloves too.

A：一定要戴上帽子和手套。

B: I will. Thanks for reminding me.

B：我会的。谢谢您提醒我。

A: You're welcome. Stay warm!

A：不客气。注意保暖！

Scene 2 勤洗手与消毒

A: Hey, guys. Don't forget to wash your hands often and disinfect them.

A：嘿，各位。不要忘记经常洗手并消毒。

重点词汇
及表达

□ cancel v. 取消

□ miss one's turn 过号

□ re-register v. 重新登记

□ make sure 确保

□ remind v. 提醒

□ disinfect v. 消毒

B: Yeah, we got it covered. Thanks, Mrs. Lee.

A: Especially during the cold and flu season. It's a real pain in the neck.

B: Tell me about it. We'll be careful.

A: Also, cover your mouth and nose when you cough or sneeze.

B: Thanks for the heads-up. We appreciate it.

Scene 3　接种疫苗

A: Hey, have you gotten your vaccine yet?

B: Yeah, I got it last week. Why do you ask?

A: I was just wondering where you got it and how much it cost.

B: I got it at the community center, and it was free.

A: Oh, that's great. Was it easy to schedule an appointment?

B: Yeah, I just went online and booked it. It was pretty simple.

B：嗯，放心吧，我们都搞定了。谢谢李太太。

A：尤其是在感冒和流感季节。真是让人头疼。

B：可不是嘛。我们会小心的。

A：还有，咳嗽或打喷嚏时要捂住口鼻。

B：谢谢您的提醒。我们很感激。

A：嘿，你接种疫苗了吗？

B：接种了，我上周接种的。你为什么问这个？

A：我只是想知道你是在哪儿接种的，花了多少钱。

B：我是在社区中心接种的，是免费的。

A：哦，那太好了。预约方便吗？

B：方便，我只是在网上预约了一下。很简单。

居家生活

227

☐ pain in the neck 很讨厌的人 / 事　　　　☐ schedule an appointment 安排预约

☐ sneeze *v.* 打喷嚏

☐ heads-up *n.* 预先劝告

☐ vaccine *n.* 疫苗

11

Part 11　Culture and Entertainment
文化娱乐

Unit 1 Festivals 节日

Scene 1　中国春节

A: Hi, have you heard of the Chinese Spring Festival?

B: No. What is it?

A: It's the Chinese New Year. It marks the start of the lunar new year.

B: Interesting. What are some traditions?

A: There's the dragon dance, fireworks, and family gatherings.

B: Sounds exciting. What's the origin of the festival?

A: It dates back over 4,000 years to ancient times.

A：嗨，你听说过中国的春节吗？

B：没有，它是什么节日？

A：它是中国的新年。它标志着农历新年的开始。

B：很有趣。有哪些传统？

A：有舞龙、放烟花和家庭团聚。

B：听起来很令人兴奋。这个节日的起源是什么？

A：它可以追溯到 4000 多年前的古代。

230　Scene 2　春节回家

A: Stop playing with your phone. You've been on it all day.

B: I'm trying to get a ticket to go home for the Spring Festival. There are more than 1.4 billion people in China. They all travel around at this time. That's why.

A: Can't you just go home another time?

B: I can't. I have to go home during the Spring Festival. I really enjoy having a big meal with my family, watching the Spring Festival gala, and visiting all my relatives.

A: Yeah. But can't you do that any time of the year?

A：别玩手机了。你都玩了一整天。

B：我想买一张回家过春节的票。中国有超过 14 亿人口。他们都在这个时候出行。这就是为什么我一直在用手机。

A：你就不能改天回家吗？

B：不行。春节期间我必须回家。我真的很喜欢和家人一起吃大餐、看春节联欢晚会、拜访我所有的亲戚。

A：好吧。但是这些事你一年中什么时候都可以做，不是吗？

重点词汇及表达

☐ Spring Festival 春节
☐ lunar new year 农历新年
☐ fireworks n. 烟花
☐ family gathering 家庭团聚

☐ gala n. 演出，庆典
☐ visit relatives 拜访亲戚

B: I can, but it feels different during the Spring Festival. I guess this is something foreigners will never understand. You know the Spring Festival is just so important for me. And it's so important for all Chinese people, I think. We have to go home no matter how difficult it is to get a ticket. Even if it took so many days, I'd still be home. It's a family tradition.

Scene 3　春节美食

A: Oh, Lily. Thank you so much for inviting me to your home this Spring Festival. How about the next Chinese New Year, you come to the US with me?

B: Er, don't even think about it!

A: Why not?

B: Look at these dishes. Chicken soup with mushrooms, boiled fish with pickled Chinese cabbage, fried tofu, stewed pig feet, and sauteed pig liver. This is heaven! And what do you guys have in America? Fried potatoes, boiled potatoes, mashed potatoes. It's all potatoes. The best food is steak. I don't even like it. Thank you so much for inviting me. But I think I'm gonna pass on that.

Scene 4　发红包

A: Mia, here is a red envelope for you. I wish you a happy new year.

B: 可以，但是春节期间感觉不一样。我想这是外国人永远无法理解的。要知道春节对我来说太重要了。我认为它对所有中国人都很重要。不管多难买到票，我们都要回家。就算抢票花了我那么多天，我也要回家。这是家族传统。

A: 哦，莉莉，非常感谢你邀请我今年春节来你家。下一个中国新年，你和我一起去美国怎么样？

B: 呃，想都别想!

A: 为什么不去？

231

B: 看看这些菜。蘑菇鸡汤、酸菜鱼、炸豆腐、炖猪脚、炒猪肝。简直是天堂! 你们在美国都有什么？炸土豆、煮土豆、土豆泥。都是土豆。最好的食物就是牛排了，我甚至连喜欢都谈不上。非常感谢你邀请我。但我想我还是算了吧。

A: 米娅，这是给你的红包。祝你新年快乐。

文化娱乐

□ family tradition 家族传统
□ dish *n.* 菜肴
□ red envelope 红包

B: No, I don't want it.

A: Come on. I really want you to have it.

B: No, I don't want it.

A: This is enough for nice shoes.

B: I don't want it. (*false rejection)

(Mia says she doesn't want it, but her hand is pointing at the pocket, and shows how to put the red envelope into her pocket.)

A: I don't want it.

B: 不用给我，我不想要。

A: 别这样。我真的很想让你收下。

B: 别给了，我不想要。

A: 这足够买一双漂亮的鞋了。

B: 我不想要。（注：假装拒绝）

（米娅说她不想要，但她的手指着口袋，告诉对方如何把红包放进口袋。）

A: 我不想要。

Scene 5　中秋祝福

A: Happy Mid-Autumn Festival!

B: Thank you! Same to you!

A: Did you have any special celebration plans?

B: Yes, I'll be having a family dinner and eating mooncakes.

A: That sounds lovely. Enjoy your time with your family!

B: Thanks! You too!

A: 中秋节快乐！

B: 谢谢! 节日快乐！

A: 你们有什么特别的庆祝计划吗?

B: 有，我会和家人一起吃晚餐、吃月饼。

A: 听起来很不错。好好享受和家人在一起的时光！

B: 谢谢! 你也是！

Scene 6　吃粽子

A: What filling do you like for zongzi?

B: I prefer pork and mushroom.

A: I like the sweet ones with red bean paste.

B: Have you tried the salty ones with egg yolk?

A: No, but I heard they're delicious.

B: Let's make a few with egg yolk, then!

A: 你喜欢什么馅的粽子?

B: 我喜欢猪肉香菇馅的粽子。

A: 我喜欢红豆沙馅的甜粽子。

B: 你吃过蛋黄馅的咸粽子吗?

A: 没吃过，不过我听说味道很好。

B: 那我们包一些蛋黄馅的粽子吧！

重点词汇
及表达

☐ pocket *n.* 口袋

☐ Mid-Autumn Festival 中秋节

☐ mooncake *n.* 月饼

☐ filling *n.* 馅料

☐ salty *adj.* 咸味的

232

Scene 7   中国传统美食

A: Let's go to Chinatown for Chinese New Year and buy some traditional foods!

B: Sounds like a plan! When should we go?

A: How about this weekend?

B: Great idea! What are you planning to buy?

A: I want to get some dumplings, rice cakes, and candies. How about you?

B: I'm looking for some red envelopes and decorations.

A：我们去唐人街过中国新年，然后买一些传统美食吧!

B：听起来是个不错的计划! 我们什么时候去?

A：这周末怎么样?

B：好主意! 你打算买什么?

A：我想买些饺子、年糕和糖果。你呢?

B：我想买些红包和装饰品。

Unit 2 Music 音乐

Scene 1   选择平台

233

A: Hey, I really like this song. Do you know where I can listen to it online?

B: Sure. What platform do you prefer?

A: I usually use QQ Music or Apple Music.

B: It's on both platforms. What's the name of the song?

A: It's called *Dancing in the Moonlight* by Top Loader.

B: Alright, let me look it up for you.

A：嘿，我真的很喜欢这首歌。你知道我在网上哪里可以听吗?

B：知道。你更喜欢在哪个平台上听?

A：我通常使用 QQ 音乐或者苹果音乐。

B：两个平台上都有。这首歌叫什么名字?

A：是捷思者合唱团的《在月光下跳舞》。

B：好的，我帮你查一下。

Scene 2   最喜欢的歌手

A: Hey, are you into pop music?

B: Definitely! I love it. How about you?

A：嘿，你喜欢流行音乐吗?

B：当然! 我喜欢。你呢?

□ traditional food 传统食品

□ rice cake 年糕

□ decoration *n.* 装饰

□ prefer *v.* 更喜欢

□ look up 查找

□ be into 喜欢

□ pop music 流行音乐

A: Yeah, I'm a big fan. Who's your favorite pop singer at the moment?

B: Ariana Grande. She's incredible. What about you?

A: Same here! But my all-time favorite has to be Taylor Swift.

B: Nice choice! I enjoy her music as well.

A：我也喜欢，我是流行音乐的超级粉丝。你现在最喜欢的流行歌手是谁？

B：爱莉安娜·格兰德。她太棒了！你呢？

A：我也觉得她很棒！但我一直最喜欢的是泰勒·斯威夫特。

B：品位不错！我也喜欢她的音乐。

Scene 3　音乐网站会员

A: Do I need a membership to listen to music?

B: Yes, but it's easy to sign up.

A: Can you show me how to do it?

B: Sure, just go to the website and follow the steps.

A: Is it expensive?

B: It depends on the plan, but they have a free trial.

A：我听音乐需要注册会员吗？

B：需要，但是注册很容易。

A：你能教我注册吗？

B：当然可以，只要登录网站并按照步骤操作就可以了。

A：会员费高吗？

B：这要看订阅计划，不过他们提供免费试用。

234

Unit 3　Movies 电影

Scene 1　挑选电影

A: What kind of movies do you like to watch?

B: I enjoy action and comedy movies.

A: What about the new releases at the cinema?

B: I'm interested in watching the latest thriller movie.

A：你喜欢看哪种类型的电影？

B：我喜欢动作片和喜剧。

A：电影院上映的新片怎么样？

B：我想看最新的惊悚片。

要点词汇
及表达

☐ incredible *adj.* 难以置信的，极好的
☐ sign up 注册
☐ free trial 免费试用
☐ comedy *n.* 喜剧

☐ release *n.* 新发行的东西，新电影
☐ thriller movie 惊悚片

A: I prefer romantic comedies myself.

B: That's cool. Maybe we can watch one together sometime.

A：我自己更喜欢浪漫喜剧。

B：太棒了。也许哪天我们可以一起看一部。

Scene 2 网络购票

A: Can we buy tickets online?

B: Yes, you can.

A: How do we do that?

B: Go to our website and select the movie, showtime, and seat.

A: Okay, thanks. Can I use my phone?

B: Yes, you can use your phone or computer.

A：我们可以在网上买票吗？

B：是的，可以。

A：我们怎么买呢？

B：到我们的网站上选择影片、放映时间和座位。

A：好的，谢谢。我可以用手机购买吗？

B：可以，你可以用手机或电脑购买。

Scene 3 选座位

A: Hi, can I have two tickets for the 7:00 pm show?

B: Sure, would you like any snacks with that?

A: Yes, can I get a large popcorn and two sodas, please?

B: Okay, that'll be $30. What seats would you like?

A: Can we have seats in the middle, maybe Row D or E?

B: Let me check...Yes, there are two seats available in Row E.

A: Great, we'll take those.

B: Here are your tickets and snacks. Enjoy the movie!

A：嗨，我可以买两张晚上 7 点的票吗？

B：当然可以，您要买点零食吗？

A：要，请给我大份的爆米花和两瓶苏打水，好吗？

B：好的，一共 30 美元。您想选哪儿的座位？

A：我们可以选中间的座位吗？比如 D 排或 E 排？

B：我看看……可以选，E 排还有两个座位。

A：太好了，我们就要这两个座位。

B：这是你们的票和零食。祝你们观影愉快！

文化娱乐

☐ romantic *adj.* 浪漫的

☐ select *v.* 选择

☐ showtime *n.* 放映时间

☐ popcorn *n.* 爆米花

☐ soda *n.* 苏打水

Scene 4　观影感受

A: How did you like the movie?

B: It was okay, but the ending was disappointing.

A: Really? I thought it was pretty good.

B: I guess we have different tastes.

A: Yeah, I suppose so. Want to grab some food now?

B: Sure, let's go.

A：你觉得这部电影怎么样?

B：还可以，但是结局令人失望。

A：是吗? 我觉得很不错呀。

B：我想我们的喜好不同。

A：我想是的。现在想去吃点东西吗?

B：好的，走吧。

Scene 5　网络电影

A: Hey, have you watched any good movies lately?

B: Not really. Any recommendations?

A: How about we try watching something online?

B: Sure. What platform do you suggest?

A: Let's try Netflix. I heard they have some good options.

B: Sounds good. Let's do it!

A：嘿，你最近看了什么好电影吗?

B：没看。你有什么推荐的吗?

A：我们试试在网上看部电影怎么样?

B：好啊。你建议用什么平台?

A：我们试试网飞（注：流媒体播放平台）吧。我听说他们有一些不错的选择。

B：听起来不错。这就开始吧!

Unit 4 Watching Games 看球赛

Scene 1　电话购票

A: Hi, I'm interested in buying tickets for the basketball game. Can you help me?

B: Sure, you can purchase tickets online or over the phone.

A: How can I buy tickets over the phone?

A：你好，我想买篮球赛的票。你能帮我吗?

B：当然可以，您可以在网上订票或者电话订票。

A：我怎样通过电话订票呢?

重点词汇
及表达

☐ ending *n.* 结局

☐ taste *n.* 喜好

☐ lately *adv.* 最近

☐ option *n.* 选择

☐ purchase *v.* 购买

B: Just give me the game date and seat preference. I'll process the payment and email the ticket to you.

A: Great. What's the phone number to call?

B: My phone number is 5551234. Thank you for calling!

Scene 2　现场买票

A: Excuse me. How can I purchase football tickets on-site?

B: You can go to the ticket office near the entrance.

A: Can I buy them with cash?

B: Yes, you can also use a credit card or mobile payment.

A: Are there any available seats for tonight's game?

B: Let me check... Yes, there are some seats left.

A: Great. Do you know if there's any discount for students?

B: Sorry, there is no student discount for this game.

Scene 3　入场时间

A: Excuse me. What time does the baseball game start?

B: The game starts at 7:00 pm.

A: What time should I arrive?

B: You should arrive at least 30 minutes before the game.

A: Can I enter the stadium earlier?

B：您只用把比赛日期和想要的座位告诉我就可以了。我来处理付款流程，然后通过电子邮件把票发给您。

A：太好了。电话号码是多少?

B：我的电话号码是5551234。谢谢您的来电。

A：请问，我在现场怎么买足球比赛的门票?

B：你可以去入口附近的售票处购买。

A：我可以用现金买吗?

B：可以，你也可以用信用卡或手机支付。

A：今晚的比赛还有座位吗?

B：我查一下……有，还有一些座位。

A：太好了。你知道学生是否有折扣吗?

B：抱歉，这场比赛学生不享受折扣。

A：打扰一下，棒球比赛什么时候开始?

B：比赛晚上7点开始。

A：我应该什么时候到?

B：你应该在比赛前至少30分钟到达。

A：我可以早点进入体育场吗?

文 化 娱 乐

237

☐ preference *n.* 偏好

☐ process the payment 处理付款流程

☐ on-site *adv.* 在现场

☐ mobile payment 手机支付

☐ stadium *n.* 体育场

B: Yes, you can enter the stadium 1 hour before the game.

B: 可以，你可以在比赛前 1 小时进入体育场。

Scene 4   购买零食

A: Excuse me. Can I buy snacks here?

A：打扰一下，我可以在这里买零食吗？

B: Sure. What would you like?

B：可以。您要买什么？

A: Do you have any chips or popcorn?

A：有薯片或爆米花吗？

B: Yes, we have both. What size would you like?

B：有，两种都有。您要多大份的？

A: Just a small one, please.

A：请给我小份的。

B: Here you go. That'll be $3.

B：给您。一共是 3 美元。

A: Thanks.

A：谢谢。

B: Enjoy the game!

B：好好享受比赛吧!

238

Unit 5 On the Beach 在沙滩上

Scene 1   准备物品

A: Hey, are you bringing sunscreen to the beach?

A：嘿，你要带防晒霜去海滩吗？

B: Yeah, I'm bringing mine. Are you?

B：要，我要带上我的。你呢？

A: I wasn't sure if I needed it.

A：我不确定我是否需要它。

B: You definitely do. You don't want to get burned.

B：你肯定需要。你不想晒伤吧。

A: Should we also bring wetsuits for diving?

A：我们也要带上潜水服吗？

B: I don't think we need them.

B：我觉得我们不需要。

Scene 2   海滩租伞

A: Let's rent a beach umbrella.

A：我们租一把沙滩伞吧。

B: Good idea. How much does it cost?

B：好主意。多少钱？

重点词汇
及表达

☐ sunscreen *n.* 防晒霜

☐ get burned 晒伤

☐ wetsuit *n.* 潜水衣

☐ diving *n.* 潜水

A: I think it's around $20 for the day.

B: Okay, let's find a good spot first.

A: Sure, let's go closer to the water.

B: Sounds good. Let's go.

A：我想一天大约 20 美元。

B：好的，我们先找个好地方。

A：好的，我们去靠近水的地方吧。

B：听起来不错。我们走吧。

Scene 3 乘坐快艇

A: Excuse me. How much is the price for a speedboat ride?

B: It's $50 for a 30-minute ride.

A: What time does the next ride start?

B: It departs every hour from 10:00 am to 4:00 pm.

A: Are there any safety precautions we should know?

B: Please wear the life jackets provided and follow the instructions of the crew.

A：打扰一下，乘坐快艇要多少钱？

B：30 分钟 50 美元。

A：下一班几点出发？

B：上午 10 点到下午 4 点之间，每小时一班。

A：有什么我们应该知道的安全预防措施吗？

B：请穿上我们提供的救生衣，听从工作人员的指令。

239

Scene 4 潜水

A: Hi coach, could you give me some tips on scuba diving?

B: Sure, what would you like to know?

A: Are there any important safety precautions?

B: Yes, always check your equipment, and never dive alone.

A: What about decompression sickness?

B: Ascend slowly, and don't exceed your dive limits.

A: Thank you. I'll keep that in mind.

A：嗨，教练，你能给我一些水肺潜水的建议吗？

B：当然可以，你想知道什么？

A：有什么重要的安全预防措施吗？

B：有。经常检查你的装备，不要独自潜水。

A：那关于减压病呢？

B：慢慢上升，不要超出你的潜水极限。

A：谢谢，我会记住的。

□ spot *n.* 地点

□ speedboat ride 乘坐快艇

□ safety precaution 安全预防措施

□ life jacket 救生衣

□ scuba diving 水肺潜水

□ equipment *n.* 装备

□ decompression sickness 减压病

□ ascend *v.* 上升

文化娱乐

Unit 6　At the Amusement Park 在游乐园

Scene 1　订公园门票

A: Hello, I'd like to ask about a ticket reservation at your park.

B: Sure, you can make a reservation online or by phone.

A: How can I get the ticket after the reservation?

B: You can pick up the ticket at the entrance with your reservation code.

A: Great, can you tell me the price of the ticket?

B: It depends on the type of ticket. Please check our website for details.

A: Thank you. I'll check it out.

A：你好，我想问一下你们的游乐园门票怎么预订。

B：好的，您可以在网上预订或者电话预订。

A：预订后我怎样才能拿到票呢？

B：您可以用预订码在入口处取票。

A：太好了，你能告诉我门票价格吗？

B：这要看是哪种类型的票。详情请浏览我们的网站。

A：谢谢，我会看看的。

Scene 2　游乐园入口

A: Excuse me. Do you know where the entrance to the amusement park is?

B: Yeah, it's just over there.

A: Thank you! Is it easy to find once we get closer?

B: Yes, it's pretty obvious. You'll see the ticket booths and the entrance gate.

A: Great, thanks for your help!

B: No problem. Enjoy your day at the park!

A：打扰一下，你知道游乐园的入口在哪儿吗？

B：知道，就在那边。

A：谢谢! 我们走近后容易找到吗？

B：容易，入口很明显。您会看到售票亭和入口。

A：太好了，谢谢你的帮助!

B：不客气。祝您在园区玩得开心!

☐ reservation code 预约码

☐ check out 查看

☐ amusement park 游乐园

☐ ticket booth 售票处

全场景英语口语

240

Scene 3　园区洗手间

A: Excuse me. Where is the restroom?

B: It's over there, next to the food court.

A: Thank you! And is there a baby changing station?

B: Yes, there is one inside the restroom.

A: Great, thanks again!

B: You're welcome. Enjoy your day at the park!

A：打扰一下，洗手间在哪儿？

B：在那边，在美食广场旁边。

A：谢谢! 那里有给婴儿换尿布的地方吗？

B：有，洗手间里有一个。

A：太好了，再次感谢!

B：不客气。祝您在园区玩得开心!

Scene 4　走失求助

A: Excuse me. Can you help us? We got separated from our friends.

B: We're lost. Can you call her for us?

A: Her name is Lily. We were supposed to meet at the entrance.

B: We've been looking for her for half an hour.

C: Sure. What does she look like? I'll try to find her.

A: She's wearing a yellow shirt and carrying a red backpack.

A：打扰一下，你能帮助我们吗？我们和朋友走散了。

B：我们迷路了。你能帮我们打电话给她吗？

A：她叫莉莉。我们本来应该在入口处会合的。

B：我们找了她半个小时。

C：当然可以。她长什么样？ 我会尽力找她。

A：她穿着一件黄色的衬衫，背着一个红色的背包。

241

- □ court *n.* 广场
- □ get separated 分散
- □ backpack *n.* 背包

Part 12　Emotions
情绪表达

Unit 1 Comforting 安慰

Scene 1　亲人去世

A: I'm sorry for your loss.

B: Thank you. It's been tough.

A: Is there anything I can do to help?

B: Just being here for me means a lot.

A: Of course, I'm here for you.

B: Thank you. I appreciate it.

A：我对你的亲人的离世深表遗憾。

B：谢谢。我太难受了。

A：有什么我能帮忙的吗？

B：你能陪在我身边，就已经意义非凡。

A：当然，我会在这里陪你。

B：谢谢。我很感激。

Scene 2　朋友失恋

A: I'm sorry to hear about your breakup.

B: It hurts so much. I don't know what to do.

A: It's okay to feel that way. It takes time to heal.

B: I just miss him so much.

A: I understand, but remember you deserve someone who loves you.

A：抱歉，我听说你分手了。

B：我很伤心。我不知道该怎么办。

A：有这种感觉没关系。这需要时间来愈合。

B：我只是太想念他了。

A：我明白，但是记住，你值得拥有一个爱你的人。

Scene 3　家人住院

A: What's wrong?

B: My grandpa's in the hospital.

A: That's tough.

B: I'm worried about him.

A: I'm here for you.

B: Thanks. It means a lot.

A：出什么事了？

B：我爷爷住院了。

A：那太令人难受了。

B：我很担心他。

A：我会在这里陪伴你。

B：谢谢。这对我意义重大。

Scene 4　家人生病

A: Are you okay?

A：你还好吗？

重点词汇
及表达

□ loss *n.* 失去；去世

□ mean *v.* 意味着

□ breakup *n.* 分手

□ heal *v.* 愈合

□ deserve *v.* 值得

□ What's wrong? 怎么了？

B: My brother's been really sick.

A: I'm sorry to hear that.

B: It's been hard for everyone.

A: Let me know if I can do anything.

B: Thanks. I appreciate your support.

B：我哥哥病得很重。

A：听到这个消息我很难过。

B：这让所有人都很难受。

A：如果我能做什么，请告诉我。

B：谢谢。感谢你的支持。

Scene 5 考试失利

A: Tough luck on your exam.

B: Yeah, I feel terrible.

A: Don't be too hard on yourself.

B: But I studied so hard!

A: Sometimes, it just doesn't go your way.

B: Thanks for being understanding.

A：你考试运气真不好。

B：是啊，我感觉很糟糕。

A：别对自己太苛刻了。

B：可是我学习那么努力啊!

A：有时候，事情并不会那么顺利。

B：谢谢你的理解。

Unit 2 Compliment 称赞

Scene 1 称赞手艺

A: Mmm, this meal is absolutely delicious!

B: Thank you so much. I'm so happy you're enjoying it!

A: You're such an incredible cook! How did you learn to make this?

B: Oh, thank you! I've always loved cooking and experimenting with new recipes.

A: I can tell you put a lot of time and care into this. Everything tastes so fresh and wonderful.

B: Yes, I do put in some effort, but it's all worth it to see you enjoying every bite.

A：嗯，这顿饭真是太美味了!

B：非常感谢。我很高兴你喜欢吃!

A：你真是个了不起的厨师!你是怎么学会做这个的?

B：哦，谢谢!我一直喜欢烹饪和尝试新食谱。

A：我能看出你在这上面花了很多时间和精力。每样东西尝起来都那么新鲜美味。

B：是的，我确实很努力，但看到你吃得很开心，一切都是值得的。

☐ support *n.* 支持

☐ tough luck 运气不好

☐ be too hard on sb 对某人过于苛刻

☐ experiment *v.* 做实验

☐ new recipe 新食谱

☐ put in some effort 付出努力

☐ worth *adj.* 值得的

Scene 2　称赞厨艺

A: Wow, this is delicious!
B: I found a new recipe to try.
A: You're getting really good at cooking.
B: Thanks. I'm enjoying it.
A: Keep it up. I'm impressed.

A：哇，真好吃！
B：我发现了一个新食谱来试试。
A：你的厨艺越来越好了。
B：谢谢，我很享受这个过程。
A：继续努力。我很佩服。

Scene 3　称赞新衣服

A: Your outfit is on point!
B: I want to try something different.
A: It looks amazing on you.
B: Thanks. I'm glad you like it.
A: You always know how to dress and look great.

A：你的穿搭真是一级棒！
B：我想尝试一些不同的风格。
A：你这身穿搭真是太帅了！
B：谢谢，我很高兴你喜欢。
A：你总是知道如何穿着得体。

Scene 4　称赞穿衣品位

246

A: That outfit looks great on you!
B: I just got it. What do you think?
A: It suits you perfectly.
B: Thanks. I wasn't sure at first.
A: You have great taste. Looks amazing.

A：那套衣服穿在你身上真帅！
B：我刚买的。你觉得怎么样？
A：非常适合你。
B：谢谢，一开始我还不确定。
A：你很有品位。看起来棒极了。

Scene 5　出色完成任务

A: That report you wrote was fantastic.
B: Thanks. I put in a lot of effort.
A: It really impressed everyone.
B: I'm glad. It was important to me.
A: You nailed it. Great job!

A：你写的报告太棒了。
B：谢谢。我付出了很多努力。
A：它给所有人都留下了深刻的印象。
B：我很高兴。这对我很重要。
A：你做到了。你做得很棒！

Scene 6　工作表现

A: You did an amazing job on that project.
B: Thanks. It was a team effort.

A：你在那个项目中表现非常出色。
B：谢谢。这是团队共同努力的结果。

重点词汇
及表达

- ☐ Keep it up. 继续努力。
- ☐ impressed adj. 令人印象深刻的
- ☐ on point 时尚好看
- ☐ suit v. 合身
- ☐ perfectly adv. 完美地

- ☐ fantastic adj. 极好的
- ☐ You nailed it. 你成功了。
- ☐ project n. 项目
- ☐ team effort 团队共同努力

A: You really stood out. Great work.

B: I appreciate it. We all worked hard.

A: You deserve the praise. Well done.

A：你的表现确实很突出。干得不错。

B：我很感激。我们都很努力。

A：你值得表扬。你做得很好。

Scene 7   成绩优异

A: Your GPA is outstanding.

B: Thanks. I'm really dedicated to my studies.

A: You're a star student. Amazing work.

B: It feels good to be recognized.

A: You deserve it. Keep up the great work.

A：你各科成绩的平均积分点很优异。

B：谢谢。我学习确实很专心。

A：你是个好学生。你做得非常好。

B：被认可的感觉真好。

A：这是你应得的。再接再厉。

Scene 8   奖学金

A: Congrats on getting the scholarship.

B: Thank you. I worked hard for it.

A: You're a top student. Well done.

B: I appreciate your support.

A: You're going places. Keep it up.

A：祝贺你获得奖学金。

B：谢谢。我为此学习很努力。

A：你是优等生。你做得很好。

B：谢谢你的支持。

A：你会大有作为的。保持下去。

247

Unit 3 Surprise 惊奇

Scene 1   工作邀请

A: I just got an interview invitation for my dream job!

B: Wow, that's great news! Congratulations!

A: Thanks. I'm so excited and nervous at the same time.

B: You got this! Just be yourself and show them what you've got.

A: I will. Thanks for the encouragement.

A：我刚刚收到了我梦寐以求的工作面试邀请!

B：哇，真是好消息! 祝贺你!

A：谢谢。我既兴奋又紧张。

B：你能行的! 做你自己，向他们展示你的实力。

A：我会的。谢谢你的鼓励。

- stand out 突出
- GPA(grade point average) 各科成绩的平均积分点
- be dedicated to 致力于
- star student 优秀学生
- recognize v. 认可
- scholarship n. 奖学金
- top student 优等生
- go places 成功
- interview invitation 面试邀请
- encouragement n. 鼓励

Scene 2　应聘成功

A: Holy cow! They offered me the job!

B: Congratulations! When do you start?

A: In two weeks. I can't believe it.

B: I'm so happy for you. You deserve it.

A: Thank you. I'm still in shock.

B: Well, get ready to celebrate!

A：天哪! 他们给了我这个工作机会!

B：祝贺你! 你什么时候开始上班?

A：两周后。我真不敢相信。

B：我真为你高兴。这是你应得的。

A：谢谢。我还在震惊中。

B：好了，准备庆祝吧!

Scene 3　中大奖

A: Look at this! I won the grand prize!

B: No way! What did you win?

A: A brand new car!

B: Are you kidding me? That's incredible!

A: I know. I can't believe it either!

B: Congrats, you lucky dog!

A：看这个! 我中大奖了!

B：不可能! 你赢得了什么?

A：一辆全新的车!

B：你在开玩笑吗? 简直不敢相信!

A：是的。我也不敢相信!

B：祝贺你，你真是个幸运儿!

248

Scene 4　好友告白

A: You won't believe it. My childhood friend just confessed to me! Jack just told me he has a crush on me.

B: No way! What did you say?

A: I was so surprised. I didn't know what to say.

B: You must be really happy!

A: I am, but I don't know if I feel the same way.

A：你不会相信的。我儿时的朋友刚刚向我表白了! 杰克刚告诉我他对我有好感。

B：不可能吧! 你说了些什么?

A：我很惊讶。我不知道该说什么。

B：你一定很高兴!

A：是的，但我不知道我是否对他有同样的感觉。

Unit 4　Regret 后悔

Scene 1　工作未完成

A: I can't believe I missed the deadline.

A：真不敢相信我错过了最后期限。

重点词汇
及表达

☐ offer v. 提供

☐ in shock 处于震惊中

☐ grand prize 大奖

☐ Are you kidding me? 你在开玩笑吗?

☐ lucky dog 幸运儿

☐ confess to sb 向某人表白

☐ have a crush on sb 喜欢某人

☐ miss the deadline 错过最后期限

B: What went wrong?

A: I didn't manage my time well.

B: If only you had planned better.

A: I know. I'm kicking myself for it now.

Scene 2　项目未完成

A: How did your project go?

B: I didn't finish it on time.

A: Why not?

B: I should've been more serious about it instead of wasting time.

A: Next time, try to stay focused and prioritize your tasks.

Scene 3　理财失败

A: I lost all my money in the stock market.

B: Oh no. What went wrong?

A: I didn't do enough research before investing.

B: That's tough. It's important to take the time to research before jumping in.

Scene 4　过度消费

A: I can't pay my credit card bills this month.

B: Why not?

A: I spent too much on unnecessary things.

B: It was a mistake to overspend.

Scene 5　身体不适

A: I feel awful. I think I got sick again.

B: What's wrong?

A: I haven't been taking care of myself.

B：出了什么问题?

A：我没有把时间安排好。

B：要是你提前计划就好了。

A：我知道。我现在很自责。

A：你的项目进展如何?

B：我没能按时完成。

A：为什么没完成?

B：我应该更认真一点，而不是浪费时间。

A：下次试着集中注意力，优先处理你的工作。

A：我在股市里赔光了所有的钱。

B：哦，不。出什么问题了?

A：我在投资前没有做充分的调查。

B：那太难了。在进入股市之前，花点时间进行研究是很重要的。

A：这个月我付不起信用卡账单了。

B：为什么?

A：我在不必要的东西上花了太多钱。

B：过度消费是不对的。

A：我感觉很糟糕。我想我又病了。

B：怎么了?

A：我一直没有好好照顾自己。

情绪表达

249

- □ manage one's time 安排好某人的时间
- □ kick oneself 严厉自责
- □ instead of 而不是
- □ stay focused 集中精力
- □ prioritize v. 优先处理
- □ stock market 股市
- □ invest v. 投资
- □ unnecessary adj. 没必要的
- □ overspend v. 过度消费

B: You should prioritize your health.

A: I know. I shouldn't have ignored it.

B: Let's work on improving your habits together.

B：你应该把健康放在首位。

A：我知道。我不应该忽视它。

B：我们一起努力改进你的习惯吧。

Scene 6　关系疏远

A: Hey, have you talked to your sister lately?

B: No, I haven't. I wish I hadn't ignored her calls.

A: What happened?

B: I've been so busy with work. I haven't had time for anyone else. Now, I regret it.

A: Why don't you give her a call?

B: Yeah, I will. I wish I hadn't let our relationship slip like this.

A：嘿，你最近和你妹妹聊过吗?

B：没有。我真希望我没有忽略她的电话。

A：发生什么了?

B：我一直忙于工作。我没有时间花在别人身上。现在我后悔了。

A：你为什么不给她打个电话呢?

B：哦，我会打给她的。我真希望我没有让我们的关系就这样破裂。

Scene 7　出言不逊

A: I'm so sorry for what I said earlier.

B: It's fine. Don't worry about it.

A: No, really. I feel terrible. I'm kicking myself for being so insensitive.

B: Let's just move past it and forget about it, okay?

A: Thank you for being understanding. I promise to be more careful with my words next time.

A：我为我之前说的话感到抱歉。

B：没事。别担心。

A：不，真的。我感觉糟透了。我真的对自己的迟钝感到懊恼。

B：我们向前看，忘掉这个，好吗?

A：谢谢你的理解。我保证下次说话时会小心一些。

Scene 8　后悔打孩子

A: What happened? Why do you look so upset?

B: My son broke a vase, and I hit him.

A: That's not good. You should apologize to him.

B: I did, but I still feel terrible. I'll never forgive myself for hitting him.

A：发生什么事了? 你怎么看起来这么沮丧?

B：我儿子打碎了花瓶。我打了他。

A：那可不好。你应该向他道歉。

B：我道歉了，但我还是觉得很难受。我永远不会原谅自己打了他。

250

重点词汇
及表达

☐ ignore v. 忽视

☐ improve v. 改进

☐ regret v. 后悔

☐ relationship n. 关系

☐ insensitive adj. 不敏感的，迟钝的

☐ move past 向前

☐ forget about 忘记

☐ upset adj. 难过的，沮丧的

☐ apologize v. 道歉

☐ forgive v. 原谅

A: You can make it up to him by spending more quality time with him.

B: You're right. I should focus on being a better parent.

A: 你可以多花点时间和他在一起，以此来补偿他。

B: 你说得对。我应该集中精力做一个更好的家长。

 Unit 5　Anxiety 焦虑

Scene 1　考试临近

A: I'm feeling so anxious about the upcoming exam.

B: Don't worry. You still have time to prepare.

A: But there's so much material to cover!

B: Break it down into smaller parts and focus on one thing at a time.

A: Okay. I'll try to stay calm and focused.

A: 我对即将到来的考试感到很焦虑。

B: 别担心。你还有时间准备。

A: 但是要学的东西太多了!

B: 把它分成更小的部分，一次专注于一个部分。

A: 好的。我会尽量保持冷静和专注。

Scene 2　担心考试

A: I can't stop worrying about the exam.

B: Take a deep breath and relax.

A: But I haven't even finished reviewing.

B: You still have time.

A: I hope you're right.

A: 我无法停止担心考试的事。

B: 深呼吸，放轻松。

A: 可我还没复习完呢。

B: 你还有时间。

A: 希望你是对的。

Scene 3　工作繁重

A: I'm so anxious about this workload.

B: I understand. It can be overwhelming.

A: I don't know how to finish it all.

B: Let's break it down into smaller tasks and prioritize.

A: That sounds like a good plan. Thanks.

B: No problem. We'll get through this together.

A: 我对这工作量感到非常焦虑。

B: 我理解。这可能会让人不知所措。

A: 我不知道怎样把它都做完。

B: 我们把它分成几个小任务，并确定优先顺序。

A: 这听起来是个好计划。谢谢。

B: 没问题。我们会一起渡过难关的。

☐ make up 补偿

☐ anxious adj. 焦虑的

☐ upcoming adj. 即将到来的

☐ stay calm 保持冷静

☐ take a deep breath 深呼吸

☐ review v. 复习

☐ workload n. 工作量

☐ overwhelming adj. 压倒性的，令人不知所措的

☐ get through 熬过（困难时期）

Scene 4　工作压力

A: I'm so stressed out with work!

B: Me too! It's overwhelming.

A: I can't even take a break without feeling guilty.

B: I know what you mean. It's like there's always something to do.

A: I feel like I'm drowning in work.

B: Let's try to prioritize and take it one step at a time.

A：我的工作压力太大了!

B：我也是! 这完全是压倒性的压力。

A：我甚至不能休息一下而不感到内疚。

B：我明白你的意思。工作似乎永远做不完。

A：我觉得我快被工作吞没了。

B：我们试着分清轻重缓急, 一步一步来。

Scene 5　准备做报告

A: I'm so anxious about this presentation.

B: You'll do great! Just take a deep breath.

A: But what if I forget something important?

B: Practice beforehand and make notes.

A: Okay. I'll try that. Thanks for the advice.

B: No problem. Good luck!

A：我对这次报告很担心。

B：你会做得很好的! 深呼吸。

A：但是如果我忘了重要的内容怎么办?

B：事先练习并做好笔记。

A：好的。我来试试。谢谢你的建议。

B：没问题。祝你好运!

Scene 6　做报告

A: I'm so nervous about the presentation tomorrow.

B: Did you finish the report?

A: Not really. I'm struggling with it.

B: You should have asked for help earlier.

A: I know. I'm kicking myself now.

B: Don't worry. Just do your best tomorrow.

A：明天的汇报让我很紧张。

B：你完成报告了吗?

A：还没全部弄完。我很纠结。

B：你应该早点寻求帮助。

A：我知道。我现在真后悔。

B：别担心。明天尽力就行。

Unit 6　Disappointment 失望

Scene 1　成绩不好

A: How was your test?

A：你的考试成绩怎么样?

重点词汇
及表达

- □ guilty *adj.* 内疚的
- □ drown *v.* 淹没
- □ presentation *n.* 报告，介绍
- □ beforehand *adv.* 提前
- □ struggle with 挣扎
- □ do one's best 尽力

B: It's not what I expected.

A: Did you do badly?

B: Yeah, I got a low score.

A: I'm sorry to hear that.

B: I'm so disappointed in myself.

Scene 2　面试失败

A: Did you hear back from the job interview?

B: Yeah, but they didn't offer me the position.

A: Oh no. I'm sorry to hear that.

B: It's a letdown. I was really hoping to get it.

A: Have you applied to any other jobs?

B: Yeah, I have a few more interviews lined up.

A: That's good. Keep your head up!

Scene 3　食物难吃（1）

A: This food I waited so long for is disappointing.

B: That's too bad. What's wrong with it?

A: It doesn't taste good at all.

B: Maybe we can find something else to eat nearby?

A: Yeah, let's try that.

Scene 4　食物难吃（2）

A: How's the food?

B: I waited in line forever, but it's terrible.

A: Really? That's a shame.

B: Yeah, I'm dissatisfied with it.

A: Maybe we can find something better next time.

B: Let's hope so.

B：不是我所期望的。

A：你考得不好吗？

B：是的，我的分数很低。

A：听到这个消息我很难过。

B：我对自己很失望。

A：你收到面试的回复了吗？

B：收到了，但是他们没有给我这个职位。

A：哦，不。听到这个消息我很难过。

B：真令人失望。我真的很希望得到它。

A：你申请过其他工作吗？

B：申请过，我还有几个面试。

A：很好。保持乐观！

253

A：我等了这么久的食物真让人失望。

B：那太糟糕了。有什么问题吗？

A：一点也不好吃。

B：也许我们可以在附近找点别的吃的？

A：是的，我们试试吧。

A：食物怎么样？

B：我一直在排队，但食物太糟糕了。

A：是吗？真可惜。

B：嗯，我不太满意。

A：也许下次我们能找到更好吃的。

B：希望如此。

情绪表达

□ score *n.* 分数

□ disappointed *adj.* 失望的

□ letdown *n.* 失望，沮丧

□ line up 排成一行

□ Keep your head up! 保持乐观!

□ disappointing *adj.* 令人失望的

□ shame *n.* 遗憾

Scene 5　取消演唱会

A: Did you hear? The concert's canceled.

B: No way! I was so excited.

A: I know, me too. I was really looking forward to it.

B: This is so disappointing.

A: Yeah, that's underwhelming.

B: I hope they reschedule soon.

A：你听说了吗？音乐会取消了。

B：不可能！我本来挺兴奋的。

A：我知道，我也是。我真的很期待。

B：真令人失望。

A：是啊，真令人失望。

B：我希望他们能尽快重新安排。

Scene 6　爽约

A: Hey, did you go out with Chris last night?

B: No, he blew me off again.

A: Really? That's a shame.

B: Yeah, I was looking forward to it.

A: Have you tried reaching out to him?

B: Yeah, but he never responds.

A: Well, maybe it's time to move on.

A：嘿，你昨晚和克里斯出去了吗？

B：没有，他又爽约了。

A：是吗？真可惜。

B：是的，我一直很期待。

A：你试过联系他吗？

B：是的，但他从不回应。

A：好吧，也许是时候向前看了。

254

Scene 7　工作未得到认可

A: How did it go with the boss?

B: Not great. My work wasn't acknowledged.

A: What? That's surprising.

B: Yeah, I was hoping for better.

A: Did they give any feedback?

B: Not really. Just brushed it off.

A: I'm sorry to hear that. Keep trying, though.

A：你跟老板谈得怎么样？

B：不太好。我的工作没有得到认可。

A：什么？这太令人惊讶了。

B：是啊，我本来希望结果会好一点。

A：老板有什么反馈吗？

B：没有。只是一笑置之。

A：听到这个消息我很难过。不过，继续努力吧。

重点词汇
及表达

- underwhelming *adj.* 索然无味的
- reschedule *v.* 重新安排
- blow sb off 拒绝某人，爽约
- respond *v.* 回应
- move on 向前看
- acknowledge *v.* 认可
- feedback *n.* 反馈
- brush off 置之不理

Unit 7 Dislike 讨厌

Scene 1 打喷嚏不捂口鼻

A: Did you see that guy sneezing without covering his nose and mouth?

B: Yeah, it's disgusting.

A: I hate it when people do that in public.

B: Me too. It's so rude and inconsiderate.

A: I always cover my mouth and nose when I sneeze or cough.

B: Same here. It's just basic hygiene and manners.

A：你看到那个不捂口鼻打喷嚏的家伙了吗？

B：是啊，真恶心。

A：我讨厌人们在公共场合那么做。

B：我也是。这样很粗鲁，而且不体贴。

A：我打喷嚏或咳嗽时总是捂住口鼻。

B：我也是。这是基本的卫生和礼仪。

Scene 2 被上司刁难

A: Did you see how my boss treated me today?

B: Yeah, I saw it. I can't stand how he talks to you.

A: It's like he enjoys making my job difficult.

B: I know. I can't stand seeing you treated like that.

A: I don't know how much more I can take.

B: Just hang in there. We'll find a way to deal with it.

A：你看到老板今天是怎么对我的了吗？

B：是的，我看到了。我无法忍受他对你说话的方式。

A：他好像很喜欢就我的工作找麻烦。

B：我知道。我无法忍受他那么对待你。

A：我不知道我还能承受多少。

B：再坚持一下。我们会有办法解决问题的。

Scene 3 房间脏乱

A: I can't bear how messy your room is. Can you please clean it up?

B: But I don't want to clean it.

A: I understand it's not the most fun thing to do, but it's important to keep your space tidy.

A：我无法忍受你的房间这么乱。你能把它清理一下吗？

B：但是我不想清理。

A：我知道这不是最有趣的事情，但保持你的房间整洁很重要。

情绪表达

255

☐ disgusting *adj.* 令人恶心的

☐ hygiene *n.* 卫生

☐ manners *n.* 礼仪

☐ treat *v.* 对待

☐ stand *v.* 忍受

☐ hang in 坚持下去，不泄气

☐ deal with 解决

☐ bear *v.* 忍受

☐ clean up 清理

B: Okay. I'll do it later.

A: No, please do it now. It won't take too long if you focus on it.

B: Fine, I'll clean it up now.

B：好的。我待会儿再清理。

A：不，请你现在就清理。如果你专心清理的话，不会花太长时间的。

B：好的，我现在就清理。

Scene 4　随地大小便

A: Look at that dog pooping on the sidewalk.

B: Ugh, I find that disgusting.

A: Me too. It's so unsanitary.

B: I wish people would clean up after their pets.

A: Agreed, it's such a common courtesy.

B: I can't bear to see it everywhere in the city.

A：看那条在人行道上排便的狗。

B：啊，我觉得很恶心。

A：我也这么觉得。太不卫生了。

B：我希望人们能清理宠物的粪便。

A：同意，这是一种常见的礼貌。

B：我不能忍受在城市里到处看到狗狗的便便。

Scene 5　随地吐痰

256

A: That guy just spat on the sidewalk!

B: Eww, It's so uncivilized.

A: Yeah, so disrespectful and gross.

B: I wish more people would have some basic manners.

A：那个家伙刚刚在人行道上吐了口水!

B：哎呀，太不文明了。

A：是啊，太无礼和恶心了。

B：我希望更多的人能有一些基本的礼貌。

Scene 6　流鼻涕

A: Excuse me. Do you have a tissue?

B: Sure, here you go.

A: Thanks. My nose won't stop running.

B: I hate it when that happens.

A: Me too. It grosses me out.

B: At least you have a tissue now.

A: Yeah, I'll survive.

A：打扰一下，你有纸巾吗?

B：当然有，给你。

A：谢谢，我的鼻涕流个不停。

B：我讨厌这种情况。

A：我也是。这让我觉得很恶心。

B：至少你现在有纸巾了。

A：是的，我得救了。

重点词汇
及表达

☐ unsanitary *adj.* 不卫生的

☐ courtesy *n.* 礼貌

☐ uncivilized *adj.* 不文明的

☐ disrespectful *adj.* 无礼的

☐ gross *adj.* 令人恶心的

☐ tissue *n.* 纸巾

☐ gross sb out 使人恶心

☐ survive *v.* 幸存，活下来

Scene 7　耳垢过多

A: What's wrong with your ear?

B: I'm repulsed by how much earwax I have. Look how much earwax I have. What a nuisance!

A: Gross, maybe you should clean it.

B: I tried, but it's still there.

A: Have you seen a doctor?

B: Not yet. I'll schedule an appointment.

A：你的耳朵怎么了？

B：我讨厌自己有这么多耳垢。看看我有多少耳垢。真讨厌。

A：真恶心，也许你应该把它清理干净。

B：我试过了，但它还在那里。

A：你看过医生了吗？

B：还没有。我会安排预约医生的。

Unit 8　Hesitation 犹豫

Scene 1　商品繁多

A: I can't decide which item to buy at the supermarket.

B: Is it because of the variety or price?

A: Both. There are so many options.

B: Maybe make a list of what you need and stick to it?

A: Good idea. I'll start doing that.

B: You got this! Don't stress too much.

A：我无法决定在超市买什么。

B：是因为品种多还是因为价格高？

A：两者都有。有太多选择了。

B：也许你可以列一张你需要物品的清单，然后只买这些东西？

A：好主意。我会开始这么做的。

B：你可以的！不要太紧张。

257

Scene 2　买车与否

A: I'm not sure if I should buy a car.

B: What's holding you back?

A: It's a big investment, and I'm worried about the expenses.

B: Have you compared the cost of owning a car versus using public transportation?

A: Not yet. Good point. Thanks for the suggestion.

A：我不确定是否应该买辆车。

B：是什么让你犹豫？

A：这是一笔很大的投资，我担心买车的费用。

B：你比较过私家车和乘坐公共交通工具的成本吗？

A：还没有。这是个好主意。谢谢你的建议。

□ repulse *v.* 使厌恶

□ nuisance *n.* 讨厌的东西

□ variety *n.* 多种式样

□ stick to 坚持

□ hold back 阻碍

□ investment *n.* 投资

□ expense *n.* 费用

情绪表达

Scene 3 选择专业

A: What major are you thinking about?

B: I'm not sure. I'm considering engineering or psychology.

A: What interests you about each one?

B: I like math and building things, but I also enjoy helping people.

A: It's a tough decision, but don't worry, you'll figure it out.

B: Thanks, I hope so.

A：你想学什么专业?

B：我不确定。我在考虑工程学或心理学。

A：这两个专业中让你感兴趣的是什么?

B：我喜欢数学和建造东西，但我也喜欢帮助别人。

A：这是一个艰难的决定，但别担心，你会做出决定的。

B：谢谢，希望如此。

Scene 4 是否应约

A: Hey, my friend invited me to hang out tonight.

B: Are you free?

A: Not really. I have a lot of work to do.

B: Then maybe you should decline the invitation.

A: Yeah, but I don't want to disappoint my friend.

B: It's understandable, but your work is also important.

A：嘿，我的朋友邀请我今晚出去玩。

B：你有空吗?

A：没有。我有很多工作要做。

B：那么也许你应该拒绝邀请。

A：是的，但是我不想让我的朋友失望。

B：我理解你，但是你的工作也很重要。

Unit 9 Blame 责备

Scene 1 错过电影

A: You're late! We missed the beginning of the movie!

B: I'm sorry. I got caught up at work.

A: That's not a good enough excuse.

B: I know. I should have left earlier.

A: It's not fair to the rest of us.

B: I'll make it up to you guys next time.

A：你迟到了! 我们错过了电影的开头!

B：抱歉。我的工作太忙了。

A：这可不是个好借口。

B：我知道。我应该早点出发的。

A：这对我们其他人不公平。

B：下次我会补偿你们的。

重点词汇
及表达

☐ engineering *n.* 工程学

☐ psychology *n.* 心理学

☐ figure out 想出

☐ hang out 闲逛

☐ free *adj.* 空闲的

☐ understandable *adj.* 可以理解的

☐ get caught up 被卷入

☐ excuse *n.* 借口

☐ fair *adj.* 公平的

258

Scene 2　工作落后

A: We missed our deadline because of your delay.

B: I'm sorry. I underestimated the task.

A: It's not just you. The whole team was affected.

B: I'll make sure to finish my work on time next time.

A：因为你的拖延，我们错过了最后期限。

B：抱歉。我低估了这项任务。

A：不只是你。整个团队都受到了影响。

B：下次我一定按时完成我的工作。

Scene 3　大声喧哗

A: Excuse me. Could you please keep your voice down?

B: What's the problem?

A: Your loud scene is disturbing others around you.

B: I'm sorry. I didn't realize. I'll try to be quieter.

A: Thank you. I appreciate it.

B: No problem. Thanks for letting me know.

A：抱歉，你能小声点吗？

B：怎么了？

A：你吵吵闹闹的，打扰了周围的其他人。

B：抱歉，我没意识到。我会尽量安静一点。

A：谢谢。我很感激。

B：不客气。谢谢你提醒我。

Scene 4　禁止吸烟

A: Excuse me. Did you know this is a non-smoking area?

B: Oh, sorry. I didn't see the sign.

A: Smoking is not allowed here. It's bad for people's health.

B: I know. I'll put it out right away.

A: Your smoking affects others around you. Please be considerate.

B: I apologize. I'll make sure it doesn't happen again.

A：打扰一下，你知道这里是无烟区吗？

B：哦，抱歉。我没看到标识。

A：这里禁止吸烟。吸烟有害健康。

B：我知道了。我马上熄灭掉。

A：你吸烟会影响周围的人。请体谅别人。

B：抱歉。我保证不会再发生这种事了。

☐ underestimate v. 低估

☐ loud scene 嘈杂的场景

☐ disturb v. 打扰

☐ non-smoking area 无烟区

☐ considerate adj. 考虑周到的，体贴的

Scene 5   未遵守承诺

A: You didn't show up for the trip! What happened?

B: Sorry, something urgent came up.

A: You promised to come and didn't show up. We missed out!

B: I know. I'm sorry. Can we reschedule?

A: It's not just about rescheduling. It's about keeping your promises.

B: I'll make it up to you. I promise.

A：你没有去旅行! 发生什么事了？

B：抱歉，我有些急事。

A：你答应要来的，却没有出现。我们错过了！

B：我知道。我很抱歉。我们能改期吗？

A：这不只是重新安排时间的问题，而是你要遵守承诺。

B：我会补偿你的。我保证。

260

□ show up 出现

□ urgent *adj.* 紧急的

□ keep one's promise 遵守承诺